WHEN VENTURE CAPITALISTS SAY "NO"

Elliott:

For Catherine

Your passion for technology clients must be one of Memphis' greatest assets!

Ron Peterson

WHEN VENTURE CAPITALISTS SAY "NO"

Creative Financing Strategies and Resources

Ron Peterson

Comanche Press
MD

> QUANTITY DISCOUNTS of this book are available at
> www.threearrowscapital.com

When Venture Capitalists Say "No"—Creative Financing & Strategies

Copyright © 2003 by Comanche Press MD

All rights reserved. No part of this book may be reproduced or transmitted in any form or by any means, electronic or mechanical, including photocopying, recording, or by any information storage and retrieval system, without permission in writing from the copyright owner.

Comanche Press MD
P.O. Box 565
Glen Echo, MD 20812-0565
tarrows@erols.com
www.threearrowscapital.com
(301) 229-6240; fax (301) 229-5462; toll free 887-245-3774

ISBN: 0-9728246-1-8

Cover art designed by Windhaven Press

First printing March 2003

Design & typeset by Windhaven Press: Consulting & Editorial Svs, Auburn, NH (www.windhaven.com)

Printed in the United States of America

10 9 8 7 6 5 4 3 2 1

CONTENTS

Introduction 1
1. Forming Your Business Strategy 5
2. Designing Your Business 25
3. Sources and Tactics for Financing & Organizing 50
4. Where to Turn for Help 112
5. Venture Capital 129
6. Corporate Capital and Strategic Partnerships 145
7. Business Angels 156
8. Small Stock Offerings 166
9. PR and Your Elevator Speech 180
10. Business and Marketing Plan, ... 195
11. Biotech, A Special Case 213
Appendix A: Federal Technology Transfer 239
Appendix B: Small Stock Offering Requirements 244
Glossary 248
Resources 251
Index 255
Addendum 262

To Gerry, Kirsten, Tess and Christian

INTRODUCTION

The art of raising money is the art of reducing risk.

Henry Ford became one of the world's richest men and forged an enduring legacy of building cars nearly one-hundred years ago without the facilities thought indispensable today. He didn't invent the automobile. Ford wasn't the first to market. He had no backing from deep-pocketed investment bankers. He had no network of well-to-do friends. Ford started his firm during the recession year of 1902. There were plenty of competitors. There were no venture capital (VC) firms, Small Business Administration (SBA) loans or government grants. He had never succeeded in business before. He had no experienced management team in place. He didn't have a written business plan and certainly not a Power-Point presentation. Sounds like a formula for failure, doesn't it? But just the opposite happened. Ford figured out how to get his financing and you can too. Ford developed a business model that circumvented the obstructions, determined what really mattered, and devised a way to make it happen. While other car manufacturers at the time were targeting the wealthy hobbyist, Ford looked for a different market—the mass consumer. In order to reach this market he had to have an automobile that was within this market's price range. To build cheaply he had to produce a standard model quickly. Without capital to buy parts, to build a plant, to inventory products, or hire salesmen, he had to generate capital from his operations and grow internally. Here is what he did.

After asking the people he knew—his friends and family—and following a failed first business, Ford raised a total of $40,000 from five investors whom he convinced that his business model would work. He next built a network of dealers who were eager to sell a low-priced automobile, and would pay cash when the cars were delivered (finding a way to generate cash flow). He contracted with parts suppliers and paid on a thirty-day invoice basis. With an initial ten workers who were paid $1.50 per day, he assembled cars rapidly. In July 1903 they started rolling out at the clip of one each ninety minutes, and were immediately sold to dealers for cash. He had the parts that he needed without paying for them, he booked revenues quickly, and he used the time spread between the sale of the cars and the purchase of parts to good advantage. Using this cash flow he built bigger and bigger operations, extended his dealer network, devised an assembly line process and eventually lowered his price from $850 for the original Model A's down to $500 for the Model T, introduced in November 1908.

Becoming a phenomenally rich man didn't require a fistful of cash to start but it did need serious study of opportunities and identifying what people really wanted. He went through all the steps to test the business, with the first and most important step concentrating on seeing if the cars would sell. Business after business has begun with little upside money but with a great deal of thought. Putting that thought in today and getting your idea across to potential investors will get you the capital you need. Wouldn't you want to invest in something that was as well thought out as Ford Motor Co., one that illustrated sales, showed internal financing for growth, and was conveyed to you with the passion of a true believer?

> *"Nothing is particularly hard if you divide it into small jobs!"*
> —Henry Ford

If you believe that things were different back in Ford's day and you have nothing to learn from examining hundreds of different approaches to forming and financing businesses, you should know that just a few years ago Michael Dell used a variation of Ford's financing technique to grow Dell Computer into the powerhouse that it has become. If you believe that the solution to your business growth lies in simply talking a venture capitalist or group of wealthy investors into backing your plan, and only need a list and some phone numbers, you may find yourselves in the company of empty-pocketed entrepreneurs and become frustrated at the whole process. Attracting capital today means devising an innovative business model and communicating that model to potential investors, wherever they are. If you're seeking the most creative ways of attracting capital and are willing to apply energy and thought to just what your business could and should be, this book is ideal for you. It doesn't really matter if you're an experienced businessperson or someone who has recently decided they wanted their own company—these pages are the best place to start.

Ralph Waldo Emerson told us "Build a better mousetrap and the world will beat a path to your door." Emerson was a preacher and essayist, not an entrepreneur, and following his advice has rung the death knell for countless would-be companies. You do begin with a superior product that is uniquely positioned in a niche market, but thinking you can stop there is a formula for failure. Raising capital today means you have to get out and sell the idea, and sell it hard. The pages that follow are designed to show you how to configure your business for funding success and how to tell your story. The first two chapters suggest how to organize and present your company to attract capital. The third chapter is the heart of the book and provides examples of how other companies were funded and grew. Additional sources of capital are described throughout the following chapters and the resources section contains references to tens of thousands more. Ways to gain attention and give you your best shot before potential investors as well as your business and marketing plan comprise the later chapters. I have included a special chapter on biotechnology because the long lead-time and torturous path to market in that industry suggest that if you can fund a life-sciences company you've got a good formula for nearly any industry. I have even included a chapter on venture capital despite the title of the book—if you frame your model correctly, chances of securing capital from these professional sources soar. Wherever possible I have included references to websites so you can access even more information and sources of capital. Entrepreneurs need not feel alone since so many organizations exist to help them.

I am indebted to many for their contributions to this book including: Dr. Bob Ouellette, who wanted to have better information on funding technology companies for his students; Erle Keefer, who found the innocence of entrepreneurs about the rigors of funding to be responsible for countless business deaths; Tor Soevik, who preaches that technology without an imaginative grounding in marketing, has little chance; as well as many others for their comments and suggestions such as Drew Field, Henry Hubbard, Dr. Jamie Love, Tom Mierzwa, Dr. Jennifer Miller, Dr. Robert Rosato, Susan P. Smith, Robert Steeves and Dr. Gideon Strassman.

A friend not long ago said; "I could have a proven cancer cure and

I still couldn't get financing." That's not true of course, but the difficulty of finding money can't be over-exaggerated. A number of newer CEOs spend so much time chasing money they have little time left to run their demanding companies. This is a very poor use of time since the preparation and insight that we illustrate in these pages can vastly reduce what most entrepreneurs see as the onerous task of begging from strangers. If you did everything right, money would come begging to you. You're welcome to make comments or suggestions or ask questions at www.threearrowscapital.com or via e-mail at tarrows@erols.com.

FORMING YOUR BUSINESS STRATEGY

"This is one of the classic times when startups happen. People are unemployed. They're thinking, 'I could take a job with a public company that's barely hanging on, or I could take this idea I've been working on and build a team, raise some money. What do I want to spend the next three years working on—realizing a dream or grinding away at a place where I'm as likely to get laid off as I am to get promoted?'" Venture capitalist Paul Holland in Optimize Magazine, December 2002.

What to do first.

Terminology and players shift, depending on such things as the stock market, the economy, technology, fads, etc. The investment community regularly redefines the definition of what makes an appealing investment opportunity, depending upon variables such as these. During the Internet heyday early-stage investing meant a viable opportunity, in nearly any given stage of development, if the company had an engaging business plan and an attractive management team. Today, what constitutes an opportunity is far more rigorous, and is squarely focused on revenue as a way of limiting risk and showing full proof of concept. Investors still need a business plan and are looking for an experienced management team but they also need: some protected and valuable intellectual property (IP); evidence that a reasonable path for developing the product or service exists; proof that significant progress had been made towards proving out the market and demonstrating customer interest; a significant market potential; a product or service with clearly delineated milestones in terms of achievements, launch dates and revenue; and, most importantly, paying customers. Lots of young firms don't have all these ingredients but can still find the money they need by highlighting the elements they do possess and showing how the rest are going to be found.

> *Changing emphasis may be necessary to attract capital. Atto Bio-Science had to alter its business model from making microscope accessories to developing products for the biotechnology industry in order to raise $3 million in new financing. Atto kept its older business but realized both the growth and the funding were in other arenas.*

> *Privately held Althexis and publicly traded Microside Pharmaceuticals succeeded in raising $60 million in private capital only after the two merged to form Essential Therapeutics, Inc. Cambridge Antibody Technology acquired cash-rich Oxford GlycoSciences for $177.5 million in stock while Oxford still had over $215 million in the bank!*

> *Arradial was founded in late 2000 to produce research equipment for drug companies. As established equipment makers like Applied Biosystems and Waters Corp. faltered, investors steered clear of Arradial. The CEO refocused the company, used its technology to support its own drug-discovery efforts, and was able to generate new funding.*

> *In the heyday of the Internet, Chemdex went public with a warning in its prospectus: "We have a history of losses and anticipate continued losses for the foreseeable future. We have had substantial losses since our inception. We currently expect our losses to increase in the future and we cannot assure you that we will ever achieve or sustain profitability." Machiavelli said: "Success or failure depends on conformity to the times." More recently, Gene Kleiner of premier venture capital firm Kleiner Perkins Caufield Byers said, "In a tornado, even turkeys can fly." Don't plan on being in a tornado again.*

Form a story that investors will want to hear.

During the 80s, businessmen asked themselves, "how do I position my company and gain advantage in a *known* game (an existing or at least an understandable industry structure)?" The question now has become, "how do I divine the contours of an evolving and changing industry structure and, therefore, the rules of engagement in a new and evolving game?" Industries represent a diversity of new, emerging and evolving games. The rules of engagement are written as companies experiment, adjust their approaches to competition, find marketing opportunities, and otherwise fight to survive.

> *Amgen, destined to become the most successful of the first-generation of biotech firms, went through a difficult time in the early 1980s. Having pursued several technical paths with little success, Amgen was in the early stages of developing a treatment for anemia known as recombinant human erythropoietin, which stimulates and regulates production of red blood cells. A partnership deal with Kirin, a Japanese brewing company that was looking for a way of entering the pharmaceutical industry via biotechnology, provided additional funds at a critical time, and allowed Amgen to press on with the new drug. Patented in 1989 and launched two years later under the brand name EPOGEN, it became the first blockbuster drug to emerge from a biotechnology firm.*

The best business opportunities.

Emerging technologies do more than change the technological skills needed to succeed, they change the relevant complementary assets, competitors and even customers. Technological change should be only one of the factors shaping an overall commercialization strategy. Complementary assets include access to distribution, service capability, customer relationships, supplier relationships, and related products. Any of these avenues offer a potential business opportunity. In fact, as long as the pace of technological developments stays strong and even accelerates, the number of potential businesses should grow dramatically.

> *A husband and wife team of Stanford University professors, Leonard Bosack and Sandy Lerner, needed to e-mail each other but found they couldn't because each accessed a non-compatible system. Their solution was the router, an instant hit, and they started and named the company "Cisco" to commercialize the innovation in 1984. The couple persuaded friends and relatives to work for deferred pay and financed the venture by running up bills on their credit cards. Sequoia Capital funded them in 1987, but only when they were profitable and doing over $3 million annually in sales.*

SCENDIS began in 1984 as a consulting firm on workforce diversity and sexual harassment. The two partners gained their experience as federal employees and chipped in $3,000 each to their new firm. The first product was a newsletter on their specialty that went to states, counties, cities and other organizations that were sensitive to these issues. Their big break came when SCENDIS was asked to bid on a $200,000 study by the State of Ohio. They won by carefully surrounding themselves with the experts needed to do the work, as well as production of a beautifully crafted proposal. SCENDIS formed a team with big names in the industry such as Hay Associates and Deloitte & Touche, among others, and gained the credibility they needed. On the basis of that contract they became established experts and next went to the states of New Jersey, Wyoming, and Florida, and cities such as Philadelphia and Ann Arbor. When SCENDIS next wanted a high-profile job with Mitsubishi, they figured a frontal assault would get lost. They went through the union involved with Mitsubishi and won the contract.

Natural funding sources.

You can't tell the players without a program and the first thing to look at is the sea of potential funders that could float a white knight your way. Determine these sources by classifying the nature of your offering. Does your business model have legs? Do you have a product or feature that is a stand-alone business or one that is really a feature add-on to an existing product? If the latter, your best bet is probably to pursue a licensing or partnership agreement with a company established in the industry. Most investors aren't interested in funding a "one-trick pony," especially if the market is limited.

If the technology is a product rather than a feature, is it a platform technology that other work can build upon or is it an improvement on existing platforms already on the market? Platform technologies that can sustain added products or services offer the highest potential return for a new venture, but they are also riskier and require a well-delineated set of steps to assure an investor that things will work out.

Make the sale first.

Oracle's Larry Ellison gained a reputation for selling "vapor ware" in the early days of Oracle Corp. People claimed that he would promise a product that hadn't yet been developed. His success stemmed from finding that he could work out the solution later. He delivered on his promises and delighted patient customers. Bill Gates has been similarly characterized as signing agreements for software as if it already existed and then going back to Microsoft to find a way of producing it. Mario Marino suggests, "if you're not out ahead of yourself, you're really not an entrepreneur." Marino and his co-founders began their telecommunications company with $600 each and eventually sold the business years later, for $2 billion.

You don't need to re-invent the wheel, just make a better wheel.

Turning a raw invention into an economically significant innovation requires a host of steps. Typically an extensive process of redesign, modification, and a thousand small improvements are needed to make it suitable for mass markets, for production by drastically new techniques, and by the eventual availability of a whole range of complementary activities. It's probably more important and profitable to figure out what ancillary services and products a new technology will require than trying to figure out the new technology itself (selling wheelbarrows to miners instead of panning yourself). The people who put the first computer together, the ENIAC at the University of Pennsylvania, didn't make a dime off the machine while many of the others who came later certainly did.

The real money will probably fall to enabling products and services that are needed for innovations such as information technology and biotechnology. Economic history suggests that sub-technologies, arrangements, and architectures are needed to adapt us to prime technical components. Given the potential of these two technologies alone suggests the rewards are likely to be huge. Harvard Professor Clayton Christensen suggests that the most viable sectors will be those that are not the most attractive to the established companies. Foresight and niches could pay big dividends. He says, "The first thing to find out is whether there is potential to create a new growth market, a new application, within the general industry dominated by an established company." The litmus test, "Is there a larger population of less skilled, or less wealthy, customers who could be pulled into that market? An innovation will get traction only if it helps people get something that they're already doing in their lives, done better." (Check out his website at www.innosight.com.)

Carve out a niche.

> *Phil Knight developed a plan to make low-cost running shoes in Asia and sell them in the U.S., as part of his work toward an MBA at Stanford. In 1964, Knight and his former track coach (whose hobby was handcrafting lightweight running shoes) each put in $500 to start the predecessor of Nike.*

Deloitte Consulting conducted a study of the most successful business models and concluded that most simply targeted customers whose needs had existed for some time—but were considered undesirable or unprofitable by existing firms. Instead of accurately predicting the future, they redefined the present. The Deloitte study suggests innovation is found by creatively addressing the questions of who, what and how—standards in journalism and sales. The corporate stars they looked at: (1) redefined customer segments and targeted those with under-served needs; (2) created new customer segments; and (3) changed the decision-maker within the existing customer base.

Having what customers want to buy.

Perhaps you should follow the more debatable approach of "ready, fire, aim" in order to gain feedback on your model as quickly as possible. What do you really know about your market and is it better to make some mistakes to rapidly find out what works? In order to help investors understand and share your vision it's essential that you gain a clear understanding of that market from potential customers and from experts in the field, before going further. Part of your funding proposition should be a market study that shows at least a survey of potential customers. This is really something you should do yourself and not delegate to market survey companies or others—you'll be surprised at how much there is to learn by being on the phone or in visiting possible buyers. Document the responses of your test subjects and later you may be able to solicit their help in reaching the milestones you or your investors establish. A marketing outreach can also serve longer term needs such as enlisting aid in finding capital, adding management, developing markets, looking for new applications—and especially in identifying customers. This is also a good time to make contacts with the variety of public service providers, government funding sources and other people that can help you grow the business. In the formative stages of your firm, enlist as many respondents as you possibly can—and then double that effort.

It's probably best to go out and even sell the wrong product or service so that you can determine what the right one is. Remember that each time Edison failed to make an incandescent lamp he was eliminating possibilities and getting close to the one that would work. Often, successful businesses have deviated considerably from their original ideas when opportunities presented themselves once they were up and running. It may be more important to be in business than to have the right model to begin with. Business failures can be anything but a failure if it quickens finding out what will sell. The best business ideas may not be obvious and require a failure or two to point you in the right direction. Failures become just a learning experience. Customer surveys can be invaluable but when conducted in the absence of the product itself, it makes it more difficult for the interviewee to understand just what you're offering.

> *"Fail often, fail fast, and fail cheaply."* Mia Wenjen, founder of the firm Aquent, doing $200 million in annual sales.

Matthew Haley, an executive in Accenture's Corporate Strategy and Business Architecture Group, suggests that all executives of a company should make sales calls. He's seen a lot of dumb luck that produced terrific successes because companies found out what would sell and what wouldn't. Haley says that selling involves looking for the ego need of potential buyers and that companies don't buy things, people do.

> *Don Britton found that his very first customer became an evangelist for his company, a small business computing solutions provider. That customer recommended him to friends and was responsible for bringing in the next customer and many more. When looking for capital, there is simply nothing stronger than to know that your solution will sell. This knowledge will permeate and energize any presentation—to investors or customers.*

Learn from customers.

Dell Computers is famous for listening to its customers and learning what they want. They prospered by eliminating the middleman (although they unsuccessfully once tried retail stores) and pride themselves on how close they are to their customers and what they learn about trends from this closeness. This was a fortuitous result instead of a conscious strategy since they couldn't hire middlemen to begin with anyway. They have advanced and executed the strategy beautifully, however. Much of Dell's success and their present marketing model stemmed from how they had to bootstrap themselves originally and, with few resources, needed to find substitutes. Not having access to capital and a name that opened doors proved beneficial and formed what became the heart of Dell's culture. Maybe you're better off than you think.

Gina Dubbe, a vice-president of early-stage venture capital fund Walker Ventures, and both an engineer and saleswoman by training, suggests that today you need to take a non-traditional route to get the money you need. She's a strong advocate of using public relations to get your message into the hands of potential investors. She also says you need sales and a proven marketing plan in order to get investors excited. Gina suggests that when you put your product in the hands of test customers (your beta test) you should write into the agreement a provision that your test site customer will buy the product if they really like it and keep it past the test period. When you get your first three orders, you'll have an insight into what matters most to customers and how you need to market your products. You'll be in a much stronger position to talk to venture capitalists and other investors when you can tell them that people bought and just what those customers said. Among her other suggestions are: focus on getting leads for sales from any of a number of sources; save money whenever you can to include printing brochures in black and white and having just a minimal website to start; and finding complementary companies in order to co-opt their customer base. Gina is at www.walkerventures.com.

Even when you feel that you have low expectations of funding from a particular angel group or venture capitalist, you're probably better off going through with a meeting and see what you learn from the experience. First, lightning may strike but more likely, every time you make a presentation and handle questions, objections, etc., you'll find out more about what needs to be done to convince people and your next presentation will be better.

Quitting your job and starting a company.

> *Larry Ellison was a computer programmer working on a database for the CIA (code name "Oracle") when he read an IBM paper on relational databases. He started a consulting company with two colleagues to develop these kinds of databases. A friend invested $6,000 but otherwise the young company bootstrapped itself, signing clients, doing the work, getting paid and developing the database product. They luckily wrote software in IBM's programming language, which soon became a standard, and the rest is history.*

Ellison isn't the only one who used a consulting company to generate the revenues needed to start a company. Gold Wire Technology, Inc. was begun by four MIT grads with a product they wanted to build. They didn't want to deal with VCs and give anything away (or couldn't anyway), so they started renting themselves out as consultants. They were paid well and put something like seven or eight hundred thousand dollars in the bank. Soon they could say: "Okay, you stop consulting, stay here and start developing the product. We'll go out and bring in the money to bring this thing alive." Gold Wire then added more consultants and kept peeling them off to man the company when they could afford it. By the time they had a working and demonstrable product, they could confidently shop it to the investment community and to lots of contacts they made through their consulting work.

> *Michael Dell hired high-school classmates to sell the Houston Post to newly married couples, taking in $18,000. Once in college he began selling the unsold stock of local PC dealers to businesses. He had taken apart an Apple II computer and noted that roughly $600 worth of parts made up at least a $2,000 retail price machine. With this kind of margin, he felt he had plenty of room to undercut prices and still make a profit.*

You can start from scratch or perhaps look for an existing business that you can materially augment. Maybe a company that has no marketing expert or where a businessman is tiring and could use a CEO would be good targets. Business brokers will have listings of companies. www.businesstown.com has information on selling a business and references a dozen other websites that provide opportunities and added background for this kind of effort.

Position your products or services to fit a customer's need.

Can you think differently about the market and come up with something useful? Phillips Lighting introduced a new type of fluorescent lamp that featured an extended lifetime, lessened energy usage, and a considerable savings over its life versus the competition. Marketing of the new lamp was frustrated, however, when purchasing agents in the U.S. failed to respond to the savings that were at the core of the benefits. Buyers were put off by a purchase price that was more than 25% higher than they were used to paying. It wasn't until Phillips changed its marketing emphasis, switching its target to chief financial officers, (CFOs) instead of purchasing agents, that they started to see sales. CFOs are interested in the bigger picture of corporate savings while the agents could only see the purchase cost. Phillips soon had a quarter of the U.S. market as a result of the new strategy.

If you offer a radically different approach that's difficult for people to understand and use in their daily lives, you may have more difficulty finding investors. Scott Cook needed $2 million to begin the financial software company, Intuit. A succession of "no thanks" to his pleas for money just confirmed to him that he had something truly novel. There were already at least two-dozen personal finance products on the market at the time but none of them were really simple and intuitive to use like Quicken. He had interviewed hundreds of people in the computer industry who had tried existing software to see what was wrong with these products, a technique of listening to the customer that he learned while working at Procter & Gamble. All the venture capital firms he spoke with passed, in every case finding something in the business model they didn't believe would work. He spent over $300,000 of his savings and his parent's money in the process. Investor capital finally came in from two wealthy parties referred by one of his associates, and he was on his way.

> *Thomas Edison threaded his electrical wiring through the emptied interior gas lines of homes to a bulb that sat where a gas flame burned before. He wanted to insure that buyers felt totally comfortable with the conversion and that changing to a new system wouldn't clash with their daily habits. Today we call this gradual change a "bounded equation."*

Think about taking an idea from one industry and applying it to another. Tom Stemberg organized the superstore Staples when a friend and Harvard Business School professor suggested that he apply what he had learned about distribution techniques while working in the grocery business, to another category of merchandise. The professor said that he should look for one that was growing faster and was poorly served, which turned out to be office supplies. The investment-banking firm of William Blair put up cash for its initial growth and later took the company public. Another early investor, Bessemer Venture Partners, helped the company obtain one of its biggest suppliers. Old friends and early investors, as Stemberg found, can give you a lot more besides just the money.

Become a salesperson.

When out seeking capital without a background in sales, you have an important handicap that needs to be corrected. Effective face-to-face selling is critical for entrepreneurs in all stages of growth. If you have to choose between the elegance of your technology and your ability to sell, choose the latter. Economic history is littered with stories of number two winning out because of this factor. Former IBM chairman, Thomas J. Watson, Jr., stated in a 1990 memoir: "In the history of IBM, technological innovation wasn't the thing that made us successful. Unhappily, there were many times when we came in second . . . [but] we consistently outsold people who had better technology, because we knew how to put the story before the customer, how to install the machines successfully, and how to hang on to the customers once we had them."

If you're new to sales, a good place to begin is with Dale Carnegie's "Six Principles to Make People Like You." The advice resonates today just as it did when first published in 1936.

- "Be genuinely interested in other people."
- "Smile."
- "Remember that a person's name is to that person the sweetest and most important sound in any language."
- "Be a good listener. Encourage others to talk about themselves."
- "Talk in terms of the other person's interests."
- "Make the other person feel important—and do it sincerely."

Ralph Waldo Emerson also said, "Every man I meet is in some way my superior, and I can learn of him." If there is any secret to sales it is to respect the person that you're speaking to and don't be intent on hammering them with every aspect of your business model. If you don't listen, there's precious little that you can learn. A little information is usually all it takes to elicit interest. Chapter nine in this book on public relations and elevator speeches will point you in the right direction. Another thing that you'll find about sales is that you never sell something to a person as much as you give information to them, and then they decide to buy it.

The section, "Resources," contains a number of references to sales texts that may help you but the best that I've ever seen never appears under the rubric of "sales." *The Dialogues of Socrates* by Plato illustrates the technique that Socrates used to persuade someone to alter his opinion and see things Socrates' way. All he ever does is state a fact and then ask a question. I've never seen anything more effective in making a sale. After all, a real sale means that the buyer saw the advantages and made the purchase decision himself or herself, with no one twisting their arm.

Sales books usually suggest things to say or not to say and illustrate a systematic way of conducting a campaign. Each person that you talk to or otherwise reach, and has the wherewithal to make an investment with you, is your prospect until they either finally say yes or no. Many people will want to think it over, investigate the proposition or otherwise need time to talk it over with others, etc., before they write a check. While many salesmen in fields such as automobiles will say you have little hope with these people you'll find that's not true. The best thing is to organize a way to keep in touch with anyone who has shown some interest. Regularly get back with more information, new facts, developments, or other information to keep you fresh in their mind. Drop them an e-mail with some information on the company, the market or other tidbit. I think calling people all the time is an intrusion and a simple note permits them to control their response to you and keeps a good relationship. A real sale always permits the buyer to be in control and never to feel forced in any way.

"I lost more hair doing this than I did raising children." Sandeep T. Vohra on searching for funding, netting a total of $22.4 million for his company, Optinel Systems.

Carry one other business adage with you, "If you've made the sale, shut up and get out." The theory is that once the deal has been agreed upon, the best possible outcome for you is already in the bag so the only change that could come has to be worse. Not doing so has been a mistake made hundreds of thousands of times.

Discovering investors through telephone calls or knocking on doors of people to tell them about a company has financed countless entrepreneurs. Sales cold calls are difficult for most people to make and the fear of rejection has stopped many entrepreneurs from ever getting very far. Inc Magazine's website lists a number of ways of getting over fears of making sales calls including articles on techniques for starting the conversation and what to do when you hear a "no." www2@inc.com will give you this material in a guide written by Jennifer A. Redmond. Houston, TX-based Michelle Nichols, writing in *Business Week*, has a list of "15 Power Selling Words" that she suggests using frequently and will help make your sale (includes "you" and "urgent" at www.savvyselling.biz).

Money at the outset.

While you may think there's no place you're going to get several million dollars to start and grow your firm, think that a number of companies were begun with less than $10,000. These included: Apple Computer; Mary Kay Cosmetics; Lillian Vernon; The Limited; Dell Computer; Gateway 2000; Papa John's Pizza; Nantucket Nectars; Ernest and Julio Gallo; Microsoft, and scads more.

GeneDx was started in late 1999 by two researchers at the National Institutes of Health (NIH), Sherri Gale with 16 years of experience and John Compton with 10. Neither had any business experience, both were Ph.D.s and their research was fulfilling. Their work in genetic markers for orphan diseases (those with less than 200,000 patients, or about 6,000 such diseases) showed a service they felt was essential. Believing this program was especially important, they approached NIH about expanding it—the answer was "no." They next thought about setting up a non-profit to do the same thing on the side, but NIH said they would have to forfeit their jobs. They then decided to chuck their jobs, start a company, and perform the service. They each put up $14,000 from savings, began the company, and never looked back. Their first revenue of $512 came in on opening day. GeneDx revenues come from individual tests and research contracts. They found space in a Maryland incubator and nine months later received a $141,000 award from a group known as MD BioTech (a public entity that receives royalties from the company). Gale and Compton felt they won the award because they were showing revenues. Paying themselves no effective salaries at the outset, they gradually changed that as they grew. Nine months after the MD BioTech award, Sequoia Bank extended them a $100,000 line of credit, which they have never had to use. In the second full year of operations GeneDx revenues are close to $1.2 million with margins of about 35 percent. They receive calls from venture capitalists all the time asking if they want any money, and the answer is "no, our revenues are all that we need for our growth." They have 9 people, can barely handle the business coming in, and need to hire more. Sherri Gale suggests that the incubator (which she first thought was some kind of babysitting space) has been a godsend. An incubator gave them affordable space, help right down the hall, a succession of classes on business topics and incalculable emotional and technical support.

At the same time GeneDx illustrated their beginnings during a seminar at Johns Hopkins, two other presenters talked about how they formed their companies and their experiences with an incubator. Marlenix was spun-off from a company that was losing focus, and took over a product the original company was no longer really interested in. Starting with an item that has revenues is often all that is needed to begin a company, with the notion that other products or services can come later. Marlenix is rolling more products out the door, has a couple of small business grants, and looks like a winner. The third presenter was a scientist with impeccable credentials who had been involved in three other startups. His science is associated with a new technique for recombinant DNA. He raised $7 million in venture capital, received $3.5 million in NIH SBIR grants, but was still only 18 months away from running out of cash.

Does gender make a difference? An axiom in entrepreneurship is "When a man starts a new company, the first thing he does is to rent expensive office space, get really nice furniture, and hire an attractive secretary. When a woman starts a business it's more likely that she begins on an ironing board in her basement." As a girl, Ling Chai escaped China inside a crate and later started a software company in the basement of her home (that now does $50 million in annual revenues).

Investor's perception of you.

Some businesses like Compaq and Sun Microsystems secured funding quickly because they had either strong technologies or highly experienced teams. These factors reduced their perceived uncertainty and permitted them to attract funding required to start out on a larger scale, accelerating their growth. Compaq and Sun received venture capital funding from Sevin Rosen and Kleiner-Perkins, respectively, firms in their own hometowns.

As a caveat, attempting to raise initial capital that will not be needed until after a significant milestone is passed, or really before its required in the company's growth phase, is a subtle signal to prospective investors that the entrepreneur is not confident about the future prospects of the venture. If you need a pile of cash that will be dormant until you draw upon it, does that mean your company may not be so attractive in the future?

Handling negotiations.

The best situation in hunting capital is to become such an attractive proposition that everyone wants a piece of you. Ideally, you'd like to be involved in a bidding war where several interested investors bid against one another for the right to invest. It's true that when you get one investor with a big name involved, others are likely to follow. Dennis Roberts, an experienced investment banker, said that he had a client who had an offer on the table to buy his company for $9 million. When Dennis finally joined the discussion, the offer immediately went up to $11 million, reflecting the belief by the buyer that hard bargaining by an experienced outside party was about to start. Dennis expanded the bidding by contacting other firms, and after a lengthy process the company was sold for $38 million. The interesting part of this success included the fact that not only did the final purchase price increase by a hefty multiple, but also the accepted bid wasn't even the highest figure that was finally bid. The terms of the accepted offer were more attractive than those given by the highest bidder, something Dennis has seen countless times.

There are a number of university business school courses and books on negotiation that are worth investigating. The Wharton School at the University of Pennsylvania has one of the oldest and best courses.

The book *Getting to Yes* is a must read for anyone about to embark on a serious sale. One of the most important lessons taught in all the courses and books is that when entering negotiations, you should look at it as if you were sitting in the other person's seat, not just your own. This kind of perspective allows insight into the process and will be advantageous to you.

If you've found potential investors slow to write their checks or they otherwise find reasons to stall, they probably believe they're the only interested party. Better to be seen as a short-term opportunity that's going to be snatched up by others if you don't act now. That won't occur unless you find several interested investors by spreading your net widely and making a good case. Even if one investor seems fine, try to increase the pool as much as possible. Corporations who both invest in you and offer your company partnering advantages may be a preferred source. If nothing else, the extra interest you generate may up the bidding or give you better terms than originally offered by venture capitalists, business angels or Wall Street investment banking firms. Think of whatever you can do to make yourself as attractive as possible. Have you spoken to a large number of venture capitalists or strategic partners and learned what they're interested in? Do you have a variety of funding alternatives?

It does make a difference where you locate.

> *A key element in raising money for the new biotech company, Vertex, in 1989, was the assembly of a world-class group of researchers. Founder Boger located his company in Cambridge, MA and recruited five senior faculty members at Harvard for his Strategic Advisory Board. Recruiting big names was doubly impressive since at the time nearly 200 biotech companies had emerged and were struggling. Only Genentech earned a regular profit and even that was small. Biotech wasn't in favor but Boger made an excellent case and recruited the names he needed, largely by making it easy and convenient for them to participate.*

Locating your new company among others that share your market or technology, an industrial cluster, can be valuable to any new enterprise. Talent is available nearby and often governments and universities offer cash or services to foster new businesses.

Joseph Schumpeter told us in 1934 that innovation in the form of new technologies or combinations that disrupted the prevailing equilibrium would usher in gales of creative destruction. Schumpeter said that innovation arrives in clusters and argued that newly formed firms commercialize inventions, increasing overall demand, causing economic growth, destroying the existing market structures and redistributing wealth among the remaining firms in the market. Not only does it arrive in clusters, but it also is best nurtured in a cluster.

Working with other people.

If you can avoid going it alone so much the better. A partner can be there to shoulder the burden, to bounce ideas off, and be there when things are rough. Also, Edward Roberts at MIT's Sloan School of Management found that the number one characteristic of successful companies was the early hire of a marketing person, usually not later than the number three person. There's little percentage in going it alone and much better to have someone alongside, especially if they have a feel for a market.

> *Gunther Than, founder of View Systems, Inc., was sitting in his lab at 11:00 PM one night musing about the difficulties of being an entrepreneur. He noted that he was constantly looking for money and for clients and he noted how difficult it was, even with a compelling technology. Gunther noted how lonely it was to be the only person whose shoulders bore responsibility for success or failure. He thought of the income he could have had if he had stayed as the vice-president of a technology company and the shorter hours that he would've spent. Still, he recognized how driven he was so he had no other path.*

Your formula for success.

Professor Amar Bhide, one of the leading experts in growing a company, suggests seven principles for successful startups, "get operational fast; look for quick break-even, cash-generating projects; offer high-value products or services that can sustain direct personal selling; don't try to hire the crack team; keep growth in check; focus on cash; and cultivate banks early." Bhide also argues that providing large amounts of capital to all comers leads to a misallocation of resources. In his view, much of the distinguishing features of promising start-ups derive from their capital constraints. "Meager funding forces entrepreneurs to conduct low-cost experiments that help resolve market and technological uncertainties and prepare the ground for subsequent large-scale investment."

> *An article at www.WSJ.com reported that a Taos, NM psychotherapist opened a business that offered artists a combination of gallery space, a studio and lodging with other artists, turning it into a thriving little enterprise. What makes this company interesting is that the entrepreneur was suffering from bad health and needed to find a service that fit their own physical limitations. The suggestion was that ailing entrepreneurs might expect to actually improve their health by owning a business.*

Muscular dystrophy devastated Gary LeTourneau's body but his mind is sharper than ever. He develops games that can be downloaded from cell phones and his company, www.paletsoft.com, represents a model of distribution, production and content that gives him a chance of building a real success. You can give Gary an idea or a situation and he'll probably have made a game to deal with it in just a day or two.

You'll need different types of money.

Most companies will employ a mix of financing and other strategies needed in their various phases of growth, largely as a function of their progress, what they learn, and the opportunities that open to them. Collateral Therapeutics, Inc., a San Diego, CA based cardiac gene therapy company was formed by a scientist/venture capitalist, Dr. Fred Reich, in concert with a research scientist, Dr. Rich Hammond. Hammond had developed a potential alternative treatment for cardiac problems while working at the University of California (UCSD) and a VA hospital. Reich had the big German pharmaceutical company, Schering AG lend the new firm $500,000 for startup costs and agree to millions of dollars in investments, milestone payments, royalties and other resources over a five-year term. The young company later raised an additional $3 million from the Welcome Trust in the U.K., garnered over $25 million in a Bear, Sterns-led IPO, another $10 million in a private placement and was eventually bought out by Schering for over $100 million. Not only capital, Schering was a partner in research while also providing help in regulatory matters, manufacturing, distribution and sales for any products that came out of the work. Collateral itself greatly expanded its research capabilities by licensing technologies at universities and other organizations and by paying for research to be conducted in related cardiac gene therapy fields. By raising capital in stages, like Collateral, the founding members of firms can potentially own a larger share of the venture at the end, when real progress is made.

> *GovCon, a company bought out by Vertical Net, began by putting the Commerce Business Daily, a government publication, free on the Internet. They built up a user list of 100,000 and used the demographics of that group to develop and sell contracting services. Governments have many resources that can be tapped and also help you along since your startup business costs are deductible.*

Dispel common myths about starting a business right now.

Rob Adams, the founder of incubator AV Labs and head of Austin Venture's bootcamp for entrepreneurs, has an engaging book called *A Good Hard Kick in the Ass* that illustrates myths that need to be quickly dispelled in your search for money. Simply, the following are *not* true:

- Good ideas are scarce.
- I know my customer.
- I have to ship the killer product.
- I must raise a lot of capital quickly.
- Investors fund business plans.
- Investors want their money back quickly.
- Advertising is the hallmark of a good marketing plan.
- I can use partners to sell my product.

Rob's bootcamp is a two-day session that exposes attendees to world-class venture capitalists, service providers, authors, et al. (www.garage.com/bootcamp). Bootcamps for entrepreneurs are becoming more popular and a check with your local business school may turn up something interesting. In Maryland www.mdhitech.org/Entrepreneur/Bootcamp has details that seem typical. On the West Coast, www.garage.com runs a half day camp and a full two-day session on financing.

"All we need to start a business is 150 cars, 4 employees, and 15 rented parking spaces." Stelios Haji-Ioannuou, founder of easyGroup. All his companies "are service-oriented and share a 'recession-proof business model' with the following components: a price-elastic demand curve (consumers will use the service more frequently if it costs less); high fixed costs; low marginal costs per customer; yield management that ensures assets are utilized as much as possible; no frills; the ability to outsource tasks to the customer; exceeding customer expectations ('under-promising and over-delivering'); and prices that dramatically undercut the competition's." www.hbswk.hbs.edu, 12/03/2002.

In the early 1990s small business wealth accounted for 56% of total business wealth but an SBA survey found that figure dropping to 43% by the year 2000. Economist Joel Popkin suggests that the stock market boom in the late 1990s incorrectly shifted this figure since small business wealth is privately held and is typically not listed in stock market quotes. Small businesses are more and more the wave of the future and the place to create wealth.

The German poet Goethe told us that when we fully commit ourselves, strange and wonderful things happen. Doors open and opportunities arise that never seemed obvious before. When you make the decision to pursue your vision, these doors should open for you as well. The rest of this book is devoted to ways to help open those doors.

DESIGNING YOUR BUSINESS

Jim Barksdale upon joining Netscape: "Look, if we want to be a leader, what we need to do is find a parade and jump in front of it."

Early American economic history is a tale of small business growth. When you find a product that sells or you can enhance the practices of an existing business with low revenues, you have a chance for a winning formula. The U.S. Army keeps a weapons museum at Aberdeen, MD so that researchers can reference solutions in the past. A little research on past business models can help you as well. Do you see anything here for you?

- Tom Watson took over the moribund Computer Tabulating Recording Company in 1914, renamed it IBM, and quickly doubled sales. The company had been organized 18 years earlier with good technology but poor marketing. Watson was the top salesman for National Cash Register (NCR) and started his career as a traveling organ salesman. The emphasis on sales still characterizes IBM today.
- SmithKline was a Philadelphia apothecary that supplied quinine to U.S. troops during the 1846 war against Mexico, spirits of ammonia during WW I, and amphetamines just after WWII. With impressive sales from each of these medicines, growth was a natural.
- Genentech was founded in 1976 by a venture capitalist, Bob Swanson, and a microbiologist, Herbert Boyer. Initial products were sold to other companies and they outsourced most corporate infrastructure such as manufacturing and sales until revenues were established.

- Digital Equipment Corporation, DEC, was formed by Ken Olsen, a research scientist at MIT. Olsen persuaded a Boston venture capital group to invest $70,000 in his plan to make modules for minicomputers. Olsen relates that the VCs made several suggestions, "First, they suggested that we not use the term *computer* because a recent *Fortune Magazine* article said no one was making money in computers, and no one was about to. Second, they suggested that five percent profit wasn't enough . . . so we promised ten percent. Lastly, they suggested that we promise fast results because most of the board was over eighty."
- Hewlett Packard's (HP) early years required the wives of the two founders to work at other jobs to keep the company afloat. In the 1970s their hottest product was a hand-held scientific calculator that they launched despite a marketing study that said people wouldn't buy them.
- American Home Products was organized in 1926 as a blend of nostrum makers. Their big break came in 1932 when they took Wyeth off Harvard University's hands, a gift from a deceased alumnus that the school did not know what to make of.
- Two engineers out of Texas Instruments started Compaq computer. Their inspiration began after IBM introduced the PC to what quickly became a huge market. Their idea was to manufacture a portable computer, a niche that IBM ignored.
- Warner-Lambert began as a simple pharmacy but steadily built itself through a succession of medications and consumer products.
- Nanotechnology firm MCNC in North Carolina, adapted an existing process for making synthetic polymers to make micro-actuators. They improved upon a technique that was already in widespread use and found a new application.
- Eli Lilly started mixing elixirs after the return of Colonel Lilly following the Civil War. It's been so good at not only mixing but also selling medicines that it forms the State of Indiana's biggest charity.
- Wang labs began after WWII with $600 from the founder's savings. He sold his data-storage device patent to IBM for

$500,000 and used the proceeds to manufacture electronic components and start another company.
- Microsoft's Bill Gates wrote a computer program for traffic patterns in Seattle when he was in the 10th grade that earned him $20,000. While famously called a college dropout, he argued formulas with Harvard mathematics professors while he was enrolled. Early indications were present that something was special about him and perhaps a signpost to invest in anything he touched.
- Pfizer started with a sugar cone wrapped dewormer, a blend of the first two partner's skills, one a confectioner and the other a pharmacist. What skills do you and your partners possess?
- Xerox's founder, Chester Carlson, a patent attorney and inveterate tinkerer, spent six years trying to find investors for his invention, until he finally found Battelle Memorial Institute (RCA, IBM, Remington Rand and GE all said they weren't interested). To keep his company (Haloid) alive, he constantly sold off equity until he had none left himself. The Board had to vote him shares.
- Squibb developed the first safe, reliable ether for use in anesthesia in 1858 and manufactured the product out of a small lab in Brooklyn. The profound differences in surgery that resulted gave them a base to become a giant company.
- Motorola built and installed the first commercially manufactured car radio in time for the 1930 convention of the Radio Manufacturer's Association, following a succession of failed products.
- Texas Instruments was founded in 1930 with an invention to use sound waves for oil exploration.
- Bechtel Construction started when the founder hired out his mule team to grade a stretch of railroad in Oklahoma.
- Douglas aircraft responded to a proposal by American Airlines and an upfront payment for a new aircraft that American needed to compete with United. The result was the DC-3 and a new standard for commercial aviation.
- Rockwell International began by making truck axles and used revenues and stock to help acquire over 50 other companies.
- Hughes invented an oil drilling head and the money just

rolled in. The Howard Hughes Medical Foundation is one of the largest pots of grant money in the world.
- Schering-Plough owes its success to its beginning when 16-year old Abe Plough mixed up a batch of cottonseed oil, camphor, and carbolic acid. He bottled it and sold it to door-to-door as Plough's Antiseptic Healing Oil.
- Raytheon invented a tube in 1922 that allowed radios to plug into wall sockets instead of batteries. An instant hit, the company later became known for its electrical engineering skills.
- GE received funding from J. P. Morgan to build upon its beginnings as Edison Electric.
- ITT began as an American-based firm operating public utilities in other countries. The acquisition hungry company largely coined the term "conglomerate" as it used its shares to help take over other businesses.
- 3M began early in the 20th century when St. Paul, MN was filled with adventurers and risk-takers. A group of them took a busted mining company, glued the tailings from the ore to rough paper, and became the premier sandpaper manufacturer.
- UPS began when a 19-year-old messenger boy named Jim Casey started delivering parcels for merchants with six messengers, two bicycles and a telephone.
- AT&T installed the first commercial phone exchange in New Haven, CT in 1878 and moved its headquarters from Boston to New York to be closer to the money. They got what they needed from J.P. Morgan.
- Whirlpool contracted with Sears in 1916 for the supply of two washers to be listed in the Sears catalog. They were quickly sold and Sears became a big buyer and the avenue the company needed to rapidly expand.
- Amana was founded by a religious society, cooperatively owned and operated. Their products have always had a reputation for integrity and workmanship, just like the colony itself.
- Stryker was a practicing physician who invented a mobile bed that was sold to the U.S. Army during WW II. Later he came up with a cast-cutting saw that was rapidly accepted by physicians.

- Honeywell began with a damper and an outside investment of $1,500 in 1891.
- Marion Labs prospered by marketing drugs that others developed. Their first in-house product was a calcium supplement made from crushed oyster shells.
- Donald Trump was born rich.

While many different avenues to building a really good company exist, what's most apparent is how many companies started with a fairly simple product that sold right from the start. In fact, while sales have the most credibility with potential investors, these early revenues form a base for you to find and develop other products that can sell. Roll out something fairly simple (and admittedly imperfect) and book revenues instead of waiting for the perfect product at some time in the distant future. Microsoft's first release of Windows was a far cry from ideal but each later version got better and better, all the way to the bank.

Forming your investment proposition

Startup companies with the right mix of technology, a realistic business plan and credible management are raising money even in the worst of markets, although its never easy. In order to join their ranks you need to boast a tenable, marketable, and defensible technology, often protected by patents but hopefully something more solid such as market penetration. Your investment proposition is weak when someone can easily replicate the identical item in a garage in a few months, unless you have a lot more going for you. Foremost, you need to give assurance that the company will have customers and will be able to generate revenues. An undefined market is generally unacceptable, everyone wants to know just who the customers are going to be. A veteran management team with a conservative approach to spending money is highly desirable if not essential. A big-name investor, manager or scientist is a huge advantage. 3ParData attracted $100 million because it consisted of nearly 30 engineers who came from Sun Microsystems. Given that the road to funding is so difficult, you want to be totally convinced yourself that your solution is viable and terrifically profitable. The first sale in developing your funding campaign is the one you have to make to yourself.

A checklist of factors needed to obtain institutional funding provided by one experienced venture capitalist includes: a good idea; strong management team; proof of concept—beta testing is a minimum requirement; pre-institutional financing support in place; laser like focus on customers—branded, referenceable accounts are extremely helpful; revenue traction; clear path to profitability; strategic partner; scaleable business model; industry recognized board of directors; first mover advantage or a space that is not overcrowded and undifferentiated; and a necktie (to be presentable to conservative investors).

Your idea.

> *Howard Schultz was in Milan, Italy when he realized the leisurely café model he saw there would work in the United States. The revelation caused him to literally shake with excitement and the Starbucks business model was born.*

A study by the *Financial Times* revealed that, out of 100 new business launches, 86 percent were "me-too" launches, or incremental improvements. However, these generated only 62% of launch revenues and 39 percent of profits. By contrast, the remaining 14% of launches—those that created new markets or recreated existing ones—generated 38% of revenues and a whopping 61% of profits.

> *Steve Bennett founded Software Warehouse in Birmingham, England with the help of a $60 (equivalent) weekly government grant. He sold it for over $50 million. Bennett's steps along with five other entrepreneurial stories in the U.K. are detailed at www.bvca.co.uk.*

Thomas Penfield Jackson, the judge in the Microsoft case said: "The code of tribal wisdom says that when you discover you are riding a dead horse, the best strategy is to dismount. However, at law firms and in established companies we often try other strategies with dead horses including the following: buying a stronger whip, changing riders, saying things like, 'this is the way we have always ridden the horse,' appointing a committee to study the horse, arranging to visit other firms to see how they ride dead horses, increasing the standards for riding dead horses, declaring that the horse is better, faster and cheaper dead. And finally, of course, harnessing several dead horses together to increase the speed."

Riding the right horse is the single most important thing your business can possibly do. Being on the right horse in a startup is more important than having a good CEO; it's more important than having a good team; it's more important than having good technical personnel; it's more important than having the right marketing strategy; it's more important than setting prices correctly; it's more important than venture financing. It's more important than all of those things put together because, if you are on the right horse, you will probably be able to figure out everything else. If you are on the wrong horse, you are probably dead.

Finding an opening for a niche solution.

> *Biomet was founded by managers of Bristol-Myers with the idea that major orthopedic companies, which were primarily divisions of large pharmaceutical companies, had neglected a service orientation approach to the real needs of orthopedic surgeons. Their new business proved right and they were quickly able to sell a range of support products using a network of existing distributors they knew from their prior work.*

Far-sighted business analysts suggest that business models are being transformed by four major changes in the nature of an emerging competitive landscape:

- The strategic space available to new firms is expanding. Neither products, services, nor industry structure need to remain static. You don't have to adopt a historic or conventional way to operate.
- Increasingly, the distinction between local and global business is being narrowed. All businesses will have to be locally responsive while all businesses will also be subject to the influences and standards of global players.
- Speed of reaction is critical. The concept of annual reviews is out of date and you need to think of incorporating new technologies whenever and wherever they occur, and integrate them efficiently into your organization.
- Innovation is the new source of competitive advantage. Your niche will probably disappear some day under competitors' imaginative moves and you'll be left wishing that

you had encouraged change along the way. There are many types of innovation but the ability to cut costs is one of the most powerful, as represented by firms such as Dell Computer, Southwest Airlines and Wal-Mart.

The Republic of Tea in Novato, CA received a real marketing advantage when bookseller Barnes & Noble agreed to sell its tea in their cafes.

Alternative street wear manufacturer, Dirtbag Clothing, skipped a $6,000 catalog and used a $350 website plus some guerrilla marketing to develop their $1 million revenue business.

Recognizing problems.

The most challenging financing problems are found in product innovations that require a long and expensive development period. Negative cash flows in such cases can extend over many years and last through both the development stage and even a rapid growth stage. A company may not begin to generate free cash flow for investors until the growth rate slows to a point where operating cash flows are sufficient to fund additional growth. The pattern of long development lead times followed by rapid sales growth is seen in many high-tech innovations such as pharmaceuticals, biotechnology, and some electronics. Large, well-established companies often perform much of this development activity since they have existing financing capabilities without the need to convince outside investors of the merits.

Firms that are easiest to fund externally are those with safe, predictable cash flows or assets that have multiple uses so they provide good collateral. Emerging technology firms typically have neither predictable cash flows nor good collateral. Since bankable assets are rarely available with early-stage emerging technologies, debt is usually not an attractive financing instrument.

Highlight flaws in your idea, a suggestion by Donald Sull of the Harvard Business School to help manage risk:

- *What is the phrase that pays?* The discipline of describing an opportunity in a short phrase forces the entrepreneur to strip away the peripheral aspects and distill an opportunity to its essence.

- *Why is the opportunity still here?* If it's so great, why hasn't someone done it already? Maybe it's too early.
- *What has changed to give rise to the opportunity?* Entrepreneurs need to point to specific changes in the competitive, technical or regulatory environment to explain the origin of their opportunity. They need more than the simple desire to be an entrepreneur.
- *What pain are you solving for the customer?* Opportunities to solve a customer's pain are often more robust than those that address less pressing desires.
- *How big is the market?* It's often difficult to forecast the market for a new product or service with any degree of precision. However, back of the envelope calculations can provide a rudimentary estimate of market size and provide a check on overblown ambitions.

Identify what is working.

Microsoft introduced virtually all its significant revenue-generating products after rival offerings were already on the market. Its first operating system, MS-DOS, came after Digital Research's CP/M was well established. Focusing upon what is selling well today and the right things that competitors are doing is a powerful check on your idea. If you're building your business plan for a partnership type of investment, it may not be a bad idea to highlight ways in which you can become a formidable competitor if another firm doesn't co-opt that possibility with an equity stake.

> *The impresario Billy Rose broke into the playwriting business as a young man in the early 1900s by researching successful plays at the New York Public Library. He discerned a formula, wrote a play based on that formula, and became a hit right out of the box. If you can't determine what is historically important to people, perhaps your business model needs a lot more work.*

Identify available technologies and funding.

An article in the *London Financial Times* by David Firn (6/24/2002) stated "Venture capital chief backs UK as biotech base" and notes

" . . . UK biotechnology companies raised record funds last year. Despite depressed capital markets, they raised . . . more than 25 times the amount raised a decade earlier . . . " "Brian Graves, head of physical sciences and engineering at Imperial College Innovations, London, said the government's $80 million university challenge scheme, launched in 1998 to give seed funds for spin-out companies, provide a crucial catalyst. 'The ability to fund spinouts prior to venture capital rounds is one of the most important changes,' he said. The scheme helped universities to expand their technology transfer departments and recruit people with commercial experience." University technical transfer groups in the U.S. are often seeking a licensing agreement on the basis of patents, a weak way to foster successful new companies. Both the U.S. government (through grants known as SBIRs) and the British government realize that seed funding for ventures is critical to their taking wing, something that universities, with restricted budgets, have not yet generally adopted. For a peek at some of the fantastic scientific resources the federal government provides look at www.science.gov. A number of university websites list technology available for commercialization and www.globaltechnoscan.com is a source for tech transfer marketplaces.

Intellectual property.

Author and attorney Andrew Sherman suggests that a good patent portfolio strengthens a company's attractiveness but needs to be part of a much more comprehensive business structure. Strong protected intellectual property and strategic partners who provide routes to market, brand credibility, and scalability are a few of the critical elements that investors focus on when making financing decisions. A company that successfully meets the challenges in these areas has a better chance of attracting financing. For the emerging growth startup, strategic partnering and outsourcing are key. These procedures reduce risk and make the playing field more level, especially when competing with corporate spin-offs.

> *Patents are not necessarily your most effective means of appropriating the gains from innovation. Howard Schultz, was quoted in the New York Times: "We had no lock on the world's supply of fine coffee, no patent on the dark roast, no claim to the words caffe latte apart from the fact that we popularized the drink in America. You could start up a*

neighborhood espresso bar and compete against us tomorrow . . . What we proposed to do . . . was to reinvent a commodity. We would rediscover the mystique and charm that had swirled around coffee throughout the centuries. We would enchant customers with an atmosphere of sophistication and style and knowledge . . . The best ideas are those that create a new mind-set or sense a need before others do, and it takes an astute investor to recognize an idea that not only is ahead of its time but also has long-term prospects." Starbucks relied not upon patents but on lead-time leveraged by complementary assets to appropriate the gains from its innovation.

A number of venture capitalists including a managing partner of Silicon Valley's Draper Fisher Jurvetson have advised companies not to make patents a centerpiece of their strategy. The expense involved in defending a patent can be draining and can rarely be justified for young companies. Instead of patents, think of the strength of your underlying technology and when you can be profitable. As entrepreneur Chris Carlson put it "Patents? Forget about it. Three years and $50,000 later you're spending all your time in court." Affymetrix had over 300 patents on its microarray DNA chips but a market that was growing by over 50% per year still brought in competition from firms like Corning, Mitsubishi, Motorola and 3M.

An expert in Internet law, Jonathan Bick, notes that you can obtain protection inexpensively by placing an invention in the public domain via the Web, and limit exposure to patent infringement suits. Bick, writing in the New Jersey Law Journal states: "An American Intellectual Property Law Association survey found that the nationwide median estimate of total cost through the end of discovery in patent infringement cases was $300,000 and that attorneys' fees for patent litigation could exceed $1 million. It may be possible to avoid this litigation cost by using the Internet to place an invention in the public domain. Internet publication offers two legal options to parties seeking to avoid becoming unsuccessful defendants in a patent infringement case. The first is to publish appropriate information on the Internet and use it to block the granting of a patent. The elimination of a patent grant will in turn eliminate the possibility of being a defendant in an infringement case associated with that patent. The second option is to identify appropriate information that has been published on the Internet and use it to secure a pre-emptive resolution of a patent infringement case. A pre-emptive resolution normally takes the form of an out-of-court settlement in the form of a cross-licensing agreement between the parties." Jonathan will provide the entire article with an e-mail to him at bickj@bicklaw.com. An intellectual property law information service is provided by the University of Maryland School of Law in their "Ask Art" column at www.miplrc.org. www.patentcafe.com is a comprehensive source of patent and corporate information with a special section for entrepreneurs and inventors. www.cafezine.com addresses the needs of young inventors.

Another protection is to offer a truly proprietary product. Premarin, manufactured by Wyeth-Ayerst Laboratories and one of the most prescribed pharmaceuticals in the U.S., has been off patent for decades. No generic drug firm has been able to produce a bio-equivalent version of the formulation and obtain FDA approval.

A briefing book by the law firm of McDermott, Will and Emery (www.mwe.com) outlines a process for producing intellectual capital, shows what can be protected and illustrates the kind of revenue that you could generate from IP. Some of the many corporate strategies they report include: Caterpillar, now receiving income from brand extension licensing to clothing and footwear; World Wrestling Federation with $150 million in revenues from licensed events, publications and merchandise; IBM with $2.5 billion in licensing revenue; and Greenpeace with $200 million per year from brand licensing. Nolo.com and Inc.com provide primers on patents that also illustrate what can't be patented.

Attracting investment money to you.

> *"I invest in people, not ideas. If you can find good people, if they're wrong about the product, they'll make a switch, so what good is it to understand the product that they're talking about in the first place?" Arthur Rock, a venture capitalist who helped found Apple, Intel and Teledyne, and gave $25 million to Harvard for a new entrepreneurial center*

You could have the smoothest presentation, a business plan that answers nearly every question and is beautifully prepared, and still not get funded. Investments are made in people not in business plans. The latter are necessary but money moves when an investor has confidence in the people he's entrusting his dollars to. One of the founders of the huge venture capital group, Carlyle, told the story of how he missed out on a big winner. Jim Clark, doing a road show among venture capital funds for Netscape in the mid 1990s, came through and tried to sell this huge fund on an investment in the company. Carlyle decided to pass but the founder noted that while he didn't understand anything about the Internet and what Clark was saying, he was still so impressed with Clark that he asked his partners if he could invest $75,000 of his own money in Netscape. They said O.K. but as it turned out, he was so busy he never got around to writing the check and so missed out on $14 million for himself at the IPO price. What was most interesting, however, was not just another "could have been story" but that a decision to make an investment was made without understanding the technology! What does that tell you about what you need to do to secure funding?

Nearly any investor will be thinking about how he could cash in if he invested with you. A grand vision and growing the firm to substantial size are nice, but show the investor that along the way, they'll have lots of chances to realize their profits in cash. They're giving up the liquidity of being able to buy and sell instantly some other investment on a stock exchange in order to go along with you, so remember this sacrifice and think of exit strategies for them.

> *Jeff Bezos launched Amazon.com with $300,000 from family members (including his parents) and savings from his work at Bankers Trust, followed by another $1 million from local investors in Seattle. He did this when he knew few people in the city and the Internet was largely unknown. As an investor noted: "He came off as this likable guy with an unshakable belief in what he was doing." He told investors that there was a 70% chance that the company would fail and they would lose all their money. Bezos happened onto a website in 1994 that suggested growth in Internet usage was 2,300 percent, something that hit his banker's demeanor just right. He made a list of the top ten products that should be good to sell online, opted for books, decided where he needed to be for software talent, packed his car and drove to Seattle.*

Terms for investors.

Entrepreneurs usually suggest they are willing to give up a certain percentage of their business for an equity investment of a certain size. While you need to have in mind what you're willing to do, one of the older and better negotiating adages is: "Whoever speaks first, loses." It is much better not to be explicit in your terms, if you can avoid it, and find out what investors have in mind. You may be pleasantly surprised to find out they are so enchanted with your deal that they will give more for less—but you'll never know that if you're completely up front with what you want. Also, since they have the money, they are in more of a position to dictate the rules than you are anyway. Hear them out and find a process of negotiation that eventually leaves them well satisfied but also confident that they aren't investing in a pushover.

When you're working out what the investors are going to get for a certain level of investment, you want to be logical and be able to back up what you say. If you can find comparable companies that have gone before and their valuation levels, that's a fair first step. Make sure that you can confidently forecast a certain level of sales and profits in a three to five year time frame and you can work back from there. For instance, let's say that in five years you'll be able to sell $100 million of product and realize a profit of $20 million. If the average stock multiple on the S&P 500 is twenty, your company could be worth $400 million on the public stock markets. If investors put up $5 million for twenty percent of your firm now, that twenty percent would theoretically be worth $80 million in five years. You can discount that figure back to give a super return, but remember the average venture capitalist is looking for roughly 40% compounded per year so the figures have to be good. This is a simple structure that you can manipulate to generate at least one valuation, even if it doesn't prove realistic. If your expectations need to be lowered or if you want to change the returns to your investors, you can do so arithmetically, using at least a logical model.

> *Many professional investors use a multiple of past earnings before interest, depreciation, taxes and amortization (EBIDTA), which will probably be a much smaller figure that a future revenue estimate but at least you have a place to start. Bioinformatics firm, Informax, was sold for the amount of cash that it had in its bank accounts. Many corporate buyers are offering purchase prices of 3 or 4 times annual EBIDTA and maybe just one times trailing sales.*

Your business model can outsource and permit you to focus on your strengths.

Think about out-sourcing or otherwise reducing the areas that you have to build, fund, staff and be responsible for. CEOs of new firms often stretch their skills and feel that they have to do everything themselves. Sometimes this seems like an ego trip such as when MicroStrategy's CEO once claiming that he had to know more law than the lawyers and more accounting than the accountants. Barry Michaels at Adjuvant (www.adjuvant.com) offers a range of services that out-sources nearly all the early functions of companies and permits the founders to spend more time on the science or other favored aspect of the firm.

> *Outsourcing has become more popular for businesses of all sizes. ID Software has created computer games Quake and Doom, but they outsource everything else that isn't creative and operate with only 17 employees. Himmel manages old brands such as Lavoris and Bromo Seltzer but they farm out everything but their core strengths of marketing and advertising. Your niche and how well you address it will probably determine your success, and being able to devote your energies to company strengths makes sense.*

Focus on the market.

Define the market that you're going after, not the market as others see it. Good profit margins are based on want, not need. How attractive can you make your product or services and how good does it make your user look? In any marketing program you want to address the ego needs of your target prospects.

> *Far more success stories will have the phrase "found a market niche" than ever will appear "developed a revolutionary process." In the 1980s, Hewlett-Packard salesman Jim Treybig noticed that customers were taking two HP minicomputers and wiring them end-to-end so if one failed a backup would be in place. The buyers were people who felt their applications were so mission-critical they were willing to pay for a second minicomputer as a safety factor. Treybig designed a fault-tolerant computer that had a built-in backup and sold for less than two minicomputers, giving birth to Tandem Computers and its 10,000 percent return for early investors.*

Management needs to limit itself.

Too many founders feel they can successfully run a company and many do find they are quite good. The good ones are in the minority, however, and the sooner your limitations become apparent and that people with other skills are required, the better. Just because you've started the company doesn't mean that you have to be the CEO. Plenty of founders are quite comfortable as a chairman of the board and chief technical officer, especially when they control the majority of the shares and are assured their vision will still dominate. You can have all the influence you need while alleviating many management headaches that are best left to another. Ask yourself what you're really good at and the answer could give you valuable guidance.

Companies have a difficult time trying to market too many different products or technologies. Better to focus early on with your best bet and to throw your resources behind it, while keeping your options open if things don't go that well with product or service number one. The ego of managers that feel they can do everything and roll out lots of products or services at the same time has killed many companies. It's true that companies can do many things but the question is "should they?" Whenever you spread your resources among different or even competing areas you know that the original area is going to lose some talent, money, or emphasis. Big companies can do nearly anything in theory, but their best people are involved in the business they already have.

Business ideas.

> *The Sharper Image was begun by Richard Thalheimer who noted an ad in 1977 for a digital chronograph watch in Runner's World but the ad had no indication of where to buy it. He ran a similar ad with a blank for mail order when granted permission by the manufacturer. The ad drew and the watch sold. His next watch ad used his developing promotional skills to bring in $300,000 in profits. While a graduate lawyer, his earlier training in selling encyclopedias door to door seemed his greatest business asset.*

Harley Davidson's' resurgence after its near collapse in the early 1980s was earmarked by a fundamental restructuring of its management-employee relations. A strongly participative new management style invited union involvement in decision-making and encouraged collaboration on all levels. Carl Reichardt took over Wells Fargo and tossed out the executive dining room, corporate jets and froze executive salaries for two years, ushering in a period of remarkable growth. Southwest Airlines employees are encouraged to "think like owners." Whirlpool devoted 20% of its R&D budget to launch employee-generated ideas and was rewarded with its first new brand in fifty years. A moribund existing company may need as little as enlisting the human capital that lies untapped.

> *John Chuang and two friends helped grow Aquent into a $200 million company by starting a desktop publishing company in their college dorm. The three were primarily interested in working together and went through several different businesses until they found something that worked, a talent agency for creative professionals.*

The National Technical Information Service has a website that you can search and retrieve thousands of articles on scientific, technical, engineering and business related material that have been produced by or for U. S. government agencies and worldwide sources. Many of the articles have small price tags and you can access them at www.ntis.gov.

Responding to market opportunities and changes

> *Hewlett-Packard's first product was an improvement on existing oscillator technology and their first customer helped generate the cash to spur growth. That HP customer was Walt Disney for the movie Fantasia.*

While it's essential to have a business model that plots out where you're going, the assumptions that you're making and the resources you need, things will be different when you're up and operating. Examining nearly any innovation over the last 100 years, from the airplane to the personal computer and the Internet, shows that applications grow and morph and give companies their own lives.

Most companies have changed their plans in response to what develops in the economy and certainly to new technology. Microsoft is an obvious example that has reinvented itself several times. Their original business model centered upon producing programming tools like Basic and on to producing operating systems. It was Bill Gates who was still urging Apple in 1985 to license out the Macintosh operating system.

IBM, although at a later stage of its development than Microsoft, had to make a shift from the business they had been built on, electrical tabulators, into computers. Change was a huge source of stress for them and stresses like that have been too much for many firms to handle. Intel experienced the same thing with the shift from memory chips to CPUs. Successful companies have to make that kind of transition, and startups often as well.

Netscape is an example of a company that built a product for the market they expected but found people bought and used the product for what seemed the wrong reason. The important thing is that they do buy and that the company begins to understand what the market really wants.

> *The author of the old sales book "How I Made A Million Dollars in Sales" gave the example of how he learned what his business should be. As a young man he bought a load of art prints that were good and cheap at $0.25 each and, so he felt, sure to sell. He rented a booth at a state fair, put up a sign that promised the prints for $1.00, and waited to sell out. He waited a good long time with no sales but the booth next to him was packing customers in and soon was out of product. That booth was selling clear-plastic enclosed ant farms and the busy colonies were just what everyone wanted. The author bought the business from the other entrepreneur and started on his way to his first million.*

In 1999, Pulse3d.com was riding high with animation tools for sophisticated and expensive websites that included *The Tonight Show* and customers like Warner Bros. When a downturn in the economy stopped those heady revenues, they were forced to examine their business and what sites were really profitable. They found the best cash flow came from website offerings that provided in-house employee training, online learning, service and customer relations. With this new emphasis, Pulse3d changed its offerings to a technology driven site with easy to use tools that change boring web sites into animated 3D and interactive platforms.

> *A pharmaceutical company shelved a cold medicine because they couldn't correct the drowsiness it produced. Someone renamed it NyQuil and sold it as a bedtime cold medicine. It became the largest selling cold medicine on the market. Just because your product is good doesn't mean it will sell. It must be positioned correctly. That's what marketing is able to do.*

Changes in business design are coming faster and sharper than ever before and a company's ability to make shifts can easily spell its survivability. Philadelphia-based Rosenbluth, Int'l. morphed from being a travel business to one that provides videoconferencing suites as an alternative to travel. It also sells software to buyers to help them get the lowest fares, and to sellers as well to help them get their quotes listed first.

> *A number of entrepreneurs will tell you to "find someone in pain" to indicate that you'll be able to sell your solution.*

The *New York Post* reported that buttoned down executives from IBM first met Microsoft's Bill Gates in the early 1980s when IBM was looking for an operating system for their PC. IBM staff members were dressed in blue suits while Gates and company showed up in golf shirts and loafers. At the fourth meeting, IBM reps showed up in casual clothes and loafers but Microsoft reps were now in business suits. Gates had originally suggested that IBM should investigate Digital Research's CP/M written by Gary Kildall but he quickly jumped on the bandwagon when Kildall couldn't be contacted in time for IBM's decision.

Competition

Don't be afraid of competition, especially if the main element in your market is a giant corporation. You may find that many of their customers believe they're unresponsive and simply uninterested in their needs, just the niche that you need to fill. Technology today ages quickly and corporate offerings based upon existing generations of product are potential targets. The key is people who are in touch with the market and can adapt products and services to changing needs.

> *In the 1950s, Xerox Corporation was facing heavy competition from other copying companies and profit margins had dwindled. They were developing an automatic copy machine that was truly revolutionary, but the costs of completing and introducing this machine were so heavy that going ahead formed a "bet the ranch strategy." To give themselves the best chance, Xerox commissioned two separate research companies to study the market. The conclusions from both were the same: the market is so small Xerox would never sell enough machines to be profitable. Xerox threw the studies away, introduced the machine, which sold (leased) incredibly well, and became a stock market star for the next decade. People inside the company had the vision while the outside experts could only*

survey what existed. They couldn't see the new market that the product would itself create.

Early resources.

Black and Decker started in 1910 with $1,200.

If you identify an incubator for your initial phase of growth you may be able to access a variety of resources that might otherwise be out of reach. Advantages of this route include: (1) fully built-out and equipped space, often with a focus on the needs of your industry; (2) below-market rental rates; (3) associated infrastructures such as university, corporate or government resources located on-site; (4) acceptance into an incubator gives credibility; (5) advice and referrals of staff and supporting services; (6) availability of interns, particularly in university-affiliated programs; and (7) the ability to grow gradually and without pressure from landlords. Bedfordshire, England's Cranfield School of Management established a curriculum around an incubator that also provided students access to more than $1.2 million in financing.

Neil Houghton suggests that: "*Free is usually more expensive.* As a result of our goal to deliver eyeglasses in the developing world, we have also received a lot of free help, and I appreciate that we have received it. However, there is often a hidden cost, and a reluctance to get the deal terms out and clear early, since it seems so good. But if the other side isn't in it for the long haul, or if the effort doesn't hit to the core of the other organization's mission, things get difficult or end up being counter-productive. Accountability is difficult. I think this experience can be generalized to other organizations, where something appears free but really ends up being more expensive." Harvey Mackay's book *Dig Your Well Before You're Thirsty* is a good resource on the topic and the movie *Startup.com* showed how early services that were rendered free, cost the company dearly later on.

Outside financing.

Typically, an entrepreneur seeks outside financing only after making a significant investment to develop the venture to a point where investors can estimate its value and when disclosing critical aspects of the venture to such people wouldn't result in the opportunity being easily appropriated. Usually, the assets in place are a sunken investment by the entrepreneur, while outside investment:

- Enables the entrepreneur to invest less of his or her own financial capital in the venture and to reduce overall risk by diversifying.
- Since well diversified outside investors have lower required rates of return than an entrepreneur who has put everything they own into one venture, increasing the amount of outside investment increases the present value of the venture. The entrepreneur can normally capture some of this value gain by retaining a larger ownership interest.
- An outside investor may contribute advice and information that enhances value, permitting the entrepreneur to share in the gain.

Types of financing for various stages of growth.

Generally, development financing comes from: entrepreneur; friends and family; angel investors; strategic partners; and SBIRs. Start-up capital comes from: angels; strategic partners; VCs; asset-based lenders (ABL); and equipment leasers (EL). Early growth investment comes from: strategic partners; VCs; asset-based lenders; and equipment lessors. Rapid growth capital comes from: SPs; VCs; ABLs; ELs; SBIC; Trade credit; factors; and mezzanine lenders. Exit capital comes from: mezzanine lenders; public debt; IPO; acquisition; and LBO or MBO.

The Chocolate Farm makes and distributes farm-themed chocolates and recipes and was begun in 1998 by then 17 year-old Evan MacMillan and his 14 year-old sister, Elise, with money raised from their parents.

Capital considerations.

Bootstrap financing includes: drawing down savings accounts; taking out second mortgages; using the credit line of multiple credit cards; borrowing from 401(K) plans or life insurance policies; keeping your day job or maybe using the income of your spouse, etc. A recent survey suggested that this type of financing is found in the following percentages of startups: personal savings (70%); credit cards 25%; loans from family and friends 12%; loans against property 7%; bank loans 5%; equity purchase by friends and family 2%; and other 12%.

- Venture capital can be substantial and bring with it access to needed management and other talent. It can be expensive, however, in terms of the equity that you must surrender and it is notoriously difficult to get (less than ¼ of 1% of deals submitted to VC firms are funded).
- Banks are not in the risk business and require substantial guarantees for loans. While a few banks are becoming more equity oriented, any loans provided carry the constant need for interest payments and the eventual payment of the entire loan—emerging companies need permanent equity capital that frees them from this overhanging problem.
- Angel investors are difficult to find. The networks that look to place accredited investors with entrepreneurial ventures have rarely born much fruit.
- Small stock sales to the public can be ideal since these equity investors are not as interested in the portion of the company they own as the story of where your company can go. Stock buyers are not all the same, however, and the difference between conventional stock purchasers and these affinity buyers is profound. The former seek a relatively quick capital gain in a liquid market and it is unlikely that your company can provide this—and are you ready for the possible headaches? If you need time to infuse funds and grow to reasonable benchmarks, affinity buyers are your answer since these are the ones who choose to understand your company or your industry and usually provide patient money that will stay for several years—an ideal investor without usual stock problems. Don't discount affinity stock buyers as customers, either, since the average stockholder in a company is often a loyal buyer, while also providing you an enthusiastic and unpaid sales/referral force. An SEC qualified stock elevates the status of your company and gives you worldwide credibility.

- Strategic partners could be your best kind of investor since they not only give you capital (in large sums) but they also give you resources to grow your company faster and better. They exist in related industries where they see an ability to share resources, leverage marketing infrastructure, speed product development, lower manufacturing or service costs, etc. Each dollar invested by a strategic partner rests on different economic terms than other types of investors. In theory, a strategic investor could lose $1 invested if they were able to gain $3 of profit in their existing operations by doing so—something that others can't cheerfully do.

Successful companies usually pursue all types of funding and arrive at their own formula. Generally, you should seek several different kinds of funding simultaneously since any money comes with some form of strings attached and needs to be individually examined. This kind of effort can be wrapped in one multi-faceted and economic plan, bypassing time and money hurdles that have strapped most firms. Different messages, approaches, valuations and constraints operate in each field and are separately addressed in good plans.

> *Konarka Technologies developed solar technologies for research materials at the University of Massachusetts in Lowell, MA. The University helped organize the company and securing a $2 million contract with the U.S. Army helped convince Zero Stage, a venture capital fund, as well as a number of business angels, to advance $500,000 for startup. They invested a lot more, later. It didn't hurt that a partner in the venture capital company was on the faculty, or that Zero Stage had made money on another solar company, or that another faculty member was a Nobel Laureate and agreed to join Konarka.*

Consider various forms of capital and learn from the resources you uncover.

Don't be tied to conventional sources. If your strategy is only to obtain venture capital or perhaps to have an investment banker sell stock for you, half the battle has already been lost. Imaginative financing, experimentation and an open mind are keys to the treasure chest. An amazing array of groups from churches to giant pension and mutual funds have made investment capital available for startups that are well thought out and decently presented. Other organizations such as insurance firms and capital pools such as hedge funds have also financed startups. Information on alternative investments is variously available from sites such as: www.assetnews.com; www.sdponline.com; www.marhedge.com; www.cambridgeassociates.com; www.independencefund.com; www.spectrem.com; and www.hedgeindex.com.

Sharing resources.

Along with incubators, perhaps one of your best strategies is to share resources, whether lab space or a CFO. Alliances can be formed with companies in your industry, either old or young, or with companies in a similar stage of development but with unrelated technologies. Physical sharing and incubation complexes can facilitate this process. Also, in a time when more economic power may be shifting to the consumer, being able to site yourself with similar firms may have considerable marketing value. By being part of an alliance, investors have greater assurance that peers approve of your operation and technology as well as suggesting that you are not alone in being convinced of market viability for a new technology, further lessening uncertainty. Alliances offer a variety of ways to enhance the competitive position of high-tech firms by providing:

- Opportunities to learn and acquire new technologies.
- Access to complementary technological resources and capabilities that are housed in other firms.
- Developing credentials and access to intellectual property, particularly when alliances involve universities or other research centers.
- Access to new markets.
- Minimizing costs by sharing or other access to resources.
- Possibility of influencing or even controlling technological standards.

Making the decision to go ahead.

"The unexamined life is not worth living." Socrates. A tragedy played out too often and the precursor to a tale of the person who never followed

their dream, someone who never broke out to form the company that they really wanted.

Thomas A. Stewart, writing in *Business 2.0* in November 2002, said that many entrepreneurs follow their gut instincts when making a decision. He gave a wonderful example of how Marine Corps tactics were changed when intuitive thinking by outside groups beat Marine Corps decision-making in the field. MarketFocusing is a consulting company that seeks to stimulate "bodily felt experience" as a business tool (www.marketfocusing.com).

> *Netscape co-founder Mark Andreesen in a Boston Globe interview suggests ". . . innovation always comes from the unsocialized 19-year-olds living in their parents' basement who probably haven't showered for a week and have just some idea. And these ideas happen on a pretty frequent basis—Napster was one of them. And they just come completely out of left field, they're usually super simple, and they always take everybody completely by surprise. They're always completely obvious, but only in retrospect . . . they never come out of big companies, they almost never come out of the venture-based companies. What's interesting about today, as opposed to five or ten years ago, is you're now talking about unsocialized 19-year olds in Russia and in Indonesia and in Taiwan and in China and in Czechoslovakia. And because of the Internet, they now all have equal access to all the information they would need to do anything they want to do, and they now have the distribution vehicle for their ideas." (Robert Weisman, www.boston.com, 11/11/02).*

SOURCES AND TACTICS FOR FINANCING & ORGANIZING A COMPANY

Lillian Vernon began in 1951 at her yellow Formica kitchen table in Mt. Vernon, NY, with $2,000 in cash. For $495 she bought a partial-page ad for monogrammed leather handbags and belts in Seventeen Magazine and generated $32,000 in orders by the end of the year. She built her empire as one of the first cataloguers. Hugh Hefner created Playboy Magazine in 1953 at his family's kitchen table and launched it with $600 of his own cash. Wilder systems sold one-year exclusive distribution rights for their software before even developing it and had $26,000 in firm orders before going ahead. Most companies today need a lot more cash than these examples show and the following are suggestions on how you can organize and finance yourself.

Depending upon the source of capital you pursue, you may find positioning yourself correctly is your greatest asset. Simply, what does this investor want or what interests him the most? How can you frame your proposition? This is not unlike the questions that you answer yourself concerning potential markets when you're developing products or services. Most entrepreneurs underestimate the difficulty of funding, and a narrow search and focus on limited sources and techniques is foolhardy. Lots of things impact on your success. How have your formed your company? Have you taken over something that existed in another dimension or developed an alliance? Your model is going to dictate how available capital is going to be. Although almost all companies use a combination of financing methods, depending upon their stage and capital availability, over 80 organizing and funding classes can be well defined:

1. Corporate startup.

Entrepreneurs develop their business idea or technology within a company and then develop it as a separate firm. Michael Saylor, the CEO of one-time high-flyer MicroStrategy, was employed as a DuPont engineer to mathematically model proposed new chemical plants and determine if they would pay back their investment. One day Saylor was asked to take on an extensive study for a new plant and he said that he would but he wanted to perform it outside of DuPont. Asked what it would cost, Saylor pulled a figure out of the air of $250,000, and was rewarded with the answer, "okay." That was the beginning of his company and led, before his stock tanked, to Saylor being listed as the 8th richest man in the country, while still in his thirties.

Shell Oil developed a technology for applying genetic engineering modeling to data abstraction, and spun off the technology into a new company as Kalido, Inc., with a $15 million investment. Sam Walton offered his idea for a new discount concept to his employer, JC Penney, was told they weren't interested, and started Wal-Mart. Marconi offered the chance to develop radio to the Italian Government and was also greeted with no's, only to find eager backers in Great Britain and the United States. Merrill Lynch set up an internal venture capital fund to help entrepreneurs within the brokerage firm's ranks. Merrill's emphasis is understandably upon technologies that will support and extend current financial businesses.

2. Corporate rollout of divisions.

Several years ago an entrepreneur who saw an underused asset wrote the Chairman of the Board of Eastman Kodak with a proposal to buy one of that company's divisions. Kodak responded with interest, met with the budding management group, and arranged the sale. The division had been under-performing and was really an orphan within that giant company, like so many other units of large companies. The new buyers had plans for the division and felt that it was just the revenue provider they needed to launch a more ambitious service. As it turned out, Kodak was particularly generous in their sale price and terms, and appreciated that the new company would continue to promote Kodak products. A twist on this relationship can be seen in instances when the unit in the field takes over the parent. The present day Reebok began as a distributor for a UK manufacturer but the Massachusetts-based firm was quickly showing the parent what to do. With a huge market, excellent sales and accomplished management, the distributor became the engine of the company and the logical successor. Express Scripts spun out of New York Life with 1.5 million subscribers at the beginning, later building to 10 million.

Big companies find that corporate insiders are often not the best people to run a new company since too few executives really fit an entrepreneurial mold. They often want a lifeline back to the company if the arrangement doesn't work out (failure for them is an option, unlike most entrepreneurs).

Thermo Electron and Safeguard Scientific are both companies that have spun out new firms by the dozens, and exemplify the type of company that develops a technology and wants to rapidly put it to commercial use in a new entity, a form of "skunkworks." Venture Capital firms are funding these kinds of firms, either immediately or following some added seasoning. Xytrans was spun-off from Lockheed Martin and eventually received $8 million in VC funding from SpaceVest. Lockheed and the U.S. Army had jointly invested $200 million in Xytrans' technology. Xytrans would also have the support of a $40 million Lockheed lab that came when the parent stayed on as a minority owner. Given the amount of investment that a corporation may have already made in a technology and often well-protected intellectual property, the appeal is strong. This becomes doubly so when the core technology team stays together with the new entity and when a group of customers is involved, providing immediate revenues and occasionally, even profits.

Drug-development firm Kalypsys was spun out of the Genomics Institute of the Novartis Research Foundation, and garnered $43 million of venture capital financing. Barrier Therapeutics is an independent company that was begun in a Johnson & Johnson subsidiary, licensed three dermatological products about to enter Phase III trials, and received a $16 million investment from J. P. Morgan Partners. Corporate partnerships and credentials can make it far easier to attract capital.

3. Corporate supplier or customer funding.

MicroUnity developed a computer technology for high-speed communications and persuaded several companies who wanted the technology to pay the development costs. Becton Dickinson provided $1 million to Tissue Genesis of Hawaii as part of a $4 million marketing partnership that saw the smaller company focus on products for Becton to sell. The economic climate of the time may easily lead to this kind of financing. When markets are soft and sales slow, some of your suppliers will be eager to book sales and advance funds to companies who will use the money to buy their goods.

4. Corporate diversification.

The world's second largest steel maker, Posco, in South Korea, put together a $50 million fund in 2002 to diversify and invest only in biotechnology. One of their first investments, done jointly with several venture capitalists, was in CreAgri, a neutraceutical company that developed an antioxidant from the pulp of olives. Posco is unusual because corporations faced with declining margins and entrenched competition typically find a related industry where cash in addition to their skills and resources have a chance of paying off, and biotechnology seems like a long way from steel. Perhaps the issue is irrelevant if you make money.

Corporate venture capital funds have become major sources of funding for new companies that can relate their business models to the needs of large companies. See Chapter six for a full description of these sources.

5. Purchase of corporate technology.

Xention Discovery of Cambridge, UK, was created following the acquisition of proprietary screening technology from, CeNeS, ltd. The startup, AEP Systems of Dublin, IR, in what amounted to a fire sale, purchased the hardware security business of Baltimore Technologies with venture capital money that they found was easy to raise on the security and revenues of that asset. More and more companies have been searching through their patent portfolios with the thought of uncovering some gems either for themselves or with the potential to be sold or licensed to other firms. American industry has too many stories of technologies that were passed over when a company didn't feel a discovery fit their existing business model. Corporate executives feel that a lot of these technologies are important assets that need to be harvested. An intellectual property consulting firm, Generics Group, is an incubator of upstarts and regularly combs through the patent portfolios of large firms. Looking for valuable business concepts, Generics operates out of Cambridge, UK, and has started a U.S. subsidiary to launch firms that parallel its numerous overseas successes.

6. Intrapreneurship.

A long word that means to nurture innovation outside the dead hand of a corporation's entrenched bureaucracy. Intrapreneurship is a conscious program of incubating technology outside of the firm and to profit by holding an equity position in the new entity. DuPont and Lucent among many other firms created new venture funds and groups to do just this. Xerox created the Palo Alto Research Center (PARC) in the early 1970s to develop new technology. Located a continent away from headquarters, too little of the potential from the innovations developed by PARC was ever realized by the parent. Ericsson Inc. launched a hybrid venture capital arm and small business incubator to generate new businesses for the giant Swedish telecom. Clayton Christensen's book *The Innovator's Dilemma* speaks to the problem big companies have in advancing technology and suggests such firms are poorly suited to be innovators. "No biological organism can live in its own waste products," said Alan Kay of PARC.

7. Leveraged Buy-Outs, Management Buy-Outs, Employee Stock Option Plans (LBOs, MBOs, ESOPs).

Springfield Remanufacturing Company was a money losing division of International Harvester that a number of managers felt needed to be re-directed. They became the buyers (MBO) and made it profitable, largely just by creating real incentives for the employees to speed up production. Instead of finding the cash to purchase an existing company, an arrangement is made to take over the operation of the corporation and to pay the purchase price out of future earnings—a tried and proven technique. Employees may want to be the buyers as well as the managers, or at least to own a significant portion and if so, ESOPS can be convenient sources of funding. Many companies fail to realize their potential under old and entrenched management, creating an opportunity for people with new ideas. Indian Motorcycle attracted a $45 million investment by Lazard Private Equity to expand this old brand when new management brought the company back to life.

8. Partner like a rollup.

Jonathan Ledecky used $200,000 borrowed from credit cards to start his first firm, a rollup of many small firms into one larger company that could do an IPO. The arguments he used with companies that were being bought were compelling and included lowering costs by eliminating duplication, group purchases, providing stock market liquidity to otherwise locked assets and vigorous marketing. Ledecky was able to secure investments of $3 million each from the venture arms of mutual fund giants Fidelity and Putnam. His company was up and running with the credit card money (18% annual interest) when a friend introduced him to Fidelity. Putnam kicked in when they heard of Fidelity's investment—very good investments for both, as it turned out. Rollups were in fashion on Wall Street for a while but fell from grace later when their vaunted efficiencies failed to materialize. Nonetheless, there is still something compelling about putting a lot of smaller operations together, forming a critical mass for funding or other purposes, and seeking to lower costs by eliminating overlapping functions and providing new marketing muscle. Besides, lots of smaller businesses simply have no good exit alternative and find that owning shares in a liquid company a lot better than letting things die on the vine, or possibly sold for little of their real potential.

9. Bootstrap.

Apple founders Jobs and Wozniak sold a Volkswagen to raise a little over $1,300, the cost of assembling and bringing out their first computer. Hewlett Packard began in a garage (equivalent today to the log cabin stories of presidential hopefuls in the 19th century) with $538. Building a business is an American dream and most businesses are going to be started with savings and other assets available to the entrepreneur. Its been said that you can never call yourself an entrepreneur unless you had to mortgage your house to meet payroll, but a little planning and thinking may eliminate that nightmare. Countless entrepreneurs developed their companies without salary, and many others used their earnings from a full time job to fund work on their new company, which they devoted time to on nights and weekends.

10. Friends and family.

Reader's Digest began with $5,000 from the family of DeWitt Wallace and published their first 5,000 copies with this money from their home in Greenwich Village. The price of the first issue was 25 cents apiece, sold by mail. Walt Disney turned to his Uncle Robert for the $500 that launched him into film production. Disney had lost his job as a movie extra and started the cartoon company in a Hollywood garage during a recession in the period 1923-1924. Bill Gates obtained the $50,000 he needed to license the software that became DOS by borrowing from his prosperous father.

Friends and family resources always carry special problems, however, because when things don't work out you may find good relationships become strained to the breaking point. In the brokerage industry it had always been a maxim for new stockbrokers to stay away from family and friends. While skills of new brokers will be minimal at the outset the more important reason is that people who are this close to you expect performance from you that you can't necessarily deliver. The same thing can be true for business startups. If you pursue these sources, do so with a strong and clear caveat that they may easily lose every penny they put with you (this won't necessarily quell their anger if things go sour). The average business that fails costs creditors, on average, only 9%. Investments by family and friends could be in the form of a loan to the new company, with the option to convert to stock at some pre-determined date.

11. Centers of influence.

Everyone has their own network through work, social organizations, family, etc., but not all of these networks are equal. Some people regularly connect with substantial investors or otherwise will enthusiastically join in the hunt for capital when they become enamored with a proposal. Alan Lindsay figured out an innovative way to capture rich copper ores from the tailings left by gold miners in Canada and the U.S. He configured a company to go after this resource and picked out individuals who he believed would quickly understand mining and who were well connected in the community. He arranged to see them, sold them on his deal, they invested and introduced him to others, and he was on his way. The company was eventually sold for a huge profit and Alan had established a new network of his own that consisted of happy investors. He's taken his management talents to biotechnology with a new company in British Columbia at www.mivtherapeutics.com.

12. Self fund.

Federal Express used a multi-million investment by its founder, Fred Smith, to start operations but they also soon secured venture capital, angels and several bank loans. While Federal Express is an intriguing story that extends from a graduate class idea through multiple levels of funding, several near bankruptcies and even a felony charge, the idea of using your own money to develop a business is attractive. A major problem is your inability to manage risk since you usually can't diversify your investments when you sink every cent into your new venture.

Al Wasserberger started Spirian Technologies with $5,000 and a Best Buy credit card. Spirian offers automated flat-fee IT services and now generates over $8 million in revenue. While Wasserberger didn't risk the millions that Fred Smith had to put up, he did have to quit his job and risk his career on something that no one could guarantee would ever work.

13. Borrow.

Our friendly bankers are the first ones to come to mind but think of other sources as well. Typically you're going to have to put up collateral but many companies have financed themselves with another party guaranteeing the loan. Black Entertainment Television's (BET) Bob Johnson received an investment of $180,000 from Liberty Media's John Malone but Malone also gave a third-party guarantee for a $320,000 bank loan. Johnson learned about the cable TV business while working as a lobbyist for a trade association, where he also met Malone. He felt that cable could segment and target audiences such as the black community just like print, a broadcast form of *Ebony Magazine*. He took out a $15,000 loan to start the company and found Malone to be a sympathetic listener and significant investor when the latter served on the board of the trade association. Malone was motivated in part by his belief that BET would be a good feeder of low-cost programming for his Memphis-based cable system. Malone's reputation in the industry spurred other investors later, including Taft Broadcasting, a firm also attracted by the synergies.

Silicon Valley Bank, Imperial Bank, Sequoia Bank and several others have been active lenders to high-tech firms, often companies that venture capitalists have already initially funded. These kinds of "entrepreneurial banks" have important connections with venture capitalists and other funding organizations and could provide the introductions to risk capital that you need. Other banks are reaching out to small business and one of them, SunTrust, is putting on "fairs" to show possible borrowers how to navigate through banking processes. Big Banks can be friendly to entrepreneurs and both Fleet and Chase have good reputations. Community banks offer an excellent chance for helping a young company and the Independent Bankers Association of America provides information on more than 5,000 community banks (800 422 8439).

Industrial banks are usually more accessible for business loans and insurance companies can be sources of long-term business capital. Check with your insurance agent for possible funding sources within their industry. Finance companies such as Heller Financial, The Money Store Inc., and AT&T Small Business Lending Corp., offer equipment financing money, working capital loans, and even specialized equity investments. Hundreds of smaller finance company players serve regional or specialized industries. A finance company will usually loan you more than the typical bank. Credit unions are also small business lenders and some were specifically formed to help entrepreneurs. American Express Small Business Services provides credit card holders with up to $50,000 in unsecured credit as well as equipment leasing and other funding. Merrill Lynch has a whole portfolio of small-business credit products. Capital Source at www.capitalsource.com has a history of arranging highly creative financing strategies against assets for such purposes as leveraged buy-outs, international expansion, etc. Asset-based lenders can finance firm orders and materially cut the amount of capital needed to pay for inventory, for example. The website of the Commercial Finance Association, www.cfa.com, has a long list of asset-based lenders and GE Capital has a free Guide to Asset Based Lending that can save you a lot of time while increasing your financial sophistication from www.gecommercialfinance.com. You can do some of this yourself if you sell certain assets to friends and lease those same assets back, you can arrange a fair price plus the cash infusion while your friend gets the tax deduction and income stream.

Mellon Bank invested $30 million for a one-quarter interest in a Brazilian merchant bank, but became impatient while waiting for returns. The Brazilian founder insisted that Mellon cough up another $20 million or its interest would be substantially diluted and accounting rules would require the big bank to report a 50% decline in the value of this investment on its books. Forced to bite the bullet, Mellon persuaded a wealthy family to make the investment but Mellon would put up the actual cash as a loan to them. Everyone got what he or she wanted by effectively leveraging the credit of the family, through the bank loan, and eventually were rewarded when the investment turned positive. A story that didn't have a happy ending involved a bank loan for Martha Gershun and her aspiring jewelry business. Gershun attributed her business failure and personal bankruptcy to a bank loan that had such onerous features that she couldn't maneuver to take advantage of opportunities or forestall disaster. Also, consider that starting with a loan may make later equity investments more difficult to do as the loan will have first call on corporate assets, something venture capitalists want themselves. If you rely on equipment financing, remember that high interest charges may not easily be taken out by bank loans later on, as some of the contracts will carry massive pre-payment penalties.

14. State government loan guarantees.

Maryland's Department of Business and Economic Development has partially backed loans for two pharmaceutical companies that promise to become good employers in that state. Increasingly, states realize that their power and credit ratings may easily leverage borrowed resources needed by young companies to grow, and state funds don't have to be tapped unless something goes wrong. For years, states and counties issued bonds for such things as industrial revenue facilities, hospitals, etc., where the low interest paid by AAA government borrowers could be effectively transferred to become the borrowing costs of young companies. Most of the lending was against plant and equipment that had a real value if the firm didn't make it. When Uncle B's Bagels was formed in Iowa (bagels from Iowa?) the founder used an industrial revenue bond for the money to convert an old factory into a modern baking plant. Vision Energy, a Los Angeles-based alternative energy provider, was offered financing for its mini-plants through state and county bonds that would carry interest rate costs under 3 percent. The State of Ohio is offering an approach with a $100 million venture fund for early-stage companies in the state. The money is coming from private investors but Ohio guarantees at least a 5% annual return to those investors, plus the upside, if things work out. Utah is debating a similar program, using a 5% guaranteed return in the form of a contingency tax credit. Otherwise known as "credit enhanced notes" the Oklahoma Capital Investment Board uses a tax credit-backed guarantee to borrow from banks, and the Oklahoma Development Finance Authority issues reserve fund-backed notes.

15. Export incentives.

The Export-Import Bank of the United States has several programs to assist US companies that can sell abroad and a number of states have extensive overseas offices just for this purpose. States such as California and New York as well as many smaller ones have offices in cities such as Shanghai or Milan that exist solely to help you make sales abroad. World Trade centers are located in a number of US cities as well as abroad, and house a range of services to make you an international player. Maryland will give small ($5,000) grants to firms to pay for export related visits, etc. by firms located in the state.

16. Incubators.

Andover, MA-based CMGI was an incubator that focused on Internet companies and became one of the hottest stocks of the late 1990s before taking a memorable dive, from over $170 to under 30 cents a share. Many other commercial incubators sprang up during the period with services and cash to promising new companies. When the markets became weak, commercial incubators across the country quickly closed their doors. Incubators today are thriving but they're the ones that are run by states, counties and universities, all organizations that put a profit motive well down on their list of objectives and have public funds backing their efforts. The State of Virginia has 23 incubators and the Greater Washington Initiative of the Board of Trade lists 20 more along with a list of services, contacts, etc. at www.greaterwashington.org.

www.Mdbusinessincubation.org lists the 11 incubators currently in that state. The Council for Entrepreneurial Development in Research Triangle Park, NC lists ten there along with an excellent website for money and training at www.cednc.org. You'll find similar state initiatives exist across the country. The National Incubation Association in Athens, OH has a website at www.nbia.org and can help you locate a convenient site. The Max Hansen Group keeps a directory of 486 incubators belonging to 250 parent companies around the world at www.maxhansen.com. Cordis helps you find a nearby incubator for European firms with a search through their website at www.cordis.lu and more information at http://europa.eu.int. Other quasi incubators exist such as Cal Tech's Technology Ventures Program and Stanford University's Technology Ventures Program, both teaching entrepreneurial skills to computer scientists and engineers. www.clusterdevelopment.com has worked with a number of states to design incubators.

Mindspring, one of the nation's largest Internet service providers, started at Georgia Tech's Advanced Technology Development Center, an incubator. Mapinfo was born at Rensselaer Polytechnic Institute's incubator in Troy, NY. In Texas, Austin's Technology Incubator has 50 companies that have graduated from their space and they continue to take in new ones. La Guardia Community College in Queens, NY received a $7.5 million grant from the state in 2002 to start an incubator, planned as the first of nearly a dozen for New York campuses and companies. The Springfield [MA] Enterprise Center (S.E.C.) is an incubator that routinely helps clients make contacts with potential funders. The S.E.C. also helps polish the funding pitches and Executive Director, Fred Andrews in American Venture Magazine stated, "Local bank presidents have said they are very interested in any of our clients because they know they are much more 'bankable' than other small businesses." Many incubators are highly specific to certain industries, markets or technologies, suggesting you narrow your focus when searching for a home.

17. Partnerships.

Millennium Pharmaceutical carved out some of their drug projects to leverage a small amount of venture capital into $700 million in partnership deals, selling drug development rights that didn't fit well with their current model. A number of symbiotic relationships have also worked out when the excess space of a firm was rented out to another. Law firms and investment counselors would be one example and accounting firms and insurance brokers is another. State economic development offices overseas will often help you negotiate foreign partnerships.

Variagenics, Inc., of Cambridge, MA partnered with Hyseq Pharmaceuticals of Sunnyvale, CA to create a new company through what they called a "reverse triangular merger." Variagenics' had been working to develop therapeutics based on the genetic structure of individuals but was experiencing results that were too slow and expensive. Instead of continuing their own work, they took the $60 million in cash they had left and invested it in the new company to help Hyseq's clot dissolving drug candidate through clinical trials and on to possible regulatory and commercial acceptance. Many companies with considerable assets but poor margins or uninteresting markets, should reposition themselves with a partner that could offer something exciting. Cheaper still is the route path taken by Darien Dash with his company, Digital Divide. Without access to funding sources, he built his company through partnerships with CompuServe and AOL. Dash found that he could build on top of their networks and offer specific content to subscribers. Digital later extended their partnering to offer hardware solutions with Hewlett-Packard and Applied Digital Solutions.

18. Joint ventures.

Alliance Pharmaceuticals negotiated a marketing agreement with Baxter Pharmaceuticals. Alliance would receive up-front licensing fees, milestone payments and royalties when any of their drug candidates made it through to commercialization. In high-tech industries it's common to find larger companies forming relationships with younger firms to develop products. They then use their own existing and extensive manufacturing, distributing, regulatory and marketing organizations to successfully commercialize those products. The larger company usually provides up-front financing and, in a number of instances, has bought the young company outright once development is completed. Mitsubishi-Tokyo Pharmaceuticals made a substantial equity investment in Cleveland, OH-based Quark Biotech while also promising to fund research and to collaborate with their scientists. Quark's deal calls for royalties on products they develop for Mitsubishi as well as their receipt of milestone payments from the big Japanese firm.

19. Business angels.

(See chapter seven) Wealthy individuals have played a key role in bringing technologies and good business ideas from the workrooms into the salesrooms. The example of Henry Ford given in the front of this book noted his reliance on angel financing. When Alexander Graham Bell formed the nation's first telephone company, AT&T, a Boston lawyer named Hubbard and a leather merchant named Sanders put up the money for the company. It was Hubbard's idea to use a form of franchise to generate added capital and keep the company focused on nationwide service, leaving local battles and problems to people who were on the spot. More recently, Advanced Ultrasound Imaging of Scottsdale, AZ, made presentations before five branches of the Gathering of Angels, raising about $600,000 from twenty investors. There are many angel groups in North America, a number of them referenced in the later chapter. Goodman's Angel Investor Network, for example, is a new Toronto-based angel group and others are continuing to form, often with a mixture of social and business interests. Angels will often be found in the ranks of corporate executives and as investors in hedge funds.

20. Investment clubs.

Non-traditional sources of seed business capital such as clubs can be a supplier of investment capital for you. There are tens of thousands of them in the U.S. and with a downturn in the stock market, their monthly contributions may be sitting in cash, waiting for an investment that doesn't record an instant loss on the daily investment pages. Clubs can be found in neighborhoods, churches and synagogues, or organized around any number of concepts. Many of these have been around for a long time and have significant assets. If you can make a presentation before a few clubs you automatically address a possible investment by their individual members as well, so pick fairly rich clubs.

21. Venture capital

(See chapter five). This is the funding source that more budding entrepreneurs feel is their logical backer and the one that more business school graduates believe is necessary to develop a true "A" list type of company. The truth is that venture capitalists fund only a tiny portion of startup companies and are a much better source of capital when a company has already developed and found other funding to absorb early risks. The "nos" so often heard by hopeful entrepreneurs come because venture capital simply isn't the right resource. Raven, Inc., with a world-class scientist as head, attended an annual life-sciences conference where the company was introduced to several venture capital firms. Their first $2.3 million had to come in from friends, family and former colleagues, but when it did and the concept was proving out, $20 million came in from VCs. (It helps to have revolutionary science, as Raven was able to boast). Astex Technology, a structural proteomics company co-founded by Cambridge University's head of biochemistry, raised start-up finance from a British pharmaceuticals company (Abingworth) and a US venture capital firm, simultaneously.

Venture capitalists tend to act *en masse* and being in the forefront of trends can be critical. Martin Spencer had no trouble raising money from VCs in the 1990s for an application service provider (an ASP, when they were hot) but after 4 years he still hadn't lined up any VC money for an out-of-favor robotics application. (A German robotics company with a proteomics application was able to generate $16 million in seed financing from public and private funds in that country, however, so perhaps looking for money overseas isn't a bad idea.) Sun finished their first year in the black and that impressive performance led to serious inquiry by VCs who felt this made them viable. Unlike most startups, Sun operated on a shoestring without expensive marketing, sales, support, advertising or PR, and therefore could generate more impressive numbers to show the VCs.

Venture capitalists either create a number of companies or actively solicit companies to invest in within certain areas. The entrepreneur in residence (EIR) is a concept whereby an idea is fleshed out by an experienced manager within the venture fund itself and then spun-out as a new company. A general partner at Foundation Capital said that 30 to 50 percent of their projects began as EIRs. BroadBus Technologies, Inc. was working on a new video-on-demand technology that Battery Ventures separately sought out. Before leading a $12 million investment, Battery executives went around talking to potential clients to insure that its feelings about the technology were correct. Principals of venture capital firm Draper Fisher Jurvetson went to the NIST to see what companies were receiving nano-technology funding, and then contacted those firms to see if they were good prospects for venture funding. If you can help these firms with investments they already made by presenting a model for change (and rescue), you may find a very receptive ear.

"We're doing a lot more due diligence now before we give a 'No' decision." A venture capitalist explaining why they weren't funding pre-revenue companies.

22. Foreign venture capital.

While U.S. funds have made large investments in European and Asian companies, the flow back from foreign funds has been small. Integrated Genomics of Chicago received an investment from a German venture capital fund but the U.S. company bore a strong resemblance to a European firm and was already booking solid profits. Differences exist between U.S.-based VCs and those that have sprung up overseas. Gaithersburg, MD Stem Cell, Inc. took in funds only from European based firms because those investors offered better terms than they could find domestically. Sucampo Pharmaceuticals, a U.S. company that develops drugs in gastrointestinal and other fields, has five recent venture capital investors who are all Japanese—Mizuho Capital, Diamond Capital, Fujisawa Pharmaceutical, Orix and UFJ Capital. Maryland-based Capital Genomix received $1.1 million from Korean Biotech Investment Capital and Woori Investment Capital, both in Seoul. Capital Genomix made a presentation to foreign investors at a forum in New Jersey and also found better terms and valuation overseas than domestic offers. Bartech Systems International received $10 million from European investors including Indufin and Defi Investment, without either the diluting provisions demanded by U.S. firms or other rigorous terms, characteristic of domestic VCs.

A capital fund of $70 million has been formed in London to support small businesses that are not yet attractive enough to interest major venture capital firms. The U.K. government's Regional Development Initiative collected funds from Barclay's Bank, pension funds, and the European Investment Fund, and expects to stimulate added private investment in the sector. Many young Israeli companies have felt they needed a U.S. or European location to be considered a world-class firm and have sought affiliations with funds and companies located in those areas.

Venture capitalists in Taiwan including The China Development

Industrial Bank invested $5 million in U.S. biochip startup Aviva Biosciences. The condition imposed on the founders was that they would take the technology, developed on the mainland with Beijing-based Capital Biochip, into a U.S.-based company. The U.S. was felt to be the best market as well as a better area for biotechnology startups with products that could quickly reach commercial acceptance. The People's Republic of China is investing considerable assets in biotechnology and will develop many new companies. The China Venture Capital Association (CVCA) claims they have 50 venture capital companies with a total of $40 billion under management. CVCA looks to Chinese universities for technology to launch companies or spin-offs created at the schools, and the prestigious Tsinghua University provides both technology and some investment funds. Many Chinese funds have partnered with American VCs and the founders of several first worked for American venture capitalists. Warburg made a 1,000 percent return on its investment in AsiaInfo and 300 percent on its bet with MediaNation in Hong Kong. IDG Ventures recorded a 65% profit it made on investing in over 100 Chinese companies. The law firm of Heller Ehrman sponsors seminars on establishing a wholly owned foreign enterprise in China (www.hewm.com).

The World Bank's International Finance Corporation invested $10 million to assist a California venture capital firm make information technology investments in India. New Path Ventures combines this money with traditional capital providers in an incubator model to use venture capital as a stimulus for business development in the Asian sub-continent. The Indian Venture Capital Association suggests at least $1 billion per year is being invested in new firms by local groups in India. VC firm U.S. Benchmark raised a total of $260 million for investment in Israeli-based companies involved in communications networks, chips and optic markets.

23. Venture capital rollout.

Genentech was formed as a partnership between a VC, Bob Swanson, and a scientist, Herbert Boyer of Stanford, the co-discoverer of the recombinant technique of DNA gene-splicing. Swanson simply called him up and made the proposal. Oxford Bioscience Partners provided seed funding for Avalon Pharmaceuticals, which received a Series A round six months later, and a $70 million Series B round eighteen months after that. Firms such as Kleiner Perkins, Menlo Ventures and

Greylock have helped create many successful companies. Some of the partners in VC firms think up the ideas for new companies and then look for managers and scientists to fulfill their visions.

24. Social venture capital.

Most VC firms indicate areas of specialization, geographic preference, and types of companies or technologies they seek but a number of funds are principally oriented to social or environmental arenas. Timbuk2 Design needed money for its pretty unromantic business of making messenger bags. The founder wanted to expand the reach of his website but he also wanted to increase production in his factory, located in the San Francisco Bay area. Silicon Valley Community Venture (SVCV) advanced him $2 million on the twin criteria that it made good economic sense and that it would help create jobs in a low-income section of the city. SVCV invested $250,000 in Vida furniture on the same basis, and also provided a free advisory program with mentors in finance, marketing and strategic planning. The Sustainable Jobs Fund (www.sjfund.com) in Durham, NC provided $266,000 to Container Technologies Industries in Helenwood, TN, when it demonstrated employment impact.

Community development funds were introduced in 1968 with the Kentucky Highlands Investment Corp. first out of the chute. The Community Development Venture Capital Alliance (www.cdvca.org) now lists many more including the Boston Community Venture, the Rural Development Fund in Seattle and Portland, Cascadia Revolving Fund, New York Community Investment Company, Coastal Ventures Limited Partnership and MMG Ventures. CDVCA also references a number of fund profiles including several that operate overseas. SEAF Bolivia, for instance, is an $8.6 million fund that focuses on Bolivian enterprises (e-mail the fund manager John Bays, johnbays@aol.com). Some of the current projects in Bolivia include JOLYKA, a high-quality wood looring manufacturer that sells in the U.S. and European markets, Virtualismo, an Internet portal, and Service Pro, a developer of software for the gas industry. Case studies and primers on community development investors are available from CDVCA. The Investors' Circle is a non-profit national network of angel and institutional investors, foundation officers and entrepreneurs who seek to balance financial, social and environmental returns, accessed at www.investorscircle.net.

The Investors' Circle has provided over $80 million to 120 companies and venture funds.

Columbia University in New York City has a Research Initiative on Social Entrepreneurship (RISE) under the direction of Professor Catherine H. Clark (cathy@cathyhc.com). In concert with the Lang Center for Entrepreneurship and Social Enterprise Program, she's conducting a national survey of early stage social private equity and venture capital funds across industry and social purpose areas. Professor Clark founded one social venture fund herself and advises the National Social Venture Competition, a partnership among Columbia, UC Berkeley and the Goldman Sachs Foundation to reward social ventures in the U.S. and overseas. Commons Capital is a Boston social venture fund that invests in health, energy, education and the environment. Kleiner Perkins guru John Doerr created a philanthropic fund in San Francisco for education businesses and other social venture funds operate in many cities including Washington, D.C. and Seattle, WA.

A social sector fund is planned in the U.K. as an $80 million demonstration project to show that returns—at least matching venture capital—can be generated by investing in profit-oriented companies in the education, healthcare and renewable energy sectors. Catalyst, a London venture capital firm will take the lead in a teaming launch with *The Big Issue*, a magazine that aids the homeless.

Increasing pressure on university endowments and other pools of capital to make more socially responsible investments may easily alter the direction of investing by venture capital and pension funds. Conventional investing may need to take on some aspect of meeting social needs, even if the funds aren't exclusively earmarked for such projects.

25. Regional funds.

Tazz Networks of Providence, R.I. received $7.7 million in early financing from a group of venture capital firms that included Point Judith Capital, a small Providence-based fund that focuses on Rhode Island and southeastern Massachusetts, and Slater Center, a Rhode Island technology fund. Tazz provides a platform for network service providers to improve subscriber management and services, and expects to partner for distribution. Regionally based funding groups are good places to start even though they may not have all the capital you need. Slater and Point Judith can maintain close contact with a young company and give other funds the confidence that local oversight will be in place so that they can decide to add their money as well. Similar funds exist in most parts of the U.S. and you'll probably find one in your area.

26. Government venture capital funds.

In-Q-Tel in Washington, D.C. was formed by the Central Intelligence Agency in 1999 to foster cutting edge technologies they felt would advance their own capabilities. With an early $150 million the idea was to funnel money into young firms that promised developments in areas the CIA felt would help their mission (www.cia.gov). The agency felt the government was being left behind relative to the developments in Silicon Valley and they wanted their needs to be addressed. Early companies included imagery analysis, pattern recognition, profiling agents, knowledge management and information security applications amidst many others. Companies receiving funding have a good chance of selling their completed work to the CIA and obtaining other government and commercial contracts, so an investment by this group brings special dividends.

The premise for In-Q-Tel is much like that of similar pools of capital formed by corporate America where the return on the investment is less important than finding ways to promote the mission of the parent organization. In fact, In-Q-Tel is a non-profit. The feeling in the government is positive about this experience and the U.S. Army is asking for $25 million to create a similar venture firm for power and energy technology. The Navy is developing plans for a fund as well and both NASA and the U.S. Postal Service have hopes of their own. The new Homeland Security Agency is allocating $500 million for their version of the Department of Defense's popular Defense Advanced Research Projects Agency.

27. Virtual companies.

The gene delivery company Targatech was formed within the University of Connecticut under the sponsorship of a venture capital firm. Targatech operated as a virtual company for three years before the VCs arranged for its acquisition. Without needing added rounds of investment, the founders effectively cut out the middleman and were able to receive a maximum return on the investment. The University provided most of the facilities on contract, making it virtual, and only a handful of professionals were needed to run the company.

The Virtual Company (TVC) is a different approach to the essential concept that has been developed in the U.K. at www.businesslinkwessex.co.uk. Business Link Wessex starts with the invention, the earliest idea stage, and adds managers, technicians and business development people with the inventor to form a company. The group puts together the business plan, seeks early stage funding (often with Britain's SMART program, see 41 below) and nurtures the process to a point where the company can operate on its own. A study on their website details the process, illustrates case histories, speaks to the formation of partnerships and shows the steps to obtaining grants.

28. Small Business Investment Companies (SBICs).

SBICs are a form of venture capital that uses special government-leveraged funds to make equity or debt money available. SBICs date their creation back to 1958 and today are found under the sponsorship of many banks. They have helped over 90,000 businesses move ahead including Apple Computer, Intel and Federal Express. Many of them are oriented towards making loans, often considerably smaller than mainstream venture capitalists typically want to advance, although they're looking for the same criteria of a well-developed business model and capable managers. Check out background on the program and SBICs that are near you at www.sba.gov. A number of today's most experienced venture capitalists received their early grounding by working in an SBIC.

29. Foundations.

These organizations have grant funds available for projects that fit their charters and often have good funding connections with other types of investors as well. While the great bulk of these funds go to non-profit organizations for programs in health and education, showing how effective in delivering services such as these through a for-profit company may easily win you some impressive grant money. The Gates Foundation will provide grants to profit-making companies if they are engaged in and specifically use those resources to further a charitable purpose. The Gates Foundation has targeted immunization programs among others, for its largesse. Don't shut the door on foundations if you can make a good case.

The Harvard Endowment Fund was an early investor in venture capital funds. Making a case for a direct investment when you have a link to a particular interest of such funds could make the difference for you.

30. Ethnic groups.

A partnership of Native American tribes from California and Wisconsin took some gambling proceeds and invested it in a new hotel near the Smithsonian Institution National Museum of the American Indian. The $43 million hotel will employ a number of Native Americans in both managerial and service jobs. Tribal leaders are interested in building economic bases for their members well past gambling and other reservation-based enterprises. If you have a company that can locate a manufacturing plant or other business to be convenient and opportunistic for Native Americans to find employment, you may find a willing source of money to help you. Valerie Red Horse runs an investment-banking firm, Native Nations Securities, on both the east and west coasts, that specializes in bond offerings for growing companies and has important contacts within the Native American community (Valerie@red-horse.com.) The National Center for American Indian Enterprise Development in El Monte, CA has an informative website at www.ncaied.org.

Ethnic groups provided money for members to start businesses throughout the 19th and 20th centuries in the U.S. and, to a lesser extent, are still doing so today. Pooled savings plans operate as a rotating-credit arrangement where members can access funds that are aggregated from the weekly or monthly contributions of members. Korean immigrants call their associations Kyes. Pakistanis call them Kommittis. Ethnic Chinese form Huis in the U.S. and Tontines in France. A number of banks including Chase Manhattan and Fleet Boston recognize these deposits as a measure of creditworthiness for a new firm. Following the 1992 Los Angeles riots, a Korean-American bank in Los Angeles offered existing customers loans of up to $50,000 without collateral to stimulate economic growth. Not one of the fifty who accepted defaulted.

The Indus Entrepreneurs (TIE) is a decade-old group of South

Asians that forms an influential network in Silicon Valley. Hispanic-Net is a new organization in Silicon Valley that has been responsible for several companies but is seeking to mobilize their community for a real presence in the years ahead. The Latin Business Association in Los Angeles, CA has a website at www.lbausa.com. Also in Los Angeles, the Asian Business Association is at www.aba-la.org and Black Business Association at www.bbala.org. The U.S. Chamber of Commerce has initiated a new "Access America" program to facilitate the growth of minority firms and extend Chamber programs.

The Milken Institute in Santa Monica, CA and the Commerce Department's Minority Business Development Agency (MBDA) reported that approximately 2% of private-equity money was earmarked for investment in minority-owned firms. Seeking to increase that proportion, MBDA has developed an Equity Capital Access Program in concert with the Emerging Venture Network, to bridge the gap between venture capitalists and minority business owners. The program is competitive and features classes on how to attract venture capital investments and other forms of preparation for making a funding pitch. The focus from one recent panel was on networking, developing a good business story and upon closing a deal. Of the 15 business owners who participated in the program in 2001, six received venture investments and the rest were reported to be in talks with possible funders.

The West Coast's Making It television show illustrates many minority business success stories and their website at www.makingittv.com has links to financial resources, corporate diversity departments, entrepreneurial training, incubation, certification, etc. Black Enterprise Magazine and Hispanic Business Magazine have growing followings in the minority communities. www.hispaniconline.com has links to organizations and exchanges to connect Hispanic businesses. An Internet community for Black IT people was formed by Anita Brown and is accessed at http://dc.internet.com. A Jewish community business network site is found at www.tribeofangels.com. General guidance for minority groups can be found at www.tmaonline.net and at the MBDA website www.mbda.gov. The MBDA website also lists seventeen types of loan or loan program.

31. Women-centered sources.

Flatiron Future Fund in New York and the Flatiron Foundation provide capital for ventures that serve minorities, women and children.

Ground Floor Ventures is an incubator in Hoboken, NJ geared to women business owners and in San Francisco, CA the Women's Technology Center does the same thing. www.womensforum.com is a partnership network of women who founded Internet businesses. Women-centered venture capital firms include Isabella Capital in Cincinnati, Axxon Capital in Boston and Viridian Capital in San Francisco. We regularly get reports that women have trouble being taken seriously by many traditional funding organizations even though women own 38% of all U.S. businesses. The National Foundation for Women Business Owners in Washington, D.C. conducts research and lobbying for women entrepreneurs. The Forum for Women Entrepreneurs and the National Women's Business Council sponsor conferences that have resulted in significant venture capital financing for female entrepreneurs. The Women's Business Center of Northern Virginia holds an annual conference for women entrepreneurs to come in contact with funding sources and gain help in marketing, etc., and can be accessed at www.wbcnova.org. Springboard Enterprises (www.springboardenterprises.org) does the same with a national focus, along with regular boot camps and some terrific success in aligning investment capital with new companies (40% of its graduates have raised capital from VCs and angels). Springboard is also developing an online Learning Center for women entrepreneurs and has recently added a program called Next Wave Alumni Conferences and one called VC Tune-Ups. The National Association of Women Business Owners has a website at www.ncaied.org and the National Association for Female Entrepreneurs indicates a number of financing sources at www.nafe.com. The Ewing Marion Kauffman Foundation and its Center for Entrepreneurial Leadership funded Springboard as well as grants to colleges for student internships. Kauffman funded the Women's Entrepreneurial Leadership Program at George Washington University, a set of course offerings that concentrate students on new venture problems.

The Diana Project from www.entreworld.com explored venture capital access by women-owned firms in a study examining eight common myths. The study provides a number of websites and organizations (WomenAngels.net, Seton Hall College's National Education Center for Women in Business, etc.) that support these companies along with statistical data that illustrates their potential. www.womenstechcluster.org has an array of services for both profit and non-profit organizations. The Women's Technology Cluster was formed by philanthropist Catherine Muther and her entrepreneurial foundation, Three Guineas, to create economic opportunities for girls and women (www.3gf.org).

Tara Godfrey runs a financial education company in New England for children and parents called "Independent Means." Among the variety of services she offers are "Camp $tart-Up$" where teenage girls spend two-weeks putting together a business plan and another, "Noise," to introduce teenagers to the business of music. In the heart of Silicon Valley, The Girl's Middle School of Mountain View, CA, provides an Entrepreneurial Program for seventh graders under the mentorship of eighth graders. The middle-schoolers form business plans, present to venture capitalists, and run businesses. The Co-Director of the Program, Donna Fedor, says "We've never had a company that didn't make a profit." Across the country, Youth Entrepreneurship Springboard Awards for talented teens are available in the 13-state Appalachian region with details at www.arc.gov/entrepreneurship.

32. Religious communities and non-profits.

An order of Catholic nuns took part of their pension fund and invested it in a Hollywood film in the 1990s and made a reasonable return. While it's always difficult to figure net profits in the movies, especially with overseas, video and DVD revenues looming larger and larger, this was a decent business proposition and the nuns proved receptive to the idea. (A matchmaking service for media and investors is run by www.starlightexchange.com.) A group of Trappist monks in Chimay, Belgium regularly invests a portion of their brewing profits in local businesses. You may have been turned down by venture capital firms and other traditional sources of capital but if you consider non-traditional sources of funding and a little more creative thought along with a terrific business proposition it could resonate with many different groups, including charitable order pension and other funds.

Educational Systems Corp. was a non-profit government contractor that provided support services for the federal Office of Economic Opportunity. Later, as other work came their way, they formed a for-profit sister company called Executive Systems Corp., and dumped commercial contracts into the new venture. The first company provided the platform, experience, facilities and marketing to launch the second.

33. Public sector pension funds

State employee retirement funds have more than $2 trillion in assets and have been frequent investors in venture capital funds. With the meltdown in venture capital returns in the early 2000s, they may increasingly be sources to make direct investments. Retirement Systems of Alabama (RSA) is a multi-billion dollar repository of investment money that aggressively seeks high returns to fund their obligations. They also have their eye on placing money where it can help the state economy. RSA bid $240 million for just over a third of U.S. Airways and provided loans and a rescheduling of leases for the ailing airline. They feel that 59 million passengers make for a good investment but also that future US. Air operations will be moving to Alabama. The Retirement System has a superior history of investing in downtrodden assets that later generate huge profits and they are willing to take a chance. RSA provided early funding for a Hispanic radio and television network that grew into a nationwide and profitable network.

The Wisconsin State Employees Retirement System has been directed to make a $60 million investment in state life-science companies to help mold a biotechnology industry there (see chapter 11). The State of Virginia normally has 5% to 10% of its money in venture type investments and in early 2002, with the stock market in poor shape, still had 6% of its money committed in this way. The biggest pension fund of all, CalPERS put as much as 4% of their funds into venture capital. CalPERS has also made direct investments including $122 million in Sports Capital Partners, an affiliate of sports marketing firm IMG, the group that represents Tiger Woods, among many others.

34. Labor union pension plans.

Labor union funds control hundreds of billions of dollars and are increasingly making alternative investments. Charlie Schoenhoeft was going hat in hand among venture capital firms with his broadband services provider offering. The economy had weakened, venture capital was held back and investor enthusiasm was a distant commodity. A private equity firm in Washington DC that represented union pension plans was willing to come up with the $5 million needed, once Schoenhoeft passed the due diligence test. As you could expect, union investments come with requirements for a generous equity plan for employees, training programs, workforce safety and other benefits aligned with the labor movement.

35. Investment banks.

Wall Street firms such as Warburg Pincus, JP Morgan, Goldman Sachs and many others regularly put together companies just like many venture capitalists, or otherwise run their own venture capital funds. Entrepreneurs may think of them only for the IPO route but they are active in private placements, mergers and acquisitions, and have impressive credentials and contacts throughout technical and capital communities. Houston-based investment banking firm Sanders Morris Harris formed an $11 million fund just to invest in functional genomics and proteomics companies, but has another $3 billion under management. Many smaller investment banks have come into being as talent has left the big firms to strike out on their own. New firms like Catapult Advisors and Revolution Partners have handled mid-level transactions and startups and are approachable, something their big brothers usually are not. America's Growth Capital was formed in Boston, MA by bankers out of huge firms that were acquired, and is newly focused on the New England market. The firm of William Blair in Chicago, IL has excellent Wall Street credentials yet remains accessible to young companies. If you have connections with some of the larger firms, you may prefer those with a solid commercial banking affiliation (or ownership) so that if an IPO market disappears they may have a funding alternative for you in-house.

36. Independent broker-dealers

Largely ignored by their well-known bigger brothers such as Merrill Lynch, the thousands of small broker-dealers that are found across North America (with good overseas connections as well) constitute an important funding avenue. These firms usually consist of less than thirty brokers but can house important specialties and access funding niches that prove ideal for emerging companies. Perhaps most importantly, while big firms won't give you the time of day, these people are accessible. Norman Swanton, CEO of Warren Resources, raised tens of millions of dollars by making presentations to broker-dealers through an organization known as FSX (Financial Services Exchange, www.FSX1.com). Smaller broker-dealers often have been formed by talented brokers who chose not to remain with big firms. Their doors can also house many registered investment advisors.

37. Commercial bank equity.

Your banker could be a source of investment capital as well as giving a line of credit or loan. Some of the most visible banks that make venture capital investments or "merchant banking" activities have been Chase, Bank of America, Fleet and First Union but many smaller banks are active as well. Honolulu, Hawaii-based City Bank formed a $7.5 million venture capital fund to stimulate small businesses in the islands. Large banks may operate separate VC companies such as First Union Capital Partners while others will have a restricted form of investing, depending upon their regulatory environment. The important thing is to get to know your bankers and use their knowledge to facilitate your funding needs. One banker with good international connections arranged to guarantee a company quick payment but arranged for their overseas customers to extend their credits over a number of months.

38. Small stock offerings (SSOs)

(See chapter eight) Registered stock offerings such as IPOs or Direct Public Offerings (DPOs), like Oregon's Willamette Valley and Jim Bernette, have been perfect fund raising tools for a number of companies. Bernette used thirteen of these small stock offerings to finance a successful winery and then a number of breweries across the country. The founder of Control Data, William Norris, and Dr. Ed Land of Polaroid, purportedly both personally sold stock on the streets of Minneapolis and Boston, respectively. Tom Ling began the giant LTV by selling stock out of a booth at a Texas state fair. Ross Perot used a small stock offering for EDS as well. Robert Kopstein, CEO of Optical Cable in North Carolina, used a DPO and became the best-performing public offering of 1996. After going through the registration process, two investment bankers backed out of the deal and told Kopstein that the stock couldn't be sold at $7.50 a share. He offered it directly at $10 instead, raised about half of what he was looking for, and then watched the stock go as high as $136.

More Americans as well as people around the world now own shares in companies than they ever did before. About half the households in the U.S. own stocks. Many of these holdings are in retirement funds, suggesting that most people are long term oriented and put their faith in the prospects of these companies. When bear markets surface and portfolios sink in value, it becomes ever more difficult to hold on, even when people are convinced they're right. One of the beauties of investing in private placements or in small companies directly that don't put their shares on a stock exchange is that the investor is freed from the vagaries of the markets and the disappointments and difficulties that daily fluctuations in price bring to the holder. This is one of the many reasons that investors should examine shares in companies that don't qualify yet for exchange listings, but have business models that can be truly visionary.

Private offerings are regularly used to secure funding for firms where existing connections to investors can be demonstrated. Grey Eye Glances is a Philadelphia "adult alternative" band that raised several hundred thousand dollars for a new album by selling interests in the album to part of its fan base.

39. Internet.

Using the Internet to find investors or make an offering provides an alternative to the traditional method of offering registered stocks to the public and can eliminate many costs for young companies. One of the biggest of these costs is printing and mailing and, since the registration statement can be placed on a website, can effectively eliminate this cost while speeding transactions. California Molecular Electronics sold stock through its own website and used the proceeds to further leverage a grant, and later a private placement. Many organizations will list your offering at special sites on the Internet but experience suggests that technique alone won't produce many investors unless separate and extensive efforts are made to make people aware of your company. This entire area remains uncertain and it is best to check with your attorney before launching any efforts. The SEC provides guidance as well at www.sec.gov.

40. Franchises.

Paychex, Inc. bootstrapped itself through a combination of joint ventures and the sale of franchise agreements, an enviable source of up-front capital. AT&T sold telephone rights to local carriers and countless other entrepreneurs have looked for similar front-end money. Tarid Faraq of Edible Arrangements is expanding his fruit offerings out of East Haven, CT by selling franchises for between $60,000 and $120,000, including a $25,000 fee and a 4% royalty. You can be either a seller or a buyer of a franchise, depending on whether you want to introduce your own business model or use someone else's idea. Many formal franchises are bankable commodities and you may find that lenders are more than willing to put up a good chunk or even most of the money needed to buy and operate a proven business franchise. I've seen instances where an experienced businessperson contracting for five or more franchises had to put up none of their own money.

41. Government grants.

This is a multi-billion dollar resource for young companies and is concentrated in Small Business Investment Research (SBIRs) and Technical Transfer Grants, detailed for you at www.sba.gov/sbir, program specifications at www.eng.nsf,gov/sbir and open solicitations at www.SBIRworld.com. PLI Systems in New Jersey couldn't raise the $5 million it was looking for from the venture capital community but obtained $1 million from the Department of Energy (DOE), $200,000 from the NJ Commission on Science and Technology, and $2 million in grants from the National Institute of Science and Technology (NIST) Advanced Technology Program (ATP, www.atp.nist.gov, see Appendix A). PLI convinced the feds they could save U.S. companies $75 billion a year and bring in an additional $10 billion in improved productivity with a software program to predict corrosion, not a bad promise. NIST is an agency within the Department of Commerce that makes a wide variety of grants oriented to improving businesses processes and new technologies. $2 million went recently to Cinea, Inc. from NIST to develop a technology that could foil media pirates who use a video camera to record movies right off the big screen. ATP awards are intended to accelerate technology research, but they're not designed to support product development work—that's supposed to come from you. You may also have to show research or technical affiliation with a university, a way of ensuring cooperation between academia and industry. SBIRs and ATPs have often been suggested as the best path for ideas that have little formal organization at the outset, but need nurturing. Links to all of the agency pages for SBIRs are at www.win-sbir.com/related.html.

Noesis, Inc. teamed with researchers at the University of Virginia to develop advanced metal fiber brushes for generators on U. S. Navy submarines. Receiving both Phase I and Phase II SBIR awards, the company developed the technology, earned a $9.5 million Navy contract, and now is actively commercializing the technology.

ATP has been called the federal government's first venture capital firm. They operate with a provision that any applicant has to demonstrate that they couldn't receive funding from conventional VCs. ATP solicits grant proposals from companies involved in innovative but high-risk research that have a reasonable path to commercialization. A number of companies involved in a promising area such as nanotechnology have received funding, including eSpin Technologies, Inc., receiving $2.5 million for a system that will let it manufacture nanofibers much more inexpensively than at present and in substantially greater volume.

Britain's Department of Trade and Industry (www.dti.gov.uk) operates a grants program known as SMART awards that closely parallels the SBIR process and permits small British companies access to funding from as little as $4,000 (equivalent) to over $600,000. The idea is to foster commercialization of technology and the formation of new companies. Background on fund availability in the U.K. is detailed at www.sbs.gov.uk/finance along with help on getting funding at www.localpartners.org.uk, www.nfea.com and www.smallbusinessadvice.org.uk.

The SCORE program of the SBA provides counselors and the SBA has hosts business articles including Small Business Financing Options at www.score.org. Most entrepreneurs have heard about SBA loans, etc., as a potential source of capital but don't know the many separate categories that money is made available for. Exports, seasonal inventory needs and defense conversion are several areas in which special SBA programs exist. Loans are usually made following establishment of the business and at least a little history. Valencia Roner, the founder of VXR Enterprises of Culver City, CA, started her PR and marketing company with $5,000 of savings. She was confident that a good-sized contract was coming her way and felt good about taking a loan risk. That contract never materialized but she went ahead and obtained several smaller assignments and used that income to justify a $50,000 loan through the SBA. With those funds in hand she bid and won a $250,000 City of Los Angeles Workforce Investment Board contract and was well on her way. Her key was approaching the SBA lender with actual contracts and letters of intent in hand, demonstrating that she was a going business instead of just an idea.

42. Government technical transfer.

Beginning in the 1960s with the National Aeronautics and Space Administration (NASA), government agencies sought to justify their research spending in part by demonstrating that their discoveries have commercial application. Marketplace success would mean that the new firms would pay these investments back through taxes, employment, licensing fees, etc. Technical transfer programs are common with government research laboratories, universities, independent research organizations, and even companies that are seeking to harvest their patent portfolios for products they can use, sell or spinout.

You can view patents the government has available at www.uspto.gov. The U.S. Defense Department is an excellent source for technology as are university programs such as those of MIT, Stanford, etc. Try www.DARPA.mil for a list of technologies that the military is looking for as well as a source of funding, if you have a solution to their needs. Los Alamos National Laboratory (LANL) in the Department of Energy has generated technology to found almost seventy companies in the last five years and has over a dozen employees on entrepreneurial leave. LANL technologies included a process for creating high-density microchips and one on complexity science techniques to help financial institutions predict economic crises. The Lab has recently launched a separate effort to develop an informatics cluster. LANL's sister lab at Oak Ridge, TN cut an innovative deal with Nanotech Capital LLC of Tryon, NC to commercialize nanotech research taking place at that lab. Nanotech Capital consists of just four entrepreneurs who seek to raise capital on the strength of this affiliation and use a network of universities to help develop commercial products.

The National Institutes of Health spends over $25 billion annually on biomedical research and actively promotes transfer of discovered and developed technologies to the commercial sector. The NIH website at http://ott.od.nih.gov will help lead you through the maze and you can talk to their staff about SBIR and other funding avenues. A number of prospective licenses and technical opportunities are listed at www.tarius.com.

The FDA has an orphan drug program that promotes treatments

for rare diseases, and can provide as much as $300,000 in funding per year for 3 years in competitive grant funding, federal income tax credits for 50% of all expenditures for human clinical trials, and a waiver of user fees. The most sought after incentive is the seven-year orphan marketing exclusivity. Enzon, Inc. was formed out of a Ph.D. thesis at the Rutgers School of Pharmacy on a polyethylene glycol (PEG) process to enhance existing therapies through coatings. The target disease was a rare immunodeficiency malady commonly called "Bubble Boy Disease," an affliction that represented only 40 to 50 cases in the world. The young company's initial market was tiny but the enzyme-replacement therapy technique it used became a platform that was extended to other applications and allowed the company to grow to $75 million in 2002 revenues with an eye-popping 60% profit margin (2003 revenues expected to be $120 million).

> "Amgen, Biogen, Enzon, Genentech, Pathogenesis and Sigma Tau all were founded upon an initial drug product which had 'orphan' status in an FDA program to develop orphan products." Robert F. Steeves, FDA. Genzyme is one of a few profitable biotech companies and owes its success to its orphan drugs Cerezyme to treat Gaucher's disease and Fabrazyme for Fabry's disease. Biogen generated revenues of nearly $1 billion in 2002 sales of Avonex, an orphan drug now used to treat multiple sclerosis.

The Robert C. Byrd National Technology Transfer Center supports tech transfer generally from its website www.ntte.edu at Wheeling Jesuit University in West Virginia. A weekly online magazine on technology transfer is found at www.globaltechnoscan.com with information and articles on business opportunities, licensing, research financing, patents, venture capital and general finance along with links to international technology and professional services. A magazine covering NASA tech transfer www.nasatech.com and technologies for all NASA centers is found at www.teccenter.org. TSI TelSys Corporation was begun with NASA encouragement by people who had worked on satellite IT at the Goddard Space Flight Center.

43. Foreign government technical transfer.

Overseas opportunities need to be examined in a global economy. The UK's leading biological and chemical defense research center, the

Defence Science & Technology Laboratories (DSTL) west of London, has worked with a local venture capital company, Circus Capital, to set up four commercial companies so far and promise a good deal more. One of the technologies developed was a rapid test for bacterial contamination in food and formed the basis for the new company Alaska Food Diagnostics. DSTL and Circus Capital are hoping to commercialize another technology that was developed to protect troops from a biological attack but also permits fabrics to become nearly 100% resistant to stains. Cotton shirts repel water better than raincoats and goggles don't fog up, reports the *Financial Times*. In Germany, the Fraunhofer Institutes conduct open research benefiting entire industries as well as contracted research for large companies.

The European Molecular Biology Laboratory (EMBL) in Heidelberg, Germany, formed a technology transfer arm known as EMBLEM in 2001. They also announced a new life sciences incubator and a $50 million venture capital fund for European startups. The incentive for EMBLEM has been Lion Bioscience, a company that was formed out of EMBL, had an IPO in 2000 and was felt to be a perfect model for other new biotechs. The European Patent Organization set up an Internet service called esp@cenet to give researchers free access to technical information. Information on competitors, company patent portfolios, geographic coverage of a patent and technology generally is available at www.european-patent-office.org/espacenet/info.

Oxford Innovation, Ltd., of the UK plans on opening an innovation center in North Carolina for biotech ventures. The model they're exporting has been developed in 13 centers in the UK, launching over 200 new ventures. Oxford Innovation intends to make this foray into the New World a mechanism for two-way technical transfer between foreign and domestic engineers and scientists as well as the making of a biotech industrial cluster that mates manufacturing and development. Other countries around the world are also looking to commercialize their research products and may be a source for both technology and funding.

44. Non-profit technical transfer.

The Charles Stark Draper Laboratory in Cambridge, MA organized Navigator Technology Ventures as a fund to provide seed money and help in organizing companies around technology that stemmed from its mostly defense-oriented work. Dr. Raanan Miller developed a tunable chemical filter spectrometer to test air for chemical warfare agents while working at the lab, with many other applications. Miller published a technical paper on the process and was swamped with responses from potential customers in a number of fields. Seeking to commercialize the technology he founded Sionex Corp. as a spin-off from Draper and received funding from two private venture capital funds as well as Navigator. The Applied Physics Lab of Johns Hopkins University has used licensing agreements to create six startup companies.

45. Venture capital technical transfer.

Michigan-based EDF Ventures focuses on commercializing research from universities. Typically these young companies are short on capital and business skills but their intellectual property, research labs and faculty make them a rich source for new companies. The early success of the Seges Fund at Vanderbilt University prompted plans for a $75 million follow-on fund for life sciences and information technology that would farm the work of higher education institutions throughout the world. ITU Ventures of Beverly Hills, CA runs a $40 million fund for spinouts from the University of California and Stanford University. ITU had two earlier funds in which they made initial investments of between $100,000 and $500,000 in campus-based companies.

A startup in Blacksburg, VA, Luna Innovations, worked with Virginia Tech University to spin-off five companies and attracted $70 million in outside funding and contracts. Luna expects to replicate its technology transfer and research functions to enable new companies to be spun out from other universities.

46. States and counties.

Increasingly, government units have established funds that are earmarked to aid companies in selected industries that promise employment within their borders. Michigan is spending $50 million per year for 20 years to build a life sciences corridor, Pennsylvania set-aside a large amount as well and a total of 41 states have announced similar initiatives. States are particularly interested in recruiting biotech companies and offer tax incentives, abundant office and lab space, a nearby university and new venture funds. The average state economic development budget is just over $2 million (www.ncoe.org), in part to pay service providers to help entrepreneurs with questions.

Loan insurance is provided through the Maryland Industrial Development Financing Authority and most states have a program to back the debt of a number of companies. Direct funding is usually carried out by a state-created corporation. In Maryland, for example, the Technology Development Corporation (TEDCO) doles out: $20,000 grants for CRADAs at federal laboratories; $50,000 for university-owned technologies; $50,000 for technology transfer; and $50,000 for technologies associated with naval aviation. If you decide to apply for this type of funding anticipate at least an eight-week review process and know that they are highly competitive.

New Jersey has recently funded a business support organization for nanotechnology. The New Jersey Nanotechnology Consortium is a nonprofit corporation headquartered at Lucent Technologies' Bell Labs and wants to leverage that center's decades of experience commercializing technology. Groups from government, universities and corporations have banded together for this effort and have pledged to meet an annual operating budget of over $10 million. Other regional groups focusing on this technology include Albany NanoTech in upstate New York and most university engineering departments.

North Carolina recently allocated $40 million from their tobacco settlement, administered by the Golden LEAF Foundation, for biotechnology investments. Funds will be directed through two venture capital groups, BioVista and Aurora, in Durham, NC. Their focus is upon companies that could eventually build manufacturing facilities and provide jobs in the state but their charters are broad. The Iowa Cooperative is planning on building a $40 million processing plant for specialty crops associated with biotechnology such as pharmaceutical grains. South Dakota has an economic development grant program that offers up to $30,000 for collaborative development efforts between entrepreneurs and state universities. Alaska's Governor hopes to use the state's $23 billion Permanent Fund to invest in companies that are willing to relocate jobs there. Check with the economic development agency where you're located and they will give you a list of similar organizations and funding sources.

The State of South Carolina induced Pilot Therapeutics to move there from North Carolina, largely in return for $10 million of various incentives including $3 million in cash. North Carolina did everything they could to get them to stay, including an offer of a $2 million cash equity infusion—all for a company with only 14 employees, albeit excellent prospects for expansion.

47. Government incentives.

In addition to cash, governments are looking at nearly any kind of program to help entrepreneurs, a truly extraordinary resource that should be checked out. Connecticut's Office of BioScience has a program that guarantees 30% of any bank's lending that is directed towards helping biotech companies buy machinery and equipment. The idea is that once banks find these types of companies to be reliable borrowers, banks will step up their lending and other assistance. Vermont's Economic Development Agency lends money to entrepreneurs at below market rates, using their tax-free and good credit risk to bring in low-cost money. You may find that city, county and state officials are more than happy to help you develop your business. In some cases they have funds earmarked in numerous ways when you utter the magic phrase "job development." Political races are run on promises to create economic growth and you could be a part of that growth—so they owe you something.

48. Foreign governments.

In certain areas such as biotechnology, governments around the world are committing funds to develop high technology companies on their shores. If you find that you could conduct business just as well in Saudi Arabia or Malaysia (among many others) you could be an attractive candidate for funding. Japan set aside $720 million for biotech to include importing technologies and companies for their development in that country. British PM Tony Blair said, "The science of biotechnology is likely to be, to the first half of the 21st century, what the computer was to the second half of the 20th century." Many governments share this belief and it illustrates why they are prepared to make extensive sacrifices in order to participate in the expected growth.

49. Public-private

Cooperative funds that merge taxpayer and private monies have been created to facilitate growth. Innovation Philadelphia is a publicly and privately funded economic development organization that has sponsored a fund for wealthy individuals to invest in startups. In Germany, large pharmaceutical companies have pooled funds with state and federal monies to jointly establish numerous biotechnology companies. One German entrepreneur described the loan program as: "the defibrillator that was put to the biotech chest." Asia Venture Partners in Alexandria, VA, supports industrial firms and venture capital groups in South Korea that are seeking relationships with US high technology firms and new markets here and abroad. The government of South Korea has provided funding for the infrastructure and both manufacturers and venture capital groups in that country provide investment funds (www.asia-venture.org). The United Kingdom has tied public and private funds together including smaller pension fund investments by forming regional investment pools in each of nine English regional development agencies.

The Israeli Industry and Trade Ministry made a $10 million contribution for seed-stage investments that are earmarked for six venture capital funds. The Israeli funds themselves have to make a matching contribution so it can be seen as either doubling the money available or lessening the risk for the VCs and encouraging them to make more early stage investments. The Israeli government had previously helped establish a venture capital industry in that country in the 1990s by forming a state-owned company to match VC investments, which peaked in 2000 at $3.2 billion. With wonderful timing, the government sold off its stake in 1999. The definition of a seed-stage company in Israel is one that has been in existence for less than six months and has spent less than $160,000 since getting started.

50. Government specialized funds.

Many federal agencies not commonly associated with funding have money available for technology development. The U.S. Fish and Wildlife Service, for example, has $2.1 million for technologies that promote their mission. The USDA has Rural Business Enterprise and Rural Business Opportunity Grants programs, both of which can be counted on as sources of capital in largely agricultural areas. Igen International inked a cooperative research agreement with the USDA's Agricultural Research Service, leading to the development of a rapid test to detect E.coli in U.S beef shipments—a process that leverages research facilities of both organizations while speeding up the commercial process.

The National Science Foundation (NSF) is probably the place to go with an early-stage proposal, an idea that is searching for a home. In the Plant-Genome area alone, for example, they have a $35 million program that is deliberately seeking unconventional and high-risk approaches. They offer three forms of awards: virtual-center for large-scale collaboration at up to $2 million per year; individual laboratories and small-group awards between $300,000 and $500,000 per year; and young-investigator awards that go up to $350,000 per year. Details at www.nsf.gov.

An amazing variety of federal funding and assistance is available from groups located within agencies. A place to start examining these sources would be www.fedmoney.com/grants.

51. University technical transfer.

It's been estimated that if Howard Florey's work on penicillin for Oxford in the 1930s had been patented, that institution would have been self-supporting for years. The University of Florida reaped tens of millions of dollars by having a license with Gatorade. Lita Nelsen directs MIT's Technology Licensing Office, a famously successful venture that returns a lot of money to the school and other universities such as Stanford, Wisconsin, UC Berkeley and Columbia receive impressive tech transfer revenues. Stanford and UC San Francisco have shared $250 million from their joint patent on gene splicing technology. Iowa State realized $30 million from a fax patent and Michigan State earned $200 million from two anti-cancer drugs. MIT produces over 400 inventions each year, signs at least 100 licenses, and is responsible for about 25 startup companies annually. The University of Minnesota involves its president in promoting workshops on technology transfer opportunities with the school. Universities now receive over $1 billion per year from technical transfer, a process that was mostly empowered by the Bayh-Dole Act in 1983 that gave the schools IP rights for federally funded work done at their institutions. The Association of University Technology Managers can be accessed at www.autm.net for a look at programs in various schools. MIT's consulting arm, MITRE Corporation, has its own technology transfer program at www.mitre.org. And Oxford, a little late perhaps, formed Isis Innovation as that university's technical transfer arm. Johns Hopkins appointed an experienced venture capitalist to direct its newly-organized Enterprise Development Office. These are incredible sources of technology and associated funding for entrepreneurs.

Too many schools are seeking funds from the entrepreneur to pay for patent and other costs, however, and lose sight of the need to have entrepreneurs take their technologies and try to build something worthwhile with them. University technical transfer offices have often been staffed by lawyers and academics: people who may not have had a clue about what is really required to sustain a young business. Their hope has been that Fortune 500 companies will license what comes out of school labs and pay lucrative fees back to the school while maintaining the ivory tower nature of their personnel, a model of up-front fees and downstream royalties. Are they afraid that many of their most talented instructors and researchers would much prefer to join a young company and make a lot of money than continuing to labor for the good of the school? When a technical transfer program is pushing for fees to be paid from an entrepreneur right away, their first order of priority may be to justify their budgets to sponsors and have little insight into business development. Former investment banker Larry Robertson of Lighthouse Consulting feels the few spectacular success stories in technical transfer have led to a totally unrealistic valuation by many university technology offices. This should still be one of the first places you look when considering a new business, however. When you obtain rights to technologies developed by recognized scientists and use the enormous research facilities and brainpower of our universities, you have an immediate asset in terms of the intellectual property as well as being able to place the development costs behind you.

The Stanford Research Institute (SRI) has been independent of Stanford University since 1970 but still holds a close relationship to the school for research and forming new companies. SRI has spun-off dozens of companies and maintained equity that climbed in value to hundreds of millions of dollars. Their relationships with nearby venture capital companies greatly facilitated technology transfer and funding while the lab itself emphasized market-ready proposals and even nascent management teams.

52. University assistance.

Tasty Delite International Ltd. received legal advice they needed from the University of Chicago's Institute for Justice Clinic. The Clinic incorporated the business, drew up a nondisclosure agreement to protect IP, reviewed contracts, helped them write a business plan and pushed them to apply for grant assistance.

Innovation Philadelphia is a publicly and privately funded economic development organization that has sponsored a fund for wealthy individuals to invest in startups.

Schools like Cal Tech arrange for equity instead of demanding upfront payments for IP from the entrepreneur, believing that startup money is just too precious to use for something that can be deferred. The University of Edinburgh in Scotland does the same thing. Immersion Corp., posts its research engineers in ivory towers like Harvard to work on government-sponsored projects that it finds too speculative to investigate on its own dime. The University of Minnesota teams technical faculty to experienced management who then are responsible for raising funds for new companies. In the UK, the government set-aside nearly $100 million to fund companies involved in transferring biotechnologies from university labs. M.I.T. carried the costs of the journal *Cell* for faculty member Benjamin Lewis until it finally broke even. The eventual sale of the publication provided Lewis with funds for his other ventures. Graduate stipends for up to $21,500 are available from the National Science Foundation and could provide some income while you're working on technology you want to commercialize someday.

53. University spinout.

Inpharmatica was formed by London's University College, based upon human genome work conducted there and raised $45 million from Dresdner Kleinwort Capital and others. Boston University has a long history of funding university spinouts with money from their Community Technology Fund. More and more schools are realizing they have the ingredients for growth in terms of technology, personnel and funds. It may be an uncomfortable world for them but the lure of new revenue streams is really too strong to pass up. The University of Maryland at Baltimore prided itself on its number of startups and other schools have a good relationship with young companies by lending their graduate students to projects that benefit both the company and the student.

Gene-Prot (proteomics) was spun out of the University of Geneva, bypassed VCs, and raised $100 million from institutions. Babson College in Boston and Duke University's Fuqua School are actively seeking to spin-off companies that will make a profit for the parent institution. Early efforts for Duke are on the educational side, looking to use cheaper technology and teachers than they could access in-house.

A startup biotech in Spain, Oryzon Genomics, was spun out of the University of Barcelona and received funding from the Spanish Foundation, the Ministry of Science and Technology, and the Center for Information and Business Development. Oryzon focuses on DNA chips and rice production from its home in the Barcelona Science Park. In both France and Switzerland, university researchers are allowed to take up to six years' leave of absence to form a new company with a guarantee of jobs and tenure when they return. Sweden gives university researchers sole ownership of their discoveries. In the United Kingdom, the Cranfield School of Management and Conference Center have generated continuous profits by spinning off new companies.

54. University funding.

Oxagen, a UK genomics start-up, obtained seed finance from Oxford University, where the researchers had done their work, along with funds from the Wellcome Trust and two private investors. The University of California has a $20 million program called BioSTAR to match industry investments in UC research (88% of the partnering companies have been small businesses). The University of Maryland began their New Markets Growth Fund (NMGF) with $20 million that is earmarked for early-stage ventures in the mid-Atlantic. Headquartered at their School of Business, NMGF invests between $100,000 and $1 million in companies that can commercialize innovative products into good-sized markets while creating new jobs and economic diversity (www.newmarketsfund.com). NMGF is demanding, however, and sets rigorous criteria to include: experienced management teams; sustainable competitive advantages; obtainable annual returns of over 30%; identified exit options; enterprise values under $10 million; net annual after-tax profits not exceeding $2 million for the previous two years;

and either located or willing to relocate to designated low-income geographic areas.

A new entrepreneurship program at M.I.T. was funded with a $20 million donation by Gururaj Deshpande, the founder of Sycamore Networks. The money provides seed funding to faculty members whose research could give rise to a new generation of local technology companies. Ignition grants of up to $50,000 are designated for projects in conceptual stages and innovation grants of up to $250,000 are made available for those that have a demonstrated R&D path and intellectual property strategy. The Chancellor's Fund was formed through a $10 million investment by Vanderbilt University's endowment to invest in high-tech firms that were begun by faculty, students or alumni. The Chancellor's Fund invested in 16 companies that rose to a value of $50 million and prompted the University to organize parallel efforts with a new company, Seges Capital Management. In the United Kingdom, British Technology Group Ltd. and the technology transfer unit of King's College London, KCL Enterprises, are flagship organizations for funding university spinouts. British Technology's antecedents date back to 1949.

The University of Rochester in New York State and Trillium Group jointly operate an $8 million University Technology Seed Fund to commercialize technologies. Rochester is targeting funding between the $100,000 to $250,000 level. Harvard Medical School created a Medical Science Partners fund and A.R.C.H. is a combination funding approach between Argonne National Laboratory and the University of Chicago. Venture Economics reported that over 100 schools in the U.S. had or were creating similar funds, usually in association with their technology transfer offices. The *Wall Street Journal* noted that two-thirds of American universities hold stock in startup companies that were begun within their walls.

Startup e-Cognita Technologies Inc., a maker of transaction–management software for the mortgage industry received the investment capital they needed from the University of Michigan. The University of Kentucky put part of its endowment into two regional venture capital firms, helped form an incubator, set up an entrepreneurship center and formed a club to have business students work with faculty. Under the Kentucky Innovation Act, companies can use up to $200,000 over two years to pay for R&D at any accredited university in the state (www.tig.kstc.com). Case Western Reserve sponsors an annual competition that awards up to $100,000 for the best technology and bioscience models out of that university (www.tiime.cwru.edu/bizlaunch).

Yale University launched a small venture capital fund named Sachem Ventures, LLC, run entirely by MBA students. The fund is oriented to job and wealth creation in New Haven, CT's business sector and combines funds from Yale, the New Haven Savings Bank and Zikha Venture Partners. Along with money, the Yale Entrepreneurial Society (YES) provides workshops and a meeting place for new business interests of students, faculty and alumni from its undergraduate and professional schools (www.yes.yale.edu). YES is the most popular student-run organization at Yale and has an impressive roster of speakers on campus along with alumni networking forums around the country.

55. University angels.

Some alumni groups sprang up during the boom years of the Internet and offered an investment network for technology businesses that had old school ties. A call to your alumni office may turn up names and lists of similar affiliations. The Harvard Biotechnology Club in Boston, MA regularly matches industry veterans with aspiring entrepreneurs and maintains a list of resources at their website, www.thebiotechclub.com. Numerous directories that can put you in touch with people who share some history with you are published by www.alumniconnections.com. The alumni idea isn't unique to schools either with consultancies such as Price Waterhouse Cooper and KPMG actively promoting connections between the firm and former employees. KPMG has 18,000 alumni just in the U.K. Boston Consulting Group feels that their alumni provide another way to develop valuable intellectual capital and serve as a real-world laboratory and development group. Bain consultants find a lot of their new business comes from alumni referrals.

56. Community colleges.

These convenient facilities often began as sources for technically trained employees but they have been expanding in many directions. Programs have been added to help entrepreneurs and the colleges are sponsoring more and more events to facilitate access to capital and expert services. Of the 1,200 community colleges in the U.S. most have business training classes and about ten percent now sponsor some form of entrepreneurial venture as well. The National Association for

Community College Entrepreneurship (www.nacce.com) was formed at the Springfield, MA Technical Community College and serves as an early guide to help new businesses. The Macklin Institute at Montgomery College received an endowment of over $1 million from the retired head of investment banking at Hambrecht & Quist, Gordon Macklin, to facilitate this kind of work. Under Jerry Feigen, who served as Executive Director of the Venture Capital Institute, the Macklin program calls for: coursework; counseling; conferences and symposia on planning and creating new businesses; executive level training; support for CEOs and their teams; and other services to support entrepreneurs. They already provide entrepreneurial boot camps and a class on commercialization that drew 450 NIH researchers. Future offerings will include technology transfer and technology entrepreneurship daylong programs as well as a new technology and incubation park. Macklin expects to make this a model for other community colleges to emulate and bring small business services closer to home.

Close behind the community colleges and nearer still, high schools are increasingly offering entrepreneurial training. Former courses in business law are being supplanted or augmented by special offerings on entrepreneurship. A course offered at Montgomery County, MD's Wootton High School in Entrepreneurship/Small Business Management requires parents to discuss the student's work and student production of a business plan containing separate sections on marketing, finance and growth along with an executive summary. Both Bill Gates and Michael Dell showed real business ability while still teenagers so perhaps identifying and supporting our future business leaders as early as practicable is a reasonable strategy. Atlanta, GA-based YoungBiz Inc. publishes a magazine and offers business seminars for teen entrepreneurs. Finance Academies in a number of states teach business skills to high-school students under the sponsorship of the National Academy Foundation (www.naf.org), a non-profit run by the cream of American businessmen.

57. Licensing.

Seattle Computer Products sold 86-DOS to Microsoft for $50,000 in 1981 and provided the technology for the spectacular growth of Microsoft. Isis Pharmaceuticals licenses its technology to large pharmaceutical companies and derives significant revenues from the deals to support its ongoing research. Celera does the same although it hopes to use more of what it produces to develop drugs on its own turf. Biopure of Cambridge, MA needed $45 million to continue operations and launch its human-blood substitute, Hemopure. In a tough funding market Biopure licensed the rights to develop and market the product in Asia for $30 million in cash, going a long way towards solving its money problems. BitzMart Inc. licensed a technology that protects digital files from being copied, from the developer, the University of Miami. BitzMart didn't have to spend a dime of its startup capital for the product it needed to grow its business.

Licensing is always a two-way street. Microsoft needed special software to fulfill demands of their big new client, IBM, and the quick way to get that technology was to license an existing product. Isis and Celera use licensing as a revenue stream while they seek to develop their companies into full-scale drug development. ChromaDex needed chemical giant Bayer's toxicity screening technology to develop tests for the food and vitamin markets. Bayer agreed to the license in return for an equity stake instead of fees, effectively funding the company's intellectual property. Bayer spends over $2 billion a year on R&D with only 10% of that actually ending up in products they can sell, potentially a rich resource of technology for young companies. Procter & Gamble (P&G) has 100 technologies available for licensing or sale that are listed on an online marketplace, www.yet2.com.

A growing practice involves corporate gifts of unused intellectual property to universities and other non-profits. Companies get tax write-offs and the beneficiaries hope they can license out the technology. While there's room for abuse of the tax system in this tactic, interesting technology applies to markets that are too small for corporate giants but could fit new entrepreneurial ventures. Some of the examples include: DuPont's gift of a drug compound manufacturing technique without acidic waste to the University of Florida: Boeing's optical computing logic and design to Alabama A&M; and P&G's control of skin pigmentation to the Cincinnati Children's Hospital Medical Center. Delphion, an intellectual property consulting company in Lisle, IL has tracked many of these programs.

58. Contracts and consulting services.

Essentially, this technique uses the customer to finance the firm either through upfront or progress payments, while it develops the product needed by the client or related products. Before its saphion batteries were marketed, Valence Technology earned revenues by acting as an R&D lab for Delphi Automotive Systems. Lynx Therapeutics provided cloning services for both BASF and Dupont, and was able to generate revenues of $20 million per year from these two giants. Support services are also quite salable. With expensive R&D pipelines, biofirms and biopharmas are outsourcing more specialty services, from IT support to clinical trials management.

59. Vendor financing.

This technique often takes the form of advances to companies to permit them to deliver products. Nokia loaned over $600 million to Hutchinson for product work Nokia needed done. Some times the vendors don't even know they are doing the financing. In the 19th century, the Swift meat packing company evolved by essentially kiting checks. Swift had banks and checking accounts on both the east and west coasts. They would pay for cattle with a check drawn on a New York bank that had to clear through the customer's account in San Francisco. The several weeks that it took permitted them a cash float to slaughter, sell the products, and deposit funds to cover their drafts. While that window has long since closed, variations of this type of financing may occur to you. Neiman-Marcus has taken up to four months to pay some vendors.

Vendor financing doesn't always take the form of loans and progress payments serve as well. LaVoie Strategic Communications Group in Swampscott, MA, signed their first client, requested an upfront payment of a third of the fee, which they received, and used the money to fund the company. RealTronics Corp ordered products from office equipment suppliers, sold them and received payment before they had to pay the vendors. When RealTronics outgrew the amount that suppliers would advance, they established an escrow account for payments that only the supplier could withdraw, permitting a tripling of revenues.

60. Intellectual property.

Angeion Corp. sued a competitor for patent infringement on its implantable cardiac defibrillators and later licensed its entire patent portfolio to that same competitor (Clayton Christensen suggests that if you want to elicit an aggressive corporate response, it's critical to frame any changes as being a threat to existing business). While that's an unusual use of intellectual property, a protected part of your technology can form the better part of your net worth. Ask yourself why venture capitalists usually use a convertible preferred type of ownership when they make an investment in technology companies? The answer is that even if the company goes under they still own the patents and other intellectual property and can try to sell them off or find some way to use the property to lessen their loss. The U. S. Patent and Trade Office is accessed at www.uspto.gov. The Intellectual Property Handbook from the law firm of Morgan, Lewis & Bockius is a quick reference guide you can obtain by email from the firm at mfclayton@mlb.com.

61. Simple products, early revenues.

Big Bang Products devised a new earmuff, raised $7,500 on credit cards and sold the winter warmers on campus. They next migrated to the home-shopping network, also with a good result, and later raised $2 million from investors for expansion on the basis of their revenues. Neurocrine Biosciences was faced with a nearly endless research task to develop a drug for multiple sclerosis when it happened upon a promising insomnia treatment. They bought the rights from a small New Jersey biotech as a "me-too" drug and developed it to the point of a $600 million annual potential. Neurocrine still has its interest in big research projects but picking up something smaller and simpler, right around the corner, could be its key to survival.

In the 21st century, bred as we are on scientific advances, it's easy to fall victim to taking only a high technology and long-term view of what's involved in creating commercial products. If you can find a simple item that can sell you can use profits from those items to take the risks associated with bringing complex and other long lead-time items into being. The reverse works as well. Boston-based Eleven, Inc. is a company that takes simple items that already sell well and then re-designs them to become more functional. Products include a retractable leash that avoids being wrapped around one's legs. Eleven, Inc.'s 2001 revenues were $2.5 million. Look what Starbucks did to a cup of coffee!

62. Forums.

Entrepreneurial beauty contests such as Springboard and many others have become a popular way of introducing young companies to large audiences of investors. Most of these forums provide counseling along with the chance to network and make a presentation. The founder of NewsMarket, Inc. in New York garnered $3 million from 4 of the 5 investors he met through a forum. Forums constitute a growth industry themselves, as the problem of matching young companies with money has become more and more difficult. BioVenture, a two-day conference in San Francisco gives each company ten minutes to make a pitch to 500 venture and institutional investors. 135 biotechs signed up to have the chance to do this in late 2002. The Brown Venture Forum in Rhode Island (www.brownventureforum.org) is more instructional in nature and puts on regular panel discussions including one that promised a "dozen creative financing techniques" and another entitled "fishing for venture capital: baiting the hook." A two-day venture capital forum called "SmartStart Venture" in Albany, NY drew more than 85 investors and venture capital firms to have a look at 30 upstate NY companies. SmartStart offers a forum for business plan reviews by angels, corporations and VCs. The Empire State Venture Group put together SmartStart to highlight the companies in the region, basing much of their offerings on technology developed at area schools such as Rensselaer Polytechnic Institute and the University of Buffalo. SmartStart itself is spearheaded by the Science and Technology Law Center of Albany Law School, which serves as a partner with a number of area institutions.

If you're going to use a forum, you better be good and be memorable. I once interviewed a company on their capital needs only to find out that I had been in an audience several months before when they had given an eight-minute presentation. Their message was blurred when sandwiched between so many others and it was just another boring Power Point presentation. The problem was not that this was a boring company but rather that it is so difficult to stand out when everyone uses the identical method of making their case. Look at chapter 9 for ways around this problem.

63. Professional organizations and service providers.

Some substantial pools of venture capital have been raised by executive recruiting firms on the basis that they have unusual insights and opportunities in developing companies. Christian & Timbers sponsored a $44 million VC fund (C&T Access Ventures). Spencer Stuart has two small employee-sponsored funds and a number of other firms are expected to launch their own when the market and economy begin to rebound.

Law and accounting firms may have their own internal investment funds along with a practice specialty in emerging growth companies. With a long history and extensive contacts, they can provide terrific introductions and leverage. 250 partners of Akin Gump in Houston, TX put up between $10,000 and $25,000 each to initiate a $5 million fund. Haynes & Boone in Dallas has a separate investment fund that made allocations of up to $2 million per year.

Even before the dot.com boom, many such firms had a history of making investments for their own partners in tax-advantaged programs such as oil drilling, or stock, bonds and real estate for their pension plans. A number set up internal funds that could make investments of $50,000 or less in hot startups that were brought into the firm as clients. In the heydays of the Internet stock market, many law firms in particular found they had to have venture capital-like funds to keep some of their most able professionals from jumping ship. When the legal press carried stories on partner earnings of firms in Silicon Valley that took equity in these firms—sometimes $2 million per year or more—everyone wanted to get into the act. Although that stock market has disappeared, the investment culture remains and the willingness to take a chance on a good idea or group is very much alive. Along with money and introductions, firms today will often provide professional services at reduced rates or with payment plans that make it easy for entrepreneurs to become clients of some of the biggest and well known.

In your area, you'll find attorneys, accountants and business development specialists who spend a lot of their time seeking capital for clients and solving other corporate problems. In law firms, ask for a corporate attorney. In Washington, DC, as an example of what you're likely to find in your own area, there are many such experts, but Stan Jutkowitz at Buchanan Ingersoll (www.bipc.com), Larry Koltun at www.koltun.law, Bill Weisberg at Mintz Levin (www.mintz.com), and John Tansey at JohnTansey@BileneUSA.com, to name a few, have substantial histories. Frank Mellon's Enterprise Business Law Group in McLean, VA is a firm entirely given to entrepreneurial ventures (www.eblg.com). Steve Mandell's focus is on new companies during his weekly radio program and he has helped a number of them with their funding (mandells@pepperlaw.com). Wiggin & Dana has an active practice in entrepreneurial and emerging companies with an on-line question and answer forum at www.wiggin.com. John Egan at McDermott, Will and Emery specializes in private equity financings, M&A, and IPOs (www.mwe.com) and David Zanardi at Baise & Miller has developed a special knowledge of biotech (zanardi@dclaw.net).

In business development, Herb Ezrin at Potomac Biz (hezrin@potomacbizgroup.com) has helped many young companies with seed funding and Avner Parnes (avner@attglobal.net) brings foreign technologies and companies from Israel and Europe for funding and technology partnerships in the U.S. Nanopowders Industries of Caesarea, Israel merged with the nanotechnology division of Minnesota-based Aveka Inc to bring metal nanoparticles to the market under the new corporate name Cima NanoTech. Aveka brought both their access to financial markets and manufacturing capability to the table while Nanopowders brought added technology in a deal promoted by venture capitalist Harlan Jacobs.

64. Political and other connections.

When looking for capital, politicians can help open doors or otherwise facilitate your development. Raul Fernandez formed Proxicom with $40,000 of his savings after working for former congressman and vice presidential candidate, Jack Kemp. With his own skills and what he learned on the Hill, as well as encouragement by Kemp, Fernandez met a number of venture capitalists and prominent investors who helped finance his growth. He sold Proxicom after ten years for $450 million. Entrepreneurs have become heroes to a number of politicians who see them as the wave of the economic future. Massachusetts senator, presidential hopeful and Senate Small Business Committee member, John Kerry states, "Small business, especially today, is entrepreneurial activity that has the capacity to make revolutions." The voting public seems to agree and in both Massachusetts and Virginia former venture capitalists occupy the governor's chair in 2003.

While you may have neither Fernandez' talent nor his connections, you should think of the variety of help that federal, state and local government bodies could provide to you. No one wants to work with government agencies that involve interminable delays and paperwork, but many of them have gotten much better. While daunting, you should still check them out and at least make sure that officials know about your company and what you have to offer. On the purely political side, annual appropriations bills from Congress are loaded with "pork" and framing your needs in something quite valuable to a state or congressional district could turn the trick for you. Professionals coming out of the government have terrific contacts along with insights into the funding process. Frank E. Young, M.D., Ph.D., the former commissioner of the FDA, began a consulting company to help biotech startups find money. By the end of the year 2002, Young's company, The Cosmos Alliance in Washington, D.C., (www.cblsa.com) had matched four companies up with $6.5 million.

65. Social investing.

In addition to fifty-four mutual funds that place social, environmental, humanitarian or other causes at the top of their agendas in the U.S., corporations, institutions and individuals often have such leanings. Appealing to this side can pay big dividends. The California Public Employees' Retirement System, (CalPERS) with $135 billion is the largest pension fund in the U.S., and is interested in using investments to promote social change. While their top priority is seeking maximum returns they have strong interests in creating jobs, rejuvenating inner cities, affordable housing and overseas efforts to enhance civil liberties. If you find that your company combines strong social gains with a profit opportunity, an appeal to organizations such as CalPERS seems reasonable. ABP, one of the world's largest pension funds, acquired a minority stake in Innovest Strategic Value Advisors, a move towards ethical investing.

The Yucaipa America Funds is the name of a pool of union pension fund investments. Yucaipa investment criteria specify companies that "maintain strong corporate governance practices and are sensitive to the interests of their employees." A number of mutual funds make alternative investments in new companies and, like the Calvert Group begun by Wayne Silby, have a social agenda. Roughly $1.5 trillion worldwide is invested according to social or ethical criteria. Susan Davis founded Capital Missions Co., in Elkhorn, WI to incubate investor networks that seek social and environmental returns as well as profits. Susan has started twenty companies herself and helped found the Committee of 200, comprised of the top women in American business.

66. Barter.

SAS Institute, Inc. was founded by Jim Goodnight to integrate and organize massive amounts of data that are stored in otherwise incompatible computers and to then view and mine that data. Goodnight co-developed the Statistical Analysis System at North Carolina State (NCS) as the underlying technology that could do this work and bartered with NCS for the intellectual property. NCS gave him the copyrights to the program in exchange for free updates. Goodnight's estimated net worth, decades after the agreement was signed, is estimated at over $3 billion.

Jill Lubin's PR firm, Promising Promotion in Novato, CA regularly has bartered PR services for legal expenses, website design, telephone installation and anything else they can find to trade. Lubin cautions that you need to put barter agreements in writing and also insure they are in compliance with IRS regulations. A number of barter organizations on the Internet will help you find products or services that you may find useful. Barter Systems, Inc., in Silver Spring, MD maintains a database of over 1,000 companies and individuals with services and products they provide. You form an account to credit and debit the value of services, in exchange for a 6% cash commission. The Reciprocal Trade Association and the National Association of Trade Exchange are both sources of barter information.

67. Leasing and factoring.

Instead of laying out scarce cash for equipment and other items in a new business, leasing is generally preferable. While payments will be higher than purchase, avoiding big cash outlays up front as well as possible maintenance expenses saves scare startup money. A way to limit your cash needs for further growth comes from factoring once you begin a revenue stream. Gary Honig of Creative Capital Associates notes if you're saddled with a cash hungry business, getting enough fuel to keep the fire burning is critical. Companies coming out of the boot strapping mode need to establish a useful bridge to more mainstream types of financing and new and entrepreneurial factoring firms have been fulfilling this need. A factoring company purchases the paper from completed work and advances the cash to the company performing the work. Unlike traditional lending, the factor relies on the good credit of invoiced customers instead of a profitable financial history of the young firm. Gary has a free factoring brochure available at ghonig@ccassociates.com. Pentech Financial Services specializes in leasing to firms that have received infusions of venture capital and arranges complex repayment options to include equity. A formula to compute whether to lease or buy is available at www.nebs.com.

68. Public debt issue.

Established companies with property assets such as rolling stock, buildings and equipment may find that they can refinance or otherwise free up cash by selling bond or note issues to the investing public. If wide ownership and solicitation is planned a securities registration is needed. If funds could come from a few pension funds or other large pools of capital, a private placement of securities may work. In periods of low interest rates and/or declining stock markets, such as the early 2000s, yields of 5% or 6% can be attractive to investors while a terrific deal for the company to replace credit lines at much higher rates. A Wyoming land company and a Massachusetts homebuilder both sold small bond issues to get the financing they needed, although with fairly hefty interest coupons. Investors like to receive interest or dividend payments, even if they aren't huge, so you may want to consider a hybrid that combines interest or dividends with an equity portion, such as a convertible bond or convertible preferred stock.

69. Research and development limited partnerships.

Genentech sold $50,000 partnerships in a number of their research projects during the mid-1980s in order to finance risky but potentially lucrative projects. Investors could gain important tax benefits and profit on successes by investing in these partnerships. While many companies have chosen this route, a Genentech partnership on monoclonal antibodies was re-purchased by Genentech in a stock swap several years later for close to $250,000. For companies with different and often diverse product and research interests, this is a way of packaging an investment to focus upon one topic and not necessarily the company itself.

70. Mutual funds.

Mutual funds are also a source. Funds as diverse as American Century Investments, Liberty Funds, MFS Investment Management and Scudder Kemper Investments began internal venture capital groups. Such funds are motivated by keeping abreast of changes and advantages in the financial services industry as well as by returns. There are well over 7,000 mutual funds, just in the U.S.

71. Special interest groups.

Name the activity or area of concern and you'll probably find an association or lobbying group already exists to represent interested parties. At one time, it was suggested that breast cancer survivors formed the largest special interest group among medical issues on the Internet. When Michael Milliken discovered he had prostate cancer he gave millions of dollars to research in the area. These groups are often highly impassioned people and if you have a product that could relate to their interest, they could be receptive to your story and be active investors as well.

72. Shareholder capitalization technique.

Mike Bradle felt the bankruptcy filing of USA Biomass had been prompted in part by untalented management that would be washed away by the filing, and that the company had inherent value that hadn't been realized. He organized an informal group and petitioned the bankruptcy court for permission to buy the assets of the company, with the proceeds of a private placement memorandum that he put together. Funds were raised on the basis of these assets and stock was sold for $0.12 cent per share, only to be trading in a few weeks at $0.19 per share. It was easy to raise funds since the bankruptcy court already had provided a floor for the valuation and funds were needed only to defray expenses of the new management. When and if you see a similar situation you might check with Mike at mike@bradlegroup.com and certainly check with your lawyer as well.

73. Acquisitions.

A Waltham, MA, software maker, Authentica, once was valued at $63 million but the falling stock market crushed its share price. It could, however, still use its stock to acquire a competitor, Shym Technology Inc., which had $7 million in unused venture capital funds. Authentica and Shym are both examples of companies that were hot prospects during the Internet bubble but a slowdown in the economy along with a sinking stock market made their markets soft and their future funding prospects problematic. Authentica continued to post rising revenues and sales for 2002 were 50 percent higher than for 2001, making the company a good bet regardless of the stock market. They point to prestige clients like Microsoft, Ford Motor Co., and Merck & Co. to differentiate themselves from firms that are still looking for sales. Authentica added another business while *increasing* its coffers by the $7 million. A number of companies will announce an acquisition program or have investment bankers or other service providers scout around for interesting firms. Invitrogen illustrated a $1 billion program to pick-up firms in proteomics and informatics as their major thrust for growth.

74. Thinking outside the box.

Being creative in seeking funding and developing a really good business plan will do more for an entrepreneur than any one source of funds. MagiQ Technologies Inc. received $6.9 million in seed funding from investors such as Jeff Bezos at Amazon.com and Walter Riley, Chairman of Guaranteed Overnight Delivery. The company has an unbreakable coding technology that incorporates both traditional methods of encryption and the laws of quantum mechanics. While people from industries such as bookselling and package delivery might not seem likely targets for a funding proposition involving quantum mechanics, the truth is that intelligent people can quickly see commercial opportunities in a truly engaging business model and understand the technology well enough to make an investment decision. Michael Nesmith, former cast member of *The Monkees*, the '60s TV show and band, invested in Molecular Electronics Corp.

Many large companies are struggling with their present business model, mired in highly competitive industries with steadily declining margins. If you see a way they can extend their business in new directions with better margins, show them just what you can do. Start with their problem and then show your solution. Companies as large as IBM have considerably altered their business emphasis in response to opportunities. Spend time in honing business models, don't limit funding avenues, and offer help.

75. Mentors.

Finding someone who has been there, knows people, has experience with making difficult decisions, and makes worthwhile suggestions and critiques has been an extraordinary resource for many companies. Mentors are people who hopefully fill such criteria and are generally available without charge. The problem has been where do you find them? Business schools have developed mentoring programs and actively solicit experienced entrepreneurs to devote time to interesting new firms. Blue Wave Semi began with a novel application of ultraviolet light applications for semiconductor manufacture. They sold all they produced, formed a range of other products, and won a number of grants to help them gear up for growth. Being matched with a mentor at the University of Maryland's Dingman Center provided a level of management and experience Blue Wave otherwise couldn't have tapped. The mentor provided insights on funding and helped focus the young company on marketing and finding sales avenues that wouldn't deplete Blue Wave's assets. Indigo Wild founder, Emily Voth, found Rick Krska, a mentor through the Kansas City-based Helzberg Entrepreneurial Mentoring Progam and credits his help at key decision points in her growth. In North Carolina, the Council for Entrepreneurship continually matches experienced entrepreneurs with companies that need their help. Many schools, chambers of commerce and other organizations run active mentoring programs that will provide funding contacts along with unparalleled business experience. www.aztecventurenetwork.com is a combination angel and mentoring group with close ties to San Diego State University.

While you may be unsuccessful getting a check written by angel groups or venture capital firms, it wouldn't hurt to ask if any of their members could provide mentoring for you. The few hours that a person could spare monthly might prove especially valuable for you while the mentor has a chance to become a lot more familiar with your company than they ever could from just an investment briefing.

Professor William Miller and Randy Williams were selected as "Most Mentoring Angels" by the International Angels Group in Silicon Valley (www.Angelinvestors.org) in 2002. The Silicon Valley Association of Startup Enterprises puts on a dinner program to instruct young companies in how to best use the mentoring process, with details at www.svase.org. Additionally, the people associated with these groups are a rich source of board members that can provide not only guidance but also access to funds. A number of banks have funded themselves by requiring that all board members invest a substantial amount of capital in the bank before taking a board seat, but don't expect that for other types of businesses.

74. Teaming.

Venture capitalists have looked favorably on new companies that brought together an executive team that worked well together before. Knowing each other's skills, leveraging their relationships, having common goals, etc., are important factors in success. Aruba Wireless Networks in San Jose, CA brought together eleven former employees of Alteon WebSystems, a firm that had been sold for $7 billion in a stock swap. A partner at Matrix Ventures who had also been Alteon's CTO committed $5 million to the venture and important board and executive members were easily recruited. Jennifer Files of the Mercury News, coining the term "start-agains," cites a Stanford University study that showed semiconductor start-ups having a better chance of survival when founders previously worked together. You can take teaming a step further as well and note that companies receiving investments from both venture capital and corporate groups provide a higher level of comfort to all investing parties. If a large company in your industry sees an advantage to your business model, other investors will give you the edge in credibility.

77. Community development.

Grants and other forms of economic assistance are available if you can bring jobs to depressed areas. The ideal situation is a manufacturing facility that can pay good wages and hire the people who live in the area, but other models work too. At a meeting of the Israel-Cleveland

Bioscience Technology Exchange, civic leaders in Ohio sought to lure interesting new companies to develop in the region and introduced them to venture capitalists, strategic partners, etc. States, counties and various regional economic development entities have generous programs to help you locate a company that promises to lift local economies.

Shorebank Enterprise Pacific of Astoria, Oregon is one of 600 Community Development Financial Institutions (CDFIs) in the U.S that provide funding and extensive technical assistance to new businesses. Shorebank worked with Oregon State University researchers to develop innovative technologies, increase access to capital, and open new domestic and international markets for seafood products that are landed at Astoria. Nisbet Oyster is one of dozens of companies to make use of the technical assistance skills and loan or equity funding by Shorebank. Nisbet uses a new high-pressure technology for shucking oysters that reduces bacteria, extends shelf like and lowers labor costs, permitting the company to expand its market domestically and overseas. Cash from Shorebank allowed their technology to be used for opening new markets.

Shorebank and other CDFIs (www.cdfifund.gov) are financed through the Riegle Community Development and Regulatory Improvement Act of 1994, aimed at providing incentives to traditional banks and thrifts. Total awards made over eighteen years amount to $534 million. CDFIs use flexible tools including loans and equity investments along with grants and deposits. The website for New American Communities at www.newamericancommunities.org documents many areas that sponsor community-based entrepreneurial development as well as examples of companies that have prospered by using them. Kansas Venture Capital, Inc., a CDFI, invested in 30 companies and repaid the original $5 million invested in them by the State of Kansas. The Colorado Seed Fund saw its investments dwindle, however, causing it to refocus. Community Development Funds are detailed at www.cdvca.org. Greater Rochester Enterprise (GRE) in New York is hoping to raise a local venture capital pool to facilitate economic growth in that region. GRE is itself a $14 million effort to promote job growth and business investment. Community economic development has the attention of American business interests as well, with companies such as Citigroup providing over $67 million in grants around the world, through their foundation, to facilitate financial education, building communities and entrepreneurial development.

The Rural Entrepreneurship Initiative was begun in 1999 as

a partnership between national organizations and several states to promote new businesses in rural America. A number of guides are provided through their publications including Equity Capital for Non-Metropolitan Businesses: An Introduction to Alternative Sources and Directory to Related Web Sites at www.rupri.org/pubs, the work of the Rural Policy Research Institute and Five Myths About Entrepreneurs: Understanding How Businesses Start and Grow, March 2001, authored by the National Commission on Entrepreneurship, www.ncoe.org. Development events and publications are found at www.accra.org.

78. Certified Capital Companies (CAPCOs).

The Louisiana CAPCO Program in Baton Rouge, LA and the Missouri CAPCO Program in Jefferson City, MO represent a private funding vehicle that was created by state enabling legislation. Insurance companies put up the money in exchange for 100 percent state tax credits, phased over ten-year time periods. CAPCOs must invest the money in specific industries within the states where they're organized and make some seed and startup investments. In Louisiana, for instance a number of CAPCOs were organized by large financial institutions such as Bank One and Advantage Capital. Over one ten-year period, they made CAPCO investments that averaged $1.2 million for each of 122 qualified Louisiana businesses.

79. Utilities and other cooperatives.

The Iowa Capital Corporation (I.C.C.) focuses on industries that are strategic to the electric power industry but will consider investing in firms in manufacturing sectors as well. I.C.C. has a very successful track record and has made a good deal of money while promoting young companies. Utility cooperatives are in a unique position to provide venture capital to businesses within their service area as customers. Most utility cooperatives also are in position to take a long-term view of investments, given their commitment to the region and their members' strong roots in the community. In Montana, for example, utility cooperatives made direct venture capital investments in a number of startups in their business areas.

80. Microfinance.

The category of small enterprise funding that has taken root in the third world is hardly something that a high-tech entrepreneur is going to get excited about. Still, nearly 14 million people have received funds from a pool of $7 billion provided by over 1,000 institutions. The average amount overseas is only $150 and goes mostly to women, but more substantial funds in the U.S. have been advanced. A number of firms promote crafts from these new ventures and "ethical" labeling has become widespread. EZiba.com sells handcrafted luxury foods from economically developing countries and raised $70 million from venture capital firms such as Berkshire Capital along with money from Amazon.com. Hernando DeSoto's brilliant book, *The Mystery of Capital*, indicates ways in which the industrious poor in the third world can access capital through a process of reforming laws and practices—eventually building their own best and most powerful aid programs.

Micro-loan programs are available in the U.S. and can spell the difference for people with vision and energy. A $5,000 loan from a public fund in Southwestern Virginia allowed a husband and wife team to start a cleaning business that now employs fifteen others and is growing steadily. The loan has long since been repaid with interest and the record of default on this type of finance around the world is miniscule. www.accion.org lists hundreds of micro-loan organizations in the U.S. and Latin America. U.S. sites are exclusively detailed at www.accionusa.org. The Association for Enterprise Opportunity (AEO) is an association of 500 U.S. microlending organizations at www.microenterpriseworks.org. The AEO lists fourteen sources of federal microenterprise funding including the little known Office of Refugee Resettlement as well as Community Development.

81. Royalty financing.

Peter Moore, founder of Banking Dynamics in Portland, ME arranged a financing for a software company that wouldn't dilute equity. Moore secured an advance of $200,000 against future sales of the software firm on the basis that the investors would receive 3% of the sales for ten years or until they received back a total of $600,000. The Greater Portland Building Fund and a public development organization, Coastal Enterprises, put up the money. If it took a maximum of ten years to receive all the payments they would realize a net compound annual return of 11.6%, but if it was paid off in five years the return would be a cushy 24.5%. Though the company's sales were small they were growing rapidly, making the deal attractive to the lenders.

WHERE TO TURN FOR HELP

While contacts can help immeasurably, you can't rely on those alone. Besides, things are changing. Former Treasury Secretary and Goldman Sachs Chairman, Bob Rubin, said: "Business does not happen off Rolodexes anymore." Wall Street relationships are different today than they used to be. Investment bankers have played musical chairs so often that clients are rarely attached to one banker. It's not a long-term relationship game anymore. It's a matter of who has the best ideas at the right time.

Resources are right around the corner.

You've seen that successful fund raising involves many different avenues and putting all the pieces in place for your effort can be daunting. You don't have to do it all by yourself. Countless resources exist to speed the funding and entrepreneurial process along and taking advantage of what exists right around you may be more than adequate. Each geographic area of the U.S. enjoys multiple facilities for promoting emerging, high-growth businesses. A visit or call to any of these organizations will start you on your way to many groups that can be of help (don't think that they are going to solve your problems, but they can speed things up for you). The following is hardly an exhaustive description of those resources and is meant only to suggest the type of help available, and spur you to uncover those waiting assets. (For updates, check www.threearrowscapital.com.)

The National Association of Seed and Venture Funds has a website with incredible resources at www.nasvf.org. Inc Magazine has a rich lode of information for entrepreneurs and both their website www.Inc.com and their e-zine messages should be on the checklist for any entrepreneur.

Try their "Where to Find Financing" on the website as well as information on angel investors, government programs and a special series on innovation. The *Wall Street Journal* pitches in with the *Startup Journal* at www.startupjournal.com and has an interesting test Are you qualified to be an entrepreneur by Joseph Mancuso. www.forbes.com provides a continual flow of insights. Magazines such as *Red Herring, Business 2.0, Fortune Small Business,* and *Business Week* are three of the bibles of the investing world and have online news services that continually feed you information on business models and funding. Try www.redherring.com, www.business2.0.com, www.FSB.com, and www.businessweek.com. Magazines that are growing in influence within the minority communities include *Black Enterprise* (www.blackenterprise.com) and *Hispanic Magazine* (www.hispaniconline.com).

FutureDex Magazine matches new companies with investors and is carving out a niche as a private capital marketplace at www.futuredex.com. www.capital-connection.com gives tips on pitching ideas along with connections between entrepreneurs and potential investors. www.capitalvenue.com matches business ventures with potential investors and lists a number of programs for entrepreneurs.

Several newspapers are very friendly to entrepreneurs seeking capital and many illustrations in this book stem from their reporting. Silicon Valley's *Mercury News* and the *Boston Globe* both regularly feature articles on imaginative business startups and provide continual references to capital, technology, etc. The *London Financial Times, New York Times, Washington Post* and the *Wall Street Journal* are a few other newspapers that should be searched for information relative to your own industry. www.corante.com is the website for a filtered approach to the daily press and picks up the best in such categories as venture capital, biotech, etc., while connecting you to innumerable blogs.

The Kauffman Center for Entrepreneurial Leadership, at the Ewing Marion Kauffman Foundation, publishes articles with great advice for business owners and wonderful links for money, training, alternative sources of capital, etc., at www.entreworld.com. These are also the people that bring you entrepreneurial insights on Public Radio and fund numerous entrepreneurial initiatives around the country. Kauffman provides a free comprehensive assessment of a company's financial vital signs at www.businessekg.com. Separately, The Wayne Brown Institute (WBI) at www.venturecapital.org helps with tools to raise capital, prototypes of startups, a venturing network, and a review of business plans ($395). The WBI has established connections with investment banks, venture capital funds and service providers in the funding industry that you can take advantage of at their seminars.

www.businessfinance.com has lists that include over 78,000 sources of capital, from individuals to venture capitalists. www.cfol.com provides lists of investors in addition to a membership program for other forms of startup business help. The National Association of Small Business Investment Companies can direct you to venture capital sources (703-683 1601). The Idea Café at www.businessownersideacafe.com is an interactive site with excellent information. The same site has a section on financing that includes tips, a glossary, financial resources, loan agreements and other financial documents, and a network to put money and entrepreneurs together. A good part of the IdeaCafe is to make the process of forming a business more enjoyable and less lonely.

The Chocolate Farm makes and distributes farm-themed chocolates and recipes and was begun in 1998 years ago by 17 year-old Evan and 14 year-old Elise MacMillan, with money raised from their parents.

Small Business Development Centers (SBDCs, www.sbdc.org) may offer as little as cheap copying facilities all the way up to full-fledged counseling and valuable referrals. Usually located at or in connection with colleges or universities, SBDCs are a source of classes and conferences that can be invaluable for the entrepreneur. The Wharton SBDC in Philadelphia houses a number of student entrepreneurs along with a roster of business classes, directed by Dr. M. Theresa Flaherty at www.wharton.upenn.edu.

The SBIR Program.

The Small Business Innovation Research (SBIR) program is the largest single federal source of seed capital available to small (fewer than 500 employees) high-tech businesses in the U.S. SBIRs fund innovations considered too risky for either large businesses or government-focused programs to do on their own. Each of the ten federal agencies (including the National Science Foundation) with a research or development budget of more than $100 million is mandated by Congress to set aside 2.5 percent of these funds for SBIRs. Commercialization is the intended end result of the supported R&D. Fund awards are made in two phases. Phase I contracts provide roughly $75,000 to develop a design concept over a six-month time period. Phase II contracts involve funding closer to $750,000 to develop a prototype, generally over two years. Small businesses can submit projects that support the topic areas that are posted by that agency. Some agencies have hundreds of topic areas and others have fewer but broader areas of interest. Each military service and agency within the Department of Defense has its own program. NIST's grants are listed under the Advanced Technology Program (ATP) and can run up to considerably more money.

> *Nanophase Technologies Corp., received nearly $2 million from NIST for the production of ceramic nano-particles targeted to the semi-conductor industry. The semi-conductor people proved less interested but Procter & Gamble found the particles ideal for sunscreen lotion and bought the whole company. (Check www.nanotechweb.org or the magaxine "Small Times" for insights into the development of nanotechnologies.) Engineering Animation had several million dollars from NIST for their human-body simulation and built the company to 950 people before being acquired by EDS.*

SBIR also has a "sister program" called Small Business Technology Transfer (STTR), which is similar but involves cooperative research and development with research institutions such as universities. The goal of the STTR program is to facilitate the transfer of technology developed by research institutions through small businesses. About one in twenty submissions under SBIR and STTR are funded. This may not sound like good odds but it is a far more likely prospect than ever finding venture capital.

> *Corinna Lathan, Ph.D., was awarded one of the four SBIRs that she submitted for her company, AnthroTronix, her first year, but six of the eight submitted the following year proved winners. She had experience with the grant process in academia and says while it's great funding a lot of hard work is involved.*

An SBDC, together with the Washington Emerging Technologies Center (www.wetcinc.com), offers a program in explaining the SBIR program and the steps needed to take a small technology firm through the process to a grant. Under Director Darrell Williams, they include topics such as eligibility, award phases, how to prepare a proposal, business development strategy, a checklist of needed items and a review of a project that received funding. They illustrate contents of winning SBIR proposals and even provide food and drink, in an abbreviated session for as little as $15.

Laura Ricci has been involved in dozens of SBIRs and runs a grant consulting company from her website www.1Ricci.com. With over twenty years of experience in helping scientists and engineers win grants, Ricci can be quick and reasonable along with providing a high likelihood of success. Big firms like Lockheed Martin have used her services in addition to academics around the country.

Educational and networking resources.

A free online course in equity financing is offered by the Telecommunications Fund of Washington, D.C., an investor in early-stage technology. Access the course at: www.tdfund.com. The Fund offers a similar program in corporate governance. The first offering is a lengthy but basic primer for people who are new to finance and the second is aimed at CEOs who need advice on designing a board of directors, director's liability insurance, audit committees, etc. Daniel H. Aronson of the law firm of Greenberg Traurig, LLP has a sixty-seven-page text, Raising Capital for the Emerging Business: A Primer for Entrepreneurs, that you can download from www.gtlaw.com.

Counties are frequent sponsors of business development programs, often in conjunction with SBDCs and other government agencies. Loudoun County, VA (www.loudounsbdc.org) provides a free class in the essential steps for starting a small business. Their basic teaching is a set of 21 marketing tips although you may have to sit through an insurance presentation that falls a little short of good theater. Your nearest Federal Reserve Bank has a Community Affairs Office that is charged with economic development. Even though the FED has all the money they aren't going to give you any, but they may help you find resources for a new company.

Many specialized businesses can find resources particularly directed towards their market. If you have environmental implications, check out www.epa.gov/efinpage/reg9fet.htm. You'll find a free 245 page report "Financing Environmental Technology, A Funding Directory for the Environmental Entrepreneur" prepared by the EPA in concert with the Alameda Center for Environmental Technologies.

The Center for Innovative Technology (CIT, www.cit.org) of the

State of Virginia provides a free seminar for entrepreneurs who are looking for their first round of financing. Led by a corporate attorney, an interactive business counseling session is held to provide real-time experience in the process, answer questions, learn about resources, etc. The Center sponsors seminars and recently had an imaginative series on the life sciences industry and another on finding federal funding for technology companies. CIT also provides counseling and business plan services for Virginia companies, workshops, a one-day boot camp, mentoring, substantial innovation awards, small grants (up to $5,000) to help with funding proposals to the feds, and discounts on proposal writing software.

Even the Toastmasters (www.ieToastmasters.org) recognize both your need and your contribution to the economy. The Internet Toastmasters bring together Internet-minded business professionals (and who isn't a user of the Internet in business today?) where participants improve their public speaking and leadership skills through regular practice, positive feedback and networking. Your first session is free and if you like what you see, the dues are modest.

The Emerging Business Forum (www.emergingbusinessforum.org) charges $395 for an event to help culturally diverse entrepreneurs build relationships with established companies, investors, and potential customers. Their program is directed to: "educate emerging companies by enhancing their management knowledge and confidence, support management diversity, and build awareness of the benefits of doing business with emerging businesses; accelerate access of emerging companies to funding sources and improve negotiation skills; improve marketing skills through presentation and media training; identify strategic partners among established companies, leveraging strengths in corporate and government expertise and recognizing merger and acquisition candidates." For $29.95, American Venture at www.avce.com will list your business plan with a number of their investor subscribers for a three-month period, and throw in a year's subscription to their magazine. The Business Alliance for Local Living Economies (BALLE) (www.livingeconomies.org) helps to connect capital to firms listed with them and otherwise organizes events and provides tools for local firms. Michael Shuman directs the Green Policy Institute for BALLE at shuman@igc.org.

Gender has a place in entrepreneurial development. The Women President's Educational Organization (www.womenpresidentsorg.com) has a free networking session called "Speed-Dating" to introduce you to other businesses and make connections with service providers, potential customers, etc.

Merger and acquisition firms such as the McLean Group (www.mcleanllc.com) will host sessions for young companies that explore topics in locating investors as well as cashing out once you've built your company. A recent program on "value drivers" featured a top ten list of ways to increase a company's value in the marketplace. www.trivisionpartners.com brings organizational structure, business plans, and marketing efforts to the telecommunications sector.

> *The road to raising capital is rocky, with a great number of duplicitous firms and individuals making promises but are either unable or unwilling to deliver. Its up to you to find the really helpful and ethical groups out there.*

Your local chamber of commerce (www.uschamber.com) may be much more interested in startup businesses than you think. The U.S. Chamber of Commerce along with other area societies holds a networking event for $35 called "Building Your Business" that features a panel of experts and ideas for professionals in high-technology fields. The panel shares their experiences, answers questions and suggests ways of coping with the current economic environment. The Greater Cincinnati Chamber of Commerce's CincyTechUSA is a technology development initiative that works in concert with an investment pool, Tri-State Growth Capital Fund. Tri-State has allocated money to two venture capital funds that invest in young health, life sciences, and business services firms. The Greater Reston, VA Chamber of Commerce Incubator Program graduated 14 companies in just over two years, www.restonchamber.org. Separately, the Chambers may put you in contact with a venture capital club and help to arrange a presentation before them.

Women in Technology (WIT, www.womenintechnology.org) hosts a set of $150 seminars to help educate entrepreneurs and tries to match experienced mentors to companies that need them. Over a five-month period, they provide 2½ hours per month of networking and guided discussions to help match protégés with four different and experienced mentors. Menttium is a company that runs a national business mentoring program. The costs are $4,800 to enroll but users such as Corinne Wayshak at Confoti, Inc. found it a bargain. She used her mentoring experience to bail her out of a sinking funding program and turn it into an over-subscribed investment round.

Students in Free Enterprise (SIFE), with chapters at nearly 800 colleges in the U.S. and 500 overseas, challenges students to launch small businesses and other economic projects in their home communities. The students gain invaluable experience while offering hands-on training for economic projects and new entities around the world (www.sife.org). Students from all walks of life have been turned on to business life by their early involvement in seeing how much difference a viable enterprise can make in the life of a community.

The D.C. Society of Young Professionals (www.dcyoungpro.com) charges $25 for a two-hour session with a number of service providers to help nervous potential entrepreneurs decide if they want to embark on their own. The Society offers sessions on: obtaining capital and seeking investors; marketing and advertising; tax deductions; building a website; legal requirements; operating and employment agreements; IP protection, etc. Sessions are led by an experienced venture capitalist, a serial entrepreneur, the head of a PR firm and other prominent business development experts. The Young Entrepreneurs Organization (YEO) has been around since 1987 to educate its 4,700 members and provides an array of learning and networking opportunities domestically and overseas (www.yeo.org). Local chapters of YEO could form an invaluable support system and introduce you to others who are faced with similar problems in building a business. Affinity groups like this probably have formed in a location convenient for you. In Boston, MA check out the Cambridge Business Development Center at www.cbdc.org. In Colorado you can find the Colorado Internet Keiretsu at www.wiredwest.org.

The Great Lakes Entrepreneur's Quest provides a prize of $175,000 in venture capital for the best new business idea from Michigan-based firms (www.gleq.org). The competition is managed by the University of Michigan's Institute for Entrepreneurial Studies and Grand Valley State's Seidman School of Business, with financial backing from the Michigan Economic Development Corp. A 17-member panel that includes representatives from nearly every venture capital fund in Michigan judges the applicants, and also meets regularly with entrepreneurs to provide mentoring and networking.

The MIT Forum (www.mitef.org) is one of the oldest and best places to hone your investment pitch, gain high-level suggestions on your business model, and seek funding. If selected, you'll describe your business in a twenty-minute session, listen to the comments of three highly qualified professionals, and take questions from the audience.

These sessions can be brutal on the principals but being asked difficult questions and hearing scathing comments can be just the ticket to toughen you up for the bigger journey ahead.

Plusses and minuses of getting the money now.

When you're considering the amount of money that you want to raise, consider that lots of companies have failed because they ran out of money but occasionally just the reverse proved true. During the bull market of the 1990s a company filed for a $30 million IPO. The market was so receptive that their investment bankers suggested upping the amount to $50 million. They did and the extra money was banked. The problem was that they only really needed $30 million and the extra money was idle and burning a hole in the company's pockets. Their investment banking firm brought a company to their attention that they felt was a good acquisition, for a coincidental $20 million purchase price. The deal was done but soon after proved a succession of headaches as the newly acquired technology, products and staff were a poor fit. The amount of time and energy the management had to devote to their new baby took them away from the original mission and their failure to follow up on marketing and product development opportunities in their original mission eventually caused the company to fail.

If you want to bank as much money as you can find, the extra cash will provide you with: (a) a cushion against setbacks; (b) flexibility to pursue unexpected opportunities; (c) credit from lenders and make terms from suppliers easier to get; and (d) provides a level of comfort for the founders and key employees. Keeping your cash needs low at the start, however, gives you benefits such as: (a) limiting losses if the company fails; (b) disciplines the entrepreneur to focus on the immediate objective; (c) causes the managers to develop skills in cash management; and (d) preserves more equity for the founders.

FatWire Corporation of Mineola, N.Y. was begun in 1996 with $40,000 from the credit cards of its two founders, Mark Fasciano and Ari Kahn. They ran their business from a spare bedroom in Fasciano's parents' home and saved money by doing a huge amount of service and startup work themselves. Four years later, with revenues and prestigious clients, they received the first of two rounds of venture capital funding and two years after that, they're doing about $10 million in revenues.

Fortune Small Business reports Fasciano saying, *"In contrast to a lot of software companies, we never had $100 million losses. We avoided that by not raising that much money to begin with—a factor that kept us much more disciplined."*

A study published by *Inc Magazine* suggested that companies that began with less than $1,000 were about as likely to be profitable as those that were started with more than $100,000. The same study found that firms beginning with less than $10,000 grew nearly as rapidly as those that were heavily funded at the outset.

The kids can help.

Count on students to organize a few things that can be valuable for you. A two-day student-led conference at the University of Maryland's School of Business explores technology and innovation in an economic downturn and provides networking (www.rhsmith.umd.edu/InForum). For a $40 fee, you'll have sessions in consulting; biotechnology; marketing; services; finance; and entrepreneurship. Students from graduate schools of business around the world are regularly assigned to companies for an internship and to get the background they need for a paper. The emphasis in recent years has drifted away from assignments with Fortune 500 firms and more students appreciate the chance to peek into the entrepreneurial world. If they help your company, you may get an innovative business plan, marketing suggestions, research and other services without any cost to you. If you remember the best-selling business book *Unleashing the Killer App* by Chunka Mui and Larry Downes, "Hire the Young" is right up there in the top ten things to do for the new economy. Students can provide a perspective that you may not have had time to develop.

University business schools are a tremendous resource.

Generally, it's a good idea to make a connection with your local college of business administration and talk to instructors that have an interest in your entrepreneurial area. Faculty can serve as valuable board members and provide terrific contacts.

"I hit the jackpot at Texas A&M." Marianne Bogel, Founder of

Carter-Bogel, on the quality of help that MBA students provided to her for her business plan.

George Mason University outside of Washington, D.C. sponsored their first annual small business conference named "Strategies for Your Growing business." The conference was broken down into twelve training sessions in three tracks with concentrations in funding, business planning and marketing. The program takes most of the day, costs $85 and comes with a free CD of all the sessions so the ones you missed in person are still provided.

Southern Methodist University (SMU) in Dallas has the Carruth Institute of Owner-Managed Business as their entrepreneurial center. Jerry White directs the Institute while teaching at the university and tries to foster new companies wherever he finds them. Louisiana Tech has formed a Center for Entrepreneurship and Information Technology by merging Internet interests of their engineering and business schools. The University of Dayton's Crotty Center for Entrepreneurial Leadership provides startup money for student businesses along with a forum and curriculum that exposes students to area business leaders. Students in Free Enterprise is a non-profit group in Springfield, MO that promotes entrepreneurship and seeks relationships with university business schools.

A two-day program at the University of Washington is designed to give new business owners the background to survive. Sponsored by the Northwest Entrepreneur Network and named "Entrepreneur University," business leaders, attorneys, academics, motivational speakers and venture capitalists teach a variety of skills, including one session on how to make a clear and concise pitch to investors. An area that is particularly addressed is confidence because, when questioned, entrepreneurs have often reported that the biggest problem they face is a growing fear of risk.

The Houston Technology Center (www.houstontech.org) is designed as a business accelerator that incubates emerging companies within select industries such as: energy, information technology, life sciences, nanotechnology, earth sciences and NASA-originated technologies. The Center is aligned with Rice and Baylor universities and provides a convenient merging of the substantial technical resources of the area with the needs of entrepreneurial firms.

Your nearest business school probably has a website that's a good source of business information. Some of the better around the country include: The University of Pennsylvania's Wharton School, http://knowledge.wharton.upenn.edu; www.hbsworkingknowledge.hbs.edu for Harvard Business School; Stanford's www.gsb.stanford.edu/community/bmag/sbsm.htm; and the University of Chicago's http://gsbwww.uchicago.edu/news/capideas.

Many universities have special programs to support entrepreneurs and you probably have some excellent resources nearby. As an example, the University of Maryland operates a program that helps technology inventors assess the viability and the variety of options for commercializing their discoveries. The program, Market and Technology Assessment (MTA), also gives capital providers as well as entrepreneurs separate analyses of industry sectors, current technology advances and market opportunities, on request. Their website is www.dingman@rhsmith.umd.edu and carries charges for the work of anywhere from $1,000 to $10,000. Services include: identification of market segments, size and growth rate; industry and competitor analyses; strategic alliance and partnership analyses; pricing and production cost data; development of pro-forma financial projections and a market strategy roadmap. MTA feeds into a number of other University business assistance programs including those for: technology transfer; mentoring by established entrepreneurs, accountants, attorneys, etc.; business plan review; and an incubator with space and support services. The University of Chicago (UC) is introducing a "New Entrepreneurs Program" with an intensive mentoring feature as an effort to teach first-time entrepreneurs the basics of building a new business. UC operates the program over four months and includes readings in classic texts in literature and philosophy while also incorporating concepts from fields such as music and anthropology, all while focusing on a business launch. Along with the University's program, the C of C runs a Chicagoland Entrepreneurial Center as a clearinghouse of information for emerging area companies.

Roughly 1,250 U.S. colleges and universities offer courses on entrepreneurship with 49 offering it as a degree program. The executive director of Ball State's entrepreneurship program, Don Kuratko, suggested calling and taking someone like him to lunch to talk about your company and what it can do for the area economy, students, etc., as well as its own needs. The website of the National Consortium of Entrepreneurship Centers is worth a visit at www.nationalconsortium.org. College tech transfer and other resources can be searched at portals such as www.utekcorp.com and www.techknowlegepoint.com. The

National Network for Technology Entrepreneurship and Commercialization (www.n2tec.org) helps faculty and students alike find help and resources.

The University of Maryland has designated a new undergraduate dorm just for students who want to be entrepreneurs. Of the one hundred who were accepted the first year, twenty had already begun businesses and six of those were generating revenue. The dorm resembles a corporate environment and students are expected to gain by close contact with others who share the spirit. A multi-million dollar initiative, the special dorm is also found at the California Institute of Technology.

Other sources of information to check out.

Jim Blasingame provides regular radio shows on entrepreneurial topics and distributes a free newsletter at www.smallbusinessadvocate.com. Jim is sponsored by IBM and provides a popular outlet for Big Blue's growing interest in small business. The Let's Talk Business Network provides entrepreneurial broadcasts while their website (www.LTBN.com) features articles and an expert that will respond to your business question at biztalk@itbn.com. www.entrepreneur.com extends the offerings of Entrepreneur Magazine and is particularly oriented towards small business. The Edward Lowe Foundation has an article on Unconventional Capital: Alternative Financing Options you can download at http://edwardlowe.org. A phenomenal store of financial and other information is available at www.ceoexpress.com, a site that gives both current and historical business data.

A European-based news service offers both information on Internet-related business topics and technology along with a networking option that could provide your business a lot of exposure. www.ecademy.com gives its free information service daily and connects you with sophisticated Internet users, including a separate discussion group on "Financing the Future" led by European funding veteran, Colin Allison. Part of its network development work suggests that, if you think it through, you probably have 1,000 contacts that you can quickly and easily draw upon, and the group itself numbers over 13,000. The founder of ecademy, Tom Powers, feels that the marketing mediums of TV, press, sales promotion, direct marketing and telemarketing have run their course, don't work well anymore, and that networking is going to become the soul of new marketing. Ecademy is actively promoting the use of personal online networks called "blogs," short for web logs.

Burt Alimansky runs the Master Class Forum in New York City as a cornucopia of seminars on business and investment topics. Some of the bigger names in venture capital and industry regularly make their way to his podium. www.capitalroundtable.com averages half-day sessions at around $350 but makes tapes on popular subjects available for $195, and has eight tape modules for $495. Some of the areas that tapes are available for include: "Cashing In On Your IP—How To Create New Revenue Streams"; "Effective Presentations—How to Win Business, Raise Capital, Sell Companies"; "Dealing With Family-Owned Companies—How To Overcome The Obstacles"; "HealthCare Investing—Meet Seven Top Investors"; "Renewable Energy Ventures—Meet Seven Investors"; "For Women Only—Growing Your Own Company"; and nearly one-hundred more, at: http:/store.yahoo.com/masterclass-audiotapes/.

www.DigitalHarborOnline.com is a free news service on technology and business events in the Baltimore, MD area. Nearly anywhere you live today you'll find your region is served by a similar organization. The New Jersey Technical Council runs a number of programs for entrepreneurs and puts out a good magazine on developments in the area. www.njtc.org. For the nitty-gritty details of running a company including health plans, associations, services, etc., you may want to check out the Home Office Association of America (www.hoaa.com), European Small Business Alliance (www.esba-europe.org), the Small Business Alliance (www.asbanet.org), Women's Business Alliance (www.womensbusinessalliance.com) , www.bizoffice.com or www.isquare.com.

If your company has an environmentally friendly product or service, you may wish to look at the forums sponsored by Keith Raab and the Clean Tech Venture Network, at www.cleantechventure.com. These sessions allow you to present in front of institutional investors who make investments of $1 million to $15 million. www.technologyshowcase.com is a regular New York City forum with as many as 125 companies exposed to venture capitalists and institutional investors.

In almost every city, a number of business organizations exist to help you. In Indianapolis you can try the Indianapolis Business Forum, www.Indybusinessforum.com. One of their recent offerings suggested: "Rather than shooting from the hip, learn to identify your target market, develop a strategic plan, test it, and successfully implement a tactical approach that will propel you ahead of the competition." Jim Cotterill at www.Jcotterill.com has details. In the same city you'll find www.ventureclub.org, one of many clubs around the country that promote networking for entrepreneurs among venture capitalists, bankers and service providers. The Greater Baltimore Technology Council offers programs for young businesses including new business leads, funding help; roundtables; online discussion groups, etc. Access them at www.gbtechcouncil.org. www.richtech.com is the website of the Greater Richmond, VA, Technology Council, a group providing networking and talks for area entrepreneurs.

eGrants is an online sponsor for classes in raising money for nonprofit ventures, but may still fit into your strategy. One day workshops are devoted to planning online fundraising campaigns, making websites effective, connecting with donors using email and the web, driving potential donors to websites, and expectations. Program details at www.egrants.org/services/workshops.cfm and costs of roughly $150.

The website of accounting firm Deloitte Touche has a booklet on mergers and acquisitions that can be useful. At www.deloitte.com you'll find M&A content that includes a primer, planning an endgame, public shell mergers, and putting your company on the block, among many other sections. Deloitte's guidebook series includes titles on *Raising Capital in the US—A Guide for Foreign-Owned Corporations*, *Selling Your Business*, *Writing an Effective Business Plan* and *Strategies for Going Public*. Separately, www.mergercentral.com is a source for industry merger data.

www.launchfuel.com sponsors venture capital fairs and is an information source on partnering with universities, corporations and government agencies to commercialize high potential intellectual property. They operate with both the inventor and technology transfer offices to bring together management talent, seed funding, and operating support to create new ventures. Launch Fuel CEO Mary Knebel began in PR and later helped develop a number of hot Internet companies.

Event calendars will alert you to the organizations and programs that exist in your area to aid entrepreneurs. In the Mid-Atlantic region, the Virginia Venture Calendar covers events from Delaware to Georgia and lists and describes sessions at www.cit.org/venturecal. Virginia also operates a website with technology and other resources for companies along with events in that state at www.innovationavenue.com. At the site you'll find separate headings for such areas as nanotechnology, biotechnology, business financing, international opportunities, etc. The National Commission on Entrepreneurship has a listing of events that could be useful to entrepreneurs at www.ncoe.org. The site also has a variety of reports on entrepreneurship such as From the Garage to the Boardroom, The Entrepreneurial Roots of America's Largest Corporations and Five Myths About Entrepreneurs, Understanding How Businesses Start and Grow.

Accenture, the successor to Arthur Andersen Consulting, has 25 business launch centers scattered around the country that are oriented towards startups. The centers begin with the business and marketing plans of young companies and focus on strategic planning and technology infrastructure. The Product Development & Management Association also helps young companies with advice on methodologies and discipline that help form early corporate structures.

Attorney Jonathan Bick has written articles on Internet law that may be useful in developing contracts and licenses. Bick wrote *101 Things You Need to Know About Internet Law* (Random House 2000) and provides articles at www.BickLaw.com. www.v-capital.com sells startup resources including a private placement memorandum for $75, a PowerPoint presentation of an investment pitch for $50, a non-disclosure agreement for $20 and a bridge financing agreement for $15.

www.bizjournals.com is the site to visit for newsworthy regional business information. A network of financial websites is at http://cbs.marketwatch.com. www.yet.com has a continued listing of technology offerings and technology needs. Legal forms such as employment agreements, letters of intent, and other business guides are found at www.allbusiness.com. Nolo has a wealth of legal information for small businesses that is written in a self-help format at www.nolo.com. Nolo also connects to sites on franchising, incubation, banking, women sites, etc.

Right-Hand Partners helps clients in the San Francisco Bay area meet investors and massages young companies to the point where they're in good shape to present their business models, www.rhpartners.com. Strategies Unlimited (SU) is a source of both business and high-technology information and studies. SU will evaluate your business and marketing plan from a scientific perspective if it is in the area of optoelectronics, optical networking, RF/wireless or photovoltaic sectors, accessed at www.strategies-u.com.

Greg Dutcher took his long real estate experience to the entrepreneurial world and now organizes loan and other investment packages for companies with good growth prospects. www.cficorp.com. www.getsmart.com has an affiliation with 17 banking and non-banking lenders including American Express and First Union.

4: Where to Turn for Help

VENTURE 5 CAPITAL

Joey "Bananas" Bonano claimed that he was not in the Mafia, that it never existed, and that he was a venture capitalist.

The experience of entrepreneurs who have been funded by venture capital varies widely: from those who would agree with the preceding quote to those who are nearly slavish admirers. Amazon.com CEO Jeff Bezos has extraordinary praise for the VCs who helped him grow. The founder of collaboration software provider, Approva Corp., PV Boccasam, has experienced real partnering from his VC investors. On the other hand, Doug Humphrey, who founded an early Internet Service Provider (ISP) pounded on the doors of two hundred venture firms before finding funding, and felt his overall experience was terrible. Humphrey's company eventually was bought out for $170 million so he had a good idea. The disappointment of the Cisco founders with their venture experience was so profound it was illustrated within a PBS television documentary on Internet growth.

Venture capital funds were first organized shortly after World War II when General Doriot formed American Research and Development and, in February 1946, when Jock Hay Whitney initiated J.H. Whitney & Co. Whitney had made speculative money by being one of the backers of the film *Gone With the Wind* and coined the term "venture" from a statement made by Bill Jackson, "I think the most interesting aspect of our business is the adventure." In one form or another, venture capital has always been with us—even Queen Isabella hocked her jewels to finance Columbus' expedition. Arguably, venture capital reached its peak in the late 1990s when a roaring stock market provided nearly instant profits for start-up companies and brought hundreds of new venture funds into the field. Because of the downward spiral of the stock market in the early 2000s, some analysts estimate that at least one-third of the venture capital firms will eventually disappear (and that may be optimistic). If such a shakeup occurs, seasoned VCs will probably feel the industry is better and stronger than ever. Venture capital regularly undergoes cycles and the Internet boom will undoubtedly be followed by another golden age—we just don't know when.

> *"Your path to market is your path to success. Exactly what is that path?" Ty McCoy, founder of Washington Capital Partners, a venture capital fund focused on high tech solutions oriented to the defense and ancillary communities, who wants fund seekers to cut to the chase. www.washcapitalpartners.com is one of many firms that are quite specialized in their approach to investing in companies, and are willing to consider small deals that have a good fit. Others include Patriot Venture Partners of Waltham, MA, focused on homeland security, TallWood Venture Capital in the semiconductor industry and Firelake Capital for energy technology companies, the last two in Palo Alto, CA. If you want to talk to them, first answer the question Ty poses in a comprehensive and well thought out fashion.*

Today, few venture capital firms are interested in startups. Like so many other investors, VCs want proven ideas and are looking for sales, intellectual property, and functioning businesses that need to expand. Even during the heyday of the 1990s, it was extremely difficult to get venture capital and only a tiny portion of applicants ever saw checks come their way. Nonetheless, venture capitalists are repositories of money, expertise and contacts, and if your young company decides to take this route, you need to be well prepared to meet their requirements. Don't anticipate much insight or understanding of your business model when you meet with VCs. Many entrepreneurs complain that Ivy-league business school graduates at the firms show little appreciation for their technologies and markets. I listened to one experienced venture capitalist that described the extraordinary return he generated from an early investment in Yahoo. When questioned further, he confessed that most of the money came from a covenant restricting an early sale when the company went public. Since he couldn't sell his shares during the timeframe, he got to ride along on the upward spiral of Yahoo's stock price—a lot of luck.

The turndown in the stock market in the early 2000s not only made more VCs wary of startups but less interested in investing in any kind of company, except those that had such good revenues they seemed "slam-dunks". Carlyle led a group that purchased Qwest's yellow pages for $7 billion. A number of firms still call themselves venture capitalists but really have moved on to the safer space of becoming buyout pools. Buyouts require large amounts of capital but ongoing businesses with real assets seem a better bet. Many tech companies are finding that having a publicly traded stock can be a real negative in a bear market—at one point about 150 companies with more than $50 million each in the bank were trading below their cash values—and are interested in becoming private again, a buyout strategy.

Because VCs usually have to invest as much time in due diligence and research for a small company as for a large one, they feel their resources are usually better spent in large deals. Risk plus lack of size increasingly steer VCs away from startups. Angel investors fund more of the early-stage companies and VCs are coming into play once the proof of concept and early corporate development are completed. Universities or other research labs are sitting on technology for a longer time, allowing it to become more mature before putting it on show for investment.

> *Roger Novak, one of the partners of long-established Novak-Biddle, says that he is always "looking for people who are passionate about their businesses and want to change the world." Implicit in this statement is that your potential market is large, that you have invested long and hard in developing your business model, that you know things work, that your statements are true and that you are so committed to the concept that you're going to stay and make it successful regardless of what happens. Novak is also one of the few VCs who invest in startups although they prefer a company that has demonstrated sales and marketing solutions.*

If you're going to operate in this field, you better know the jargon. VC taxonomy reflects the correlation between financing choices and development stages:

- The earliest external financing is known as seed financing. Market studies, business plan, etc. are all in place and the principle investment risks are those of discovery.
- Start-up financing covers activities from late-stage R&D to the initiation of production and sales. Main risk is cost-effective manufacturing of the technology/product.
- First-stage financing is most suitable for a company that has

initiated production and is generating revenues but usually not yet profitable. Market risk dominates at this point.
- Second-stage financing supports growth of a company from around the breakeven point.
- Mezzanine financing (debt financing) is used for a major expansion of a profitable business, usually with revenues above $10 million. Bridge financing is temporary, between later-stage and harvesting.

Some ventures have gone through as many as 16 stages of venture capital financing, with a new valuation analysis performed at each stage.

Fourteen keys to attracting seed-stage venture capital.

In today's market, an entrepreneur's "elevator speech" has become the single most important element to attracting the capital needed for growth. Can you describe your compelling value proposition in thirty seconds or less? (See chapter nine on PR and elevator speeches). Close at hand is a well thought out business plan and the presentation made of that plan (chapter ten). A major portion of the presentation should address an experienced and aligned management team. Also, clean up your books and records and avoid looking sloppy. Operate as a corporation and don't bother with an LLC. The following steps come from venture capitalists that would like to see you make the most of your time (and of course not to waste their time).

1. "Show me somebody with experience in the field who can sell something—and preferably the CEO." If you haven't structured and rehearsed an intelligent sales presentation you're wasting everybody's time. Have you thought of just what your essential selling proposition really is and how it relates to your audience's interest?
2. "Show me a bottoms-up sales projection." If you're resting on an assumption that you have a $10 billion market and you're going to get 5 percent of it, you can skip going any further because you have just demonstrated that you don't really know how you're going to achieve market penetration. Step-by-step, lay out what you're going to do to build the company. Who you expect to sell to, why, how long,

what have you done to show that this is realistic? Identify 100 customer prospects, show that 10 of these are almost definite and illustrate 5 beta test sites.

3. "Show me an unfair advantage." What is your competitive niche and how can you exploit it? Characterize your overall market, name the players who are there now and demonstrate how your strategy can earn a place at the table. Do you have something revolutionary?

4. "Show me some team skin in the game." Who comprises your management team, why have they chosen to join you and what are they bringing to the table? Members of the management team should have already invested some of their own money in the company.

5. "Show me some economic sacrifice (and low overhead)." How committed is everyone to this project and what have they done to insure that they stay through thick and thin? Also, what have you done to save money and preserve the capital that you have?

6. "Show me some passion—some fire in the belly." You don't need to give a revival-like presentation but you do need to demonstrate that this company is the most compelling economic thing in your life and that you're going to do everything to insure it's success.

7. "Show me some team depth." Indicate just how you have the personnel bases covered for the growth of your company and indicate where you're weak and the type of person you need. Show that you've really thought this out methodically.

8. "Show some reality in the financial projections." As one venture capitalist pointed out, "Of the 70 deals we have funded only one came even close to their projections so you can imagine how much we rely on the figures submitted." Don't think that high numbers are going to impress anyone but alternatively, if you can't show significant growth and a large enough market to justify risk capital, you're not going to get far.

9. "Show some valuation reasonableness." Tie the figure you're asking for into a valuation model and project the model out, demonstrating the projected growth from that capital into the next round of financing and a considerably higher valuation.

10. "Show some respect for the competition." Don't say, "there is no competition" since some competition always exists (gas-lit lamps were competition for electric lights) or will be coming along shortly. If nothing else, make up some potential competition since you need to show this for credibility. Describe the current competitive landscape and your competitor's strengths and weaknesses.
11. "Show me a segmented market." Break down your larger market into the most opportune and less opportune segments, based on your product or service, and the strength of the competition within those segments.
12. "Show me some evidence of customer interest." The latter point is close to being the most important of all since, if you can't show that people will buy what you're seeking to sell, no one will want to invest in you. Also, this evidence ties in with your marketing steps, your sales projections, your selling proposition and all the other features that you have chosen to illustrate. Go out and talk to potential buyers, seek beta sites, arrange contracts or letters of interest or otherwise paper the promises that you're making.
13. "Illustrate your intellectual property, your protection or even monopoly." Show some way that the investor can be insulated from another firm competing with you and perhaps passing you just by copying your route path.
14. "Detail your path to market." Make sure that your business plan incorporates a detailed marketing plan, one that works both forwards and backwards to provide milestones for a potential investor to monitor progress, and highlight all the critical issues.

"You need to be a little stupid to be any good at making an investment decision." Bill Hambrecht, founder of investment banking firm Hambrecht and Quist, remarking that knowing everything about a deal is tantamount to not acting.

Another long-term venture capitalist expressed his wish for a succinct but comprehensive presentation to get his interest. He suggested that if you're speaking to VCs or really any other potential investors, be prepared to answer the following questions, at a minimum:

- What is the market opportunity in this particular niche and why does it exist?
- What is your solution to the market need?
- Just how big is the opportunity and in what direction is it heading?
- What is your economic model—especially revenues and profits? Just what steps do you have to take to realize a profit and when do you expect it?
- How are you going to reach your market? How are you going to sell?
- What and who is the competition? How do you believe the competitive landscape will change?
- What is your value proposition? What are your competitors' weaknesses and your strengths? How are you going to differentiate yourself from others and how do you expect to maintain those differences?
- How are you going to execute your business plan? How do you expect to grow and to manage your business?
- What risks lie in executing your business plan? In other words, what might stop you?
- Why are you going to succeed? Why will you be successful instead of someone else?
- Who comprises your management team? Are any of them experienced with start-ups?
- How did you arrive at your valuation? What is your financing plan?
- How are we going to make money by investing with you?

Champion Ventures of Redwood City, CA enlisted former Forty-Niner and Chiefs star quarterback, Joe Montana, as the marquee name for a $150 million venture capital fund for technology investments. The fund solicited investment from high-profile athletes and hoped to use it as a vehicle to help them manage their post-playing careers.

Today, for venture capitalists and funders of all types, nothing is so attractive as profitability, or at least significant revenues. The VC appetite for risk is low. Most long-lived, high technology companies including HP, Oracle, Microsoft, Cisco and Dell have been profitable more or less from the start. e-Bay was profitable right from the gun and Yahoo turned profitable fairly quickly.

Certain industries lend themselves to different types of funding, risk levels and the investors that should be approached. In biotechnology and drug development, for example, given the number of years, hundreds of millions of dollars, and heightened uncertainly of technology, the best strategy may be a period of corporate funding, followed by venture capital, followed by an IPO, and, in the best-case scenarios, finally acquired by a large pharmaceutical company.

In Mike Southon's book, *The Beermat Entrepreneur*, he suggests that most entrepreneurs can grow organically and should stay away from venture capitalists. Many entrepreneurs will suggest venture capital is rarely appropriate in the initial stages of building your company, but has value when sales and revenues become interesting downstream, and this kind of investment enables major growth. The time and energy spent by early-stage entrepreneurs fruitlessly trying to interest venture capitalists in their companies would be better spent in securing sales and customers.

VCs are still in the market for new solutions to old problems, even with all these caveats. How are you positioning your offering? A number of law firms, business development consultants, and accounting firms tout their venture capital connections. Not a bad thing to ask about when you're interviewing prospective service providers. Remember that a lot of the announcements for VC funding you read about are really for third and fourth rounds of investment—most of the money isn't going into startups. Exceptions to this rule have been compiled by Entrepreneur Magazine (www.entrepreneur.com/listings) and separately published by Price Waterhouse (www.pwcglobatltech.com) in a compendium of the top 100 venture capital firms for entrepreneurs. The list leads off with New Enterprise Associates doing 16 early stage deals in 2001, followed by Bessemer Venture Partners, Sequoia Capital, etc., down to Paradigm Venture Partners in the bottom slot with 3.

> *"[VCs] . . . are more important for their network of connections than for their money." John Seely Brown in "Understanding Silicon Valley."*

Lessons from a venture capitalist.

- A well-known VC will receive upwards of 15,000 business plans per year and may fund 10-15 of them. If your essential message is not heard in the first seven to ten seconds

of your pitch, it is unlikely that your business plan will be taken seriously.
- Traditionally, a VC looked for a business that could produce a return of twenty-five times the money invested in a 5 to 7 year life. In today's low-attention-span environment the size of the return has remained the same but the time period is shorter.
- VC's do not like risk and they are seeking every mitigating factor to avoid losing money.
- A number of risks can be addressed and remedied by VCs including staffing, etc., but regulatory risks are entirely out of their control.
- VC's are looking for deals that have a global market but are leveraged and scalable so they can be built upwards.
- The particular qualities of a deal that most likely will lead to VC funding include: (a) potential market size; (b) management team; (c) novelty of the idea, and (d) critical thinking behind the approach.
- VC funding is growing in importance in part because corporate America relies on normal R&D fleshed out by entrepreneurs. Companies like Microsoft and Cisco have demonstrated that it's cheaper and more effective to buy a company that has solved a problem than to try to do it themselves in-house.
- The thinnest business plans get read first.
- A picture of the product or graphic of the service helps.
- Examples of excellent business plans include those written by eBay and Priceline.

> "We want to help you, so we're going to save you time: we don't finance women." A venture capitalist in the 1960s responding to Susan Davis' attempt to raise $2 million in venture capital financing.

Ten rules for obtaining venture capital funding.

1. Some of the best feedback you'll hear will come during your presentation to VCs. They'll have new insights and observations. Show yourself to be a good listener.
2. Agree on the next action step by the end of the meeting.

Don't leave the meeting without a follow-up.
3. When they ask what the valuation is, avoid offering one if possible. If you're high, they'll laugh—and if you're low, they'll run with it. Let them set your valuation.
4. When a VC calls to tell you their decision and it's negative, accept it and learn as much as you can. Ask the tough questions to learn why they turned you down and incorporate that intelligence into your next presentation.
5. Don't look to anyone to lead you. You've got to make it happen by being the driving force. If you're not passionate, it's over, get out.
6. The *presentation* of your business plan is the essential key to getting investors. Use props, demos, samples and mock-ups.
7. Contact VCs in waves. If you schedule one at a time, you'll have only one offer on the table at a time, and it'll likely be a low one.
8. Give VCs your cell phone as your contact number, and keep it turned on.
9. Never mail a business plan to a VC unless requested by one of the partners.
10. The only thing you should send someone, to whom you have not been properly introduced, is an executive summary describing your investment opportunity. A simple notepad.txt in an e-mail is best.

During the worst recession in the semiconductor industry in forty years, a startup in semiconductors received $10 million from two prominent venture capital firms. Icera had innovative technology but most prominently, the founders were three executives who previously had built a startup to a $600 million sales price. Performance speaks more loudly than any other feature.

Suggestions from venture capitalists on how to approach them.

- Recently, some venture capitalists were receiving 5 to 7 times more deals than they had a few years previously. They simply have no way of winnowing out the good from the bad. The amount of capital in each deal has gone up con-

siderably since the number of funded deals is fairly steady and the pools have skyrocketed.
- In a competitive world of information overload, your 30-second elevator speech is more important than ever. If you can't tell your story quickly, you won't get the chance to tell it at length.
- In relating your story think of drawing an analogy to a successful company or undertaking. Give your listener an immediate understanding of what you can do.
- Put together a first-class business plan. Your financial projections should be minimal, no more than 5 or 6 pages. Do your research, check your spelling and grammar, lay out an intelligent course, illustrate the competition, etc.
- Hire a PR firm.
- Find a credibility factor for your deal such as a strategic partner or customer, someone with a name.
- The CEO of the company should be the principal PR spokesperson and should head up the PR effort. Make sure that everything goes out over his or her signature and that the CEO is present at any briefing.
- Clever tactics do work.

"Out of all the companies I have monitored over the years, [more than 150] hardly any have failed because the technology does not work. The main cause of failure is management that is not responsive enough." Walter Herriott, former Barclay's Bank manager and director of St. John's Innovation Centre in Cambridge, UK.

Convertible preferred stock is the standard financing instrument for venture capital investments, providing a senior lien on any assets along with the ability to capture the upside return when successful. Venture capitalists or other lenders maintain some control by staging the financing, making it contingent on continued progress that is consistent with previously agreed upon milestones, or placing funds in an escrow account or having minimums come in. It's possible that you can arrange quite flexible terms based upon milestones and potentially give away more equity in the beginning, only to earn it back if you perform on certain promises. Other assurances that you can make could include a provision for redeemable preferred stock so if an exit event doesn't go as planned, investors will receive added stock or other compensation.

These kinds of terms make potential investors much more comfortable and build in incentives for everyone to win. You can also expect a number of covenants in VC term sheets, which give significant added control to those investors (remember, the devil is in the details).

> *John Rowles of Newport R. I. secured $500,000 from a venture capital investor to help expand his four year-old website design business. The investor decided the company should concentrate on developing e-commerce software instead, which subsequently failed, and Rowles found himself out on the street looking for a job. Reported by Michelle Kessler at the Mercury Center.*

An article in the *New York Times* described a mock negotiation by an entrepreneur and venture capital firm, designed to teach an audience of 50 just what goes on in one of these sessions. A founder of the exercise noted "If you ask a V.C. what value they add, and you get them after a few drinks, they'll say 'We replace the C.E.O.'"

Mark Frantz, a partner with $13 billion Carlyle Venture Partners, notes that while most of their deals are large, they have invested as little as $4 million in a compelling idea that was brought to them. During the heyday of the Internet a number of venture capital-type funds came into existence. meVC was a $330 million public offering of securities that was backed by prestigious Draper Fisher Jurvetson. The new fund would allow the investing public access to a deal flow that was usually reserved for the wealthy (don't feel you missed anything, the share price went right down). Technology Funding made its sixth pool a public offering over the Internet, offering individual investors the opportunity to become venture capitalists in a $100 million offering. OffRoad Capital allowed wealthier investors to invest in fledgling private companies through a Dutch auction held at OffRoad's website.

The author of *The Venture Café: Secrets, Strategies, and Stories from America's High-Tech Entrepreneurs*, Teresa Esser, suggests that you should target the six venture capital funds that are most likely to fund you. Geography, size, expertise and history are all compelling factors in narrowing down your efforts. Teresa says to contact other companies that have been funded by your target VCs and ask for a referral (www.theventurecafe.com). Studies suggest VCs will invest twice as often in companies ten miles from their offices, compared to those 100 miles away, and this is especially true for early-stage companies. VC firms with experience in a specific industry are six times more likely to repeat an investment in that industry than VCs who haven't tread in those waters before.

If you enter negotiations with a venture capital firm, make sure that you're well represented by counsel. You may want to hammer out some basic terms by yourself but don't sign anything until your lawyer gives you a green light. It has been suggested that Bill Gates became the richest man in the world by not accepting multiple rounds of venture capital. In other words, venture capital deals are complex and more than one entrepreneur regretted the fact that he didn't really understand all the innuendos of his deal and wound up with a lot less than he believed he was going to get. Also, since venture capitalists often arrange to change CEOs, if you're a founding CEO and don't want to leave, the pain of being fired from your own creation is acute.

> *Toucan Capital is an unusual venture capital fund operating out of Bethesda, MD with $120 million marked for technology deals (240 469 4060). A good chunk of the fund is designated for biotechnology and medical applications. What makes this firm different is its focus on early stage investment opportunities and a desire to work with inventors, researchers, scientists and first-time entrepreneurs who are at the beginning of their efforts to commercialize an invention or technology. Some of their areas of particular interest are: cell therapies; tissue engineering; RNA technologies; proteomics; life science platforms; data mining; information security; wireless networks; advanced batteries; fuel cells; ultra capacitors; and nanotechnology.*

While many companies owe their success to obtaining venture capital funding, a large number of VC-backed firms that never see the light of day indicates that the process may not be optimal for many young firms. You need to ask yourself if growth and very existence can only be realized with an injection of capital from the outside, do you really have a sustainable business model? Perhaps VC money should only be sought to speed the growth of a company instead of being a necessary ingredient to make the proposition work at all.

The law firm of Nixon Peabody sponsors a free annual "Venture Capital Pitch Day," allowing as many as a dozen companies to present their plans to a panel of venture capitalists, including some of the largest. You have to qualify through a review process that requires your executive summary, business plan and financials. Details are at www.nixonpeabody.com. Just like the M.I.T. forum, you may not find funds through this vehicle but every time that you can find a place to practice and perfect your pitch, as well as field the probing questions, the better executive you will become and the more likely money will eventually come. Many law firms and accounting firms have instructional papers on venture capital and other investment topics listed on their websites. Try a search under Kirkland & Ellis, Wilson Sonsini Goodrich & Rosati, Venture Law Group, Ernst & Young, KPMG, and many others. A group of attorneys at Baker & McKenzie operate a full-scale venture capital university with courses, videos, links, reviews, and legal education credits at http://vcexperts.com. Videos from this group include; "A VC's Perspective on Valuation" lasting 20 minutes and costing $15.00; "Introduction to Venture Capital," 60 minutes and costing $20.00; "Leveraged Buyouts," nearly an hour and priced at $20.00 and; "Private Placement Memorandum," 45 minutes and costing $20.00. These videos are extraordinary bargains and a good place to check out before going looking for money.

Venture capital listings can be found in both printed and on-line versions of The Directory of Venture Capital Firms by Grey House Publishing, www.greyhouse.com. The latest edition of this tome listed 1,438 U.S. firms and another 1,847 foreign funds—and they didn't list all of them by a long shot. Pricing is $450 for the print version and nearly double that for the online service. The National Association of Venture Capital Firms in Arlington, VA (703 528 4370) publishes a directory and a simple search on the Internet will turn up several additional lists. www.infon.com charges $195 for 3,500 firms, www.vcaonline.com provides background on 1,840 domestic and 1,360 foreign firms for $99.95 as well as a service to list a firm profile in their Investor Directory for six months, at $29.95. www.vc.funding.net has a free service to connect with venture capital firms but charges for listing private firms to investors. The venerable Pratt's Guide is found at www.ventureexpert.com and www.Biz4mation.com has a subscription service for a three-month membership to their base for $90. The Price Waterhouse Cooper MoneyTree VC funds are online and indicate region and type of fund at www.pwcmoneytree.com and a search option for venture capital firms that have invested in certain areas and by state is found at www.venturereporter.net. www.vfinance.com and www.fundingpost.com sell access to investors through their databases. There are also lots of firms that also call themselves venture capitalists but are really service providers.

> "To be successful, startups must anticipate the direction of personal technology—which right now is moving toward small, always-connected devices that combine several functions—and then make their products crucial to that development." Julie Landry in Red Herring Magazine, November 5, 2002, noting that venture capitalists do fund startups that provide enabling technologies, but usually not consumer products.

U.S. venture capital statistics are found at www.nvca.org and data on their European counterparts are at www.ventureone.com. A separate listing of European venture capital associations along with worldwide associations is free from the British Venture Capital Association (BWVA) at www.bvca.co.uk (yes, there are Turkish and Slovakian venture capital associations!) In Prague, the Erste bank placed the equivalent of $33 million into a new venture capital fund through Ceska sporiteina, to be managed by a Dutch firm. $45 million has been allocated for New Zealand technology companies in a new fund managed by TMT Ventures. Details on a Canadian venture capital conference that hosts companies from that country and investors from the U.S. and Canada, are found at www.ticontact.com. Roughly ten percent of all the new venture capital funds in Canada are emanating from the Canada Pension Plan and are managed through a network of conventional venture capitalists. The Business Development Bank of Canada often partners with venture capital groups to fund Canadian startups. The Asia Pacific Venture Capital Alliance groups the investment associations of nine countries in the region, headquartered in Kuala Lumpur.

www.lighthouse-consulting.com has a free Entrepreneur's Guide to Raising Private Capital that details the venture capital process. Sections include: "How Venture Capital Works," "Probability of Success," "Questions Entrepreneurs Should Ask," and nearly two-dozen more. Andrew J. Sherman compiled a report entitled Venture Capital—An Overview of the Basic Issues and Challenges for Entrepreneurs in the form of a checklist for preparing to visit this community. Sherman also wrote a popular book on raising capital and can be contacted at ajsherman@mwe.com.

Venture capitalists want to know not only how you're going to make money but, more importantly, how they're going to make money. Exit strategies for any class of investors need to be considered and put near the top of the list, in terms of importance. Bill Link of Versant Ventures suggests there are four steps in developing a smooth exit (entreworld, 2002). In step one; reverse the business plan to focus on cashing in as the primary objective and working through the business strategy to achieve this exit. In step two the focus is on satisfying a market gap, or need, giving you a clear advantage over competitors. Step three concentrates on developing the path of progress with a strategy of marketing the company to potential acquirers. The last step involves the actual execution of the exit path. Additional articles on other exit strategies are available at the Ewing Marion Kauffman Foundation website, www.entreworld.org.

> *"The secret to raising money is that you have to figure out the end point first, and that requires a long-term vision."* Bob Mulroy, CEO of Merrimack Pharmaceuticals.

According to Mei-Yun Lee, head of BuyerZone.com, Inc., attracting money needs a clear and simple message. "VCs, you'll find, aren't good listeners; the less they have to listen to, the better for you. And speaking of listeners, they demand that you be what they aren't: a good listener who processes their ideas and works them into a plan that they will eventually consider acceptable for funding." Mei-Yun started the Business Consumer Guide as a subscription-based newsletter in 1992 along with one partner, pooling $30,000 between them. Her next business was fueled by the Internet mania, generating $6.5 million of venture capital in 1999 and $15 million more the following year.

> *Bill Nguyen heads Seven Networks, a wireless software company that eventually secured funding of $34 million in venture capital. Drawing on a history of successful startups, he first made a presentation to Ignition Venture Partners that fell flat, with the thought that it just wouldn't work. Nguyen went back and worked on the technical aspects of his solution for three days straight—with no sleep— presented his business model to Ignition again and got his money*

CORPORATE CAPITAL & STRATEGIC PARTNERSHIPS

When Donna Dubinsky set out to raise money for the PalmPilot she found a lot of skepticism about her business model because of the previous failure of the Apple Newton. Venture capitalists weren't interested and corporate investors such as Compaq Computer took forever to respond. The leading modem supplier, U.S. Robotics turned out to be the right partner, investor and later, the acquirer. Following her success with U.S. Robotics and the now established PDA market, she formed Handspring to bring innovative ideas and a low priced alternative to the market she had developed.

Corporations need sources of innovation.

Corporations increasingly use entrepreneurial young companies as their innovation partners and invest funds and dedicate some of their facilities for partnership use. Unlike venture capital firms, corporations are usually motivated more by finding ways of increasing their core or ancillary businesses and extending markets by leveraging their existing sales, manufacturing, management and research assets.

During the 1970s and 1980s, Exxon Enterprises invested a total of $12 million into 18 spin-off companies and realized a return of $218 million from that investment—but still shut the operation down! Exxon felt that these new companies were unrelated to their core petroleum focus and the return didn't justify maintaining the effort.

Corporate funding is characterized by a combination of available capital with extensive internal controls. These investors undertake initiatives that require large initial capital commitments under varying degrees of uncertainty. Understandably, their bias is towards proven concepts. Corporate decision-makers require objective data on markets and the prospective firm's capabilities vis-à-vis its competitors. The role of the evaluators of new corporate initiatives is usually to try to poke holes in the case, so you better be on firm ground. This hard-nosed attitude is really an organizational remedy for the cognitive errors that individuals tend to make, including the common Pollyanna attitude of some entrepreneurs and a tendency to rely on anecdotal information. Evaluators in staff positions don't receive bonuses for endorsing ventures that turn out well. If the venture fails and they didn't follow proper procedures, they may be accused of dereliction of duty, so poorly documented proposals are going to be rejected outright. Line managers, as it turns out, have different incentives from staff and may be more receptive.

> *A Midwestern insecticide manufacturer didn't like the trends for his industry as he saw genetically modified crops using less and less of his products. Feeling that it was time to exit the business, he looked to sell his firm. He targeted the largest insecticide firm in the country and made a pitch to them for the sale. He emphasized that they would be getting a proven line that complemented their own, added new customers, and good facilities. The sale was made and he pocketed several million dollars, just in time as it turned out since insecticide use started a dramatic drop. While he felt that he made a convincing case for the sale and he brought out all the advantages that would accrue to the buyer, it wasn't until sometime later that he found the real reason that the large company bought him out. The divisional manager who took over his company received a bonus each year that depended on his sales. The easiest way to increase sales was to buy a company. Our seller was lucky but you can't be lucky unless you get out and try something. You may be wrong in a number of your assumptions but still win as you give yourself a chance to have fortune smile on you.*

It's easier to talk to companies in your own industry.

People working in companies like your own or who serve your market, are naturally going to be receptive to something they already know. They can quickly understand what you're talking about and they can see that your success could augment or promote their own business models.

Established companies don't necessarily have all the advantages over entrepreneurial ventures. Corporate fund allocations are made upon making returns that are greater than the firm's cost of capital. The adoption of emerging technologies with higher risks and potential returns requires an alternative approach to their usual way of doing business. A number of companies have deliberately put aside separate funds in their own venture groups, so that decisions can be made outside of the corporate structure. Corporate bureaucracies are typically vested in their historic products or services and markets, placing barriers against introducing something seen as competitive.

Big companies are interested in your ideas.

In 1993 the economist William Baumol stated that any technical change or innovation "will require entrepreneurial initiative in its introduction." A major difficulty for large companies is that people with an entrepreneurial spirit rarely gravitate to them. Spinning off new technologies often has to be done with outsiders.

> *In the late 1980s, Carol Latham tried to get her employer, BP, to invest in a new class of heat-dissipating polymers. BP remained uninterested so Latham, a divorced mother of three, quit to form her own company, Thermagon Inc. She raised $70,000 from family, friends and an angel investor and worked in her basement using cookie sheets and mixing bowls to find the right polymer combination. She moved into a small apartment, rented out her house and generated some income from part-time consulting. Latham now counts customers such as Dell and Sun Microsystems for her $20 million revenue company.*

Corporations respond to different messages than other investors

> *United Parcel Service put $50 million into its Strategic Enterprise Fund to "... be hand in glove with companies with cutting-edge technologies coming down the pike that might have an application for us," in the words of UPS's Bob Godlewski. "It's a nice accident if we make money."*

A corporation can have its own venture capital fund yet be totally different in the selection criteria they use from those of conventional or independent venture capital analysts. Since corporations are looking for business ideas that will complement and leverage existing assets and capabilities you'll find them open to different terms than VCs. On a stock offering for a physician management company, the biggest investors were institutions that cared most about how the young company could be in position to assist their efforts. One of those institutions, another and larger physician management company, sought the increased geographic coverage that would come from strategic partnering. A second investor, a hospital, just wanted physicians to refer patients to their beds. Neither seemed to care a hoot about the offering provisions of the deal or even its quality as an investment vehicle. Their own business interests were paramount, and their principal requirement was an audited financial statement to help show that they had done their due diligence (if things turned sour).

In-Q-Tel, the venture fund set up by the CIA, is a good example of how corporate venture funds are different from typical venture capital interests. Their mission statements read that they want to invest in promising technologies that support the parent, and returns are secondary. Instead of assessing the investment merit of the candidate company, the question becomes "what synergies exist between our needs and this venture?" The task becomes one of assessing combinations and seeing what connections between existing missions and technology can be drawn, a creative and demanding process. Talk about them, not yourself.

Deutsche Telecom revised its original $500 million venture capital fund to work more closely on technologies beneficial to the company and less oriented towards returns. The hope was to gain early access to relevant innovations in four different technology sectors that are important to the firm. Eli Lilly formed a $75 million venture capital fund to invest in early-stage biotechnology companies. Lilly BioVentures followed Lilly's earlier fund, e-Lilly, an entry to e-business companies with applications in pharmaceuticals.

> *Jim Barksdale relates how chancy the corporate environment really is, and how unpredictable the impact of a new idea can be. He said, "Thomas Edison thought he was inventing the light bulb. He was actually inventing not going to bed with the chickens."*

Advantages of corporate investing.

When a big company invests in you many more assets are in play than just the money. Think of their expertise in areas such as marketing, advertising, sales, distribution, manufacturing, human resources, licensing, legal counsel, etc., etc. When you couple access to these helping hands, along with less emphasis on the amount of equity they take, a corporate investment and strategic partnership is in the interests of more and more young companies. Effectively, larger firms are outsourcing their research and development while obtaining entrepreneurial and other talent that they could rarely nurture themselves—a good deal for them. By leveraging their existing infrastructure through the company they are investing in, they get a double for their money, talent and product!

> *KLA-Tencor of San Jose, CA had relied on internal development and acquisition to fuel its growth but formed a separate $50 million venture capital fund to accelerate the process. Eastman Kodak felt a corporate venture capital fund would help move its film business further into the digital area, and permit it to make many more and smaller bets than an internal commitment would require.*

Venture capitalists, angel investors and stock buyers are all seeking variations of the same thing, a capital gain. Strategic investors usually are not as concerned with returns, because they have other possibilities. True, they will always be thinking of returns but unlike other investors, they don't have to achieve it just from the money invested in you. Companies continue to acquire other firms, make investments in them, arrange for sharing assets, developing joint projects, etc., all with the intent of growing their own revenues and profits.

> *Aventis indicated that it is in the market to invest in or acquire bioinformatics firms or research labs that can round out its own capabilities. If you can show them how you can give them a competitive advantage they want to hear from you.*

Think first of a strategic partnership and corporate investment.

Hewlett-Packard was one of several investors in a startup genotyping maker called HandyLab. HP's interest stems from an aim to create a special-purpose PDA that will drive and control HandyLab's cartridge, and wasn't focusing on a dollar return from its investment. IBM formed a $100 million life-sciences investment fund to promote companies and technologies that could become big users of its data-processing capabilities. Genomics and proteomics, for example, are disciplines with huge computing requirements. IBM recently announced another fund for companies that are furthering this work, and IBM noted they wanted to increase their technology partnerships.

> *"Do you want us to invest in you, buy you out, prepare you for an IPO, or just continue to contract with you for services?" A client relationship Richard Paul found ideal for his video conferencing firm.*

Getting to the right person.

We have spoken with many entrepreneurs who say they have been to IBM or AT&T or a similar corporate giant, without success. They probably only talked to one person in one division who didn't understand the possibilities, had little resources or even had a personal agenda that was more important. They didn't exhaust IBM or AT&T—they didn't really talk to them. In a crowded universe of information you need to make your case to as large an audience as possible with the most compelling proposition you can configure. It often will take only one advocate for you inside a company initially to gain the funding you need—but you have to find that person.

You need a corporate visionary to understand what you can do for them.

The former director of Motorola's Eastern Corporate Venture Capital Fund, a $300 million pool, explained the way they operated. When an interesting business plan came in, her office would determine the Motorola division that was most knowledgeable in the technical or market area, and give it to them to vet. While that seems logical, there are several things wrong with the approach. First, while the division would know exactly what they were doing, it's unlikely they would be able to see the whole picture of interests in such a large company. Secondly, there's an institutional bias against things that aren't invented there. Third, if the prospective investment is in an area where a new firm could compete and maybe take market share, it might make the division look bad. Fourth, what does the reviewing division stand to gain if the new technology or approach takes off? Fifth, what happens if they give a thumbs-up and it fails?

> *Compaq Computer put $10 million into a Canadian incubator as a way of extending its reach into markets and finding companies that have new and different ideas. Compaq also becomes the preferred supplier of computers and equipment to the incubator and its clients, giving them an interesting way of increasing sales.*

Corporate investors.

Intel invested in over 60 companies by the late 1990s. Microsoft and Cisco invested in many more. Lucent Technologies poured hundreds of millions of dollars into their own venture capital unit and banks like Chase Manhattan and financial institutions like GE Capital became aggressive venture investors, until too many of their investments turned sour. In one year during the Internet boom, a majority of Chase Manhattan's annual earnings came from capital gains from these investments.

> *Artisan Entertainment, a New York producer and distributor whose marketing on the Internet helped to turn the low-budget "Blair Witch Project" into a hit movie, set up a $50 million venture capital fund. Named iArtisan, its mission was to invest in start-ups working on new-media plumbing like streaming video and digital compression. Paccar, a truck manufacturer in Seattle is pursuing technologies to improve its operations and the WPP Group is financing new media start-ups. Bertelsmann A.G., placed $1 billion into a venture fund to bankroll new media technology companies. Reuters made a smaller bet with their Greenhouse Fund and emphasized that they were looking for companies that can give Reuters a leg up in media and transaction businesses. Bayer Diagnostic teamed with venture capital firm Burrill & Company to form a $50 million fund for diagnostic research and other areas that Bayer wants to pursue.*

David Barry, senior editor of *The Corporate Venturing Report*, counts hundreds of formal corporate venture capital programs around the world that are active. Corporate venture programs accounted for $8.2 billion, or 15 percent, of the $54 billion invested by the venture capital industry in the first half of 2000. Barry said, "Corporations need a venture capital arm to stay on top of companies that may either be their future partner or eat their lunch." Barry's annual directory costs $695 but shows you what firms have formal funds, just who to contact, criteria for investing, etc., at www.assetnews.com.

A survey by PricewaterhouseCoopers asked 421 of the fastest growing U.S. businesses how they were deploying surplus cash and says 18% of them turn to external business investments. These "Trendsetter" companies, ranging in size from $1 million to $50 million in annual revenue, were mainly private or closely held. Some simply invested in the stock market, but others were pursuing synergistic strategies.

While many companies make private investments in firms with products that are attractive to their own businesses, others opt for an incubation program for a new enterprise. "CEOs need to be broader than just their own businesses" says G. Steve Hamm, a PricewaterhouseCoopers executive in Newport Beach, CA. Firms such as Senior Market Sales Inc., Omaha, Neb., a private insurance marketing outfit, reported outside investments come only after Internal growth targets are met. Milton Kleinberg, owner of Senior Market Sales, said his firm grows about 20% a year and regularly generated cash to invest.

> *GreenCross Pharmaceuticals, one of the largest drug companies in South Korea, made money investing in two early stage biotechs in the U.S. and intends to do it again. Overseas money from many quarters is attracted to the U.S., but mostly for high-tech deals. As an exception, Mitsubishi established Red Diamond Capital Partners LP as a $150 million fund to be used to overhaul management and boost profitability at underperforming companies operating in conventional industries. Mitsubishi already owned Millennia Venture Partners, a VC fund specializing in high-tech startups, as well as a private equity turnaround specialist, MC Private Equity Investment, and is the main Japanese partner in Ripplewood Holdings LLC, a private equity fund. Mitsubishi leverages their mammoth existing assets and feels that any investments made will be enhanced by their own global market skills and information. No question that Mitsubishi brings to the table enormous capabilities in such things as distribution, R&D and manufacturing. The big Japanese firm had been a cautious investor and backed other U.S. funds before they formed their own fund, and only then with the cream of American*

talent to manage the investments. Mitsubishi expected that they often have to change CEOs of the companies they buy into, and have recruited a group of potential candidates for jobs. These executives need to be able to work autonomously but also relate to the parent company and relevant divisions. Crossing so many cultures required them to set up a special executive training program as a management cadre.

In difficult markets, companies still rely on small firms for new products.

Though firms such as AOL Time Warner have shown losses of more than $100 billion in market capital through a stock market downturn that began in 2000, they remain ardent venture capital investors. The giant media company is less motivated by showing dollar returns than by making equity investments in technologies that will be needed by TV and Internet audiences of the future. Other firms quickly scaled back or stopped investing altogether, suggesting that their forays into the VC world had a short-term orientation. Agriculture conglomerate Cargill had a venture unit that flirted with software and Internet companies but reverted to its core interests of food and biotechnology, an effort to use its internal expertise. Venture Economics states that in 2000 there were as many as 2,100 corporate venture deals but that those numbers fell to just 302 in the first half of 2002. Even with a weak economy active companies remained and included Intel, Johnson & Johnson, Microsoft, Sony and Cisco. Investments by telecommunications companies, unfortunately, largely disappeared.

Shaping your message.

When you're approaching a corporation to seek funding and a strategic partnership, a little research goes a long way. By examining their most recent annual report you'll learn what emphases the company is making, where they're placing their money, how they operate, the words and phrases that are in vogue, and a host of added information to help you shape a responsive submission. The annual reports are usually on-line but otherwise they will be happy to send one out to you. Annual reports today are one of the best PR vehicles a company has and also a way to keep shareholders enthused about company prospects. Even if you don't see a direct relationship between your company and the potential investor, do your best to tie it to some of their missions and relate it with the words and phrases you find common in their statements. If you're a biotech firm, for example, the *Genome Technology* news service puts out a survey entitled "What Big Pharma Wants" and gives an insight into the needs of half a dozen major corporate partners. Similar resources are going to be found for nearly any industry and, even if they don't cause you to re-shape your business model, will certainly give you clues about how words and ways you should use to present your idea.

An Ernst & Young study found the number one reason for corporate venturing is the broad aim of gaining competitive advantage. Financial motivation ranked second and other goals such as moving into new products and increasing speed and flexibility were close behind. The failure of some corporate ventures has been attributed to: fear of risk taking; lack of imagination; the institutionalization of most executives; and a general fear of failure.

> *When Teresa Meng and John Hennessy took their technology for making wireless technology cheaper and more powerful to a number of companies for licensing they struck out. The two formed a new company, Atheros, put together a management team and secured over $90 million in financing from groups such as Fidelity Management and Research, August Capital and Bowman Capital.*

Multi-group investing.

You'll often see corporate investments made as part of an overall deal that includes several venture capital funds as co-investors. Everyone feels better having a corporate partner that knows the industry the young company is marketing to and the management oversight of the VCs probably represents comfort for the corporate partner as well. A strategic partner, and certainly an industry leader, will enhance your ability to attract institutional venture capital investments. Many investors view the participation of a strategic player as a precondition to their own investment.

www.CorporateVenturingSummit.com sponsors an annual conference in New York of corporate venture groups. Firms such as Eastman Kodak, Hewlett-Packard, Sony, Hearst and hundreds of other funds show up for this two-day program in how to manage money. The International Business Forum at www.ibforum.com does largely the same thing on the West Coast.

Corporations often have two separate forms of investment cash. The first may be designated for strategic partnerships and companies with business models that are related to the parent's mission. The second may be a pure venture capital fund that simply seeks the highest returns from any investment, although the focus area usually is within their conventional markets. As a third type of focus, Nokia began a $40 million Early Stage Technology Fund to provide financing for new business ideas made inside the company. This fund is designated to serve internal entrepreneurs and provide the seed capital to develop new businesses. Their bias remains mobile telecommunications markets and technologies, of course. Sweden's Ericsson teamed up with Merrill Lynch and several other Swedish companies to form a mobile Internet venture capital fund.

Corporate alliances have become more important for most companies. Lou Gerstner Jr. took over direction of IBM in the mid 1990s and emphasized how these business relationships can augment IBM's business. Today, nearly 100,000 companies have a partnership relationship with Big Blue and contribute one-third of IBM's revenues versus one-twentieth when Gerstner arrived.

An article on how corporate venturing works is available from Baker & McKenzie at http://vcexperts.com under the title "Structuring a Result-Oriented Corporate Venture Program."

BUSINESS ANGELS

An early Intel executive supported Apple computer in 1977 with $91,000 and a guarantee of $250,000 for credit lines. British investors provided money hundreds of years ago for canals and steam engines. Laurence Rockefeller backed Eddie Rickenbacker and the development of Eastern Airlines in the 1930s.

Angels defined.

The term "angel" was coined on Broadway to characterize wealthy individuals who invested in stage plays. Today, the term extends to people who invest anywhere from $25,000 to $2 million in startup companies. While angel groups exist across the country and a number of attempts have been made to allow entrepreneurs to access them on-line, it's still a personal way of investing that is characterized by someone that you get to know and an industry they feel comfortable with. A number of the angel sources listed in this chapter are good places to start but angel investing is specific to everyone and needs to be separately thought out by company principals.

Angels are often entrepreneurs themselves, many of whom come with a solid business background along with money, expertise and time to share with young companies. Differences exist between angels and venture capitalists including the fact they are investing their own money and not institutional funds that venture capitalists represent. You may find angels more patient, less demanding, and able to understand your business model sooner, especially if they have background in an industry related to your own. The biggest difference is the stage of company growth where they become the best source of money—early and even seed stage. While most venture capitalists are seeking fairly proven business models, angels take more chances and can be counted on for riskier funding.

Angel investors usually have time horizons that are longer than other investors and tend to make their cash rewards a lower priority than venture capitalists. Many times they are motivated by the sheer fun and adrenalin rush that's involved in developing a company.

The National Commission on Entrepreneurship (NCOE) reports that about 6% of the adult population is involved in angel investing, an extraordinarily large number for an entrepreneur to chase down. NCOE Executive Director, Patrick Von Bargen, says, "High-growth entrepreneurs account for less than 5 percent of the start-up activity out there, but in the 40-year period we studied, they created most of the new jobs in the country and nearly all of the important technology breakthroughs." High-growth entrepreneurs are the ones who expect to employ hundreds and make millions and are not exclusively high-tech, as we see by the growth of firms such as Starbucks and Jiffy Lube. A roadblock to seeing more successes is the lack of funding in the area of plus or minus one to two million dollars. The task becomes one of matching angels with entrepreneurs.

Finding angel investors.

Instead of gravitating to existing angel groups, think of how easy it really may be to get in touch with people and what your connections might be. In 1967, psychologist Stanley Milgram used a chain letter experiment to discover how people were connected to each other. He sent packages to 160 randomly chosen addresses in Kansas and Nebraska with the name and address of a stockbroker in Boston, MA. Milgram asked the recipients to send the package to the Boston Addressee but not before sending it to someone they knew who might get it closer to the stockbroker. Each link was asked to add their name to the envelope. When the packages finally arrived, Milgram found that most had taken between five or six steps, the basis for the idea of "six degrees of separation," which became the title of a play by John Gaure (illustrated in *The Tipping Point*).

Duke Chung and four other newly minted engineers out of Cornell found an angel investor who had developed and sold a company before, and was willing to put money into their firm, Cyracle, Inc. The angel had retired from a large company four years before, became bored, and knew he needed to get back into harness. He became Cyracle's chairman, provided an invaluable network for them, and has been a mentor for their growth. Cyracle has continued to use angels and now has a 20-person board of advisors, largely to extend the work of their first angel. Don Britton at Network Alliance had the same result, an angel investor who proved to be a wonderful guide and mentor.

> *Energy Conversion Devices (ECD) of Rochester Hills, MI persuaded the former chairman of General Motors, Robert Stempel, to leave retirement, take over as chairman of ECD, and help build the company to over 500 employees. It seems strange to think that the former head of one of the world's largest companies would be willing to dip down into a seeming micro-organism, but don't discount the interest people may have in the creative process that your company represents. Also, don't expect them all to be like that, as most directors are more passive and often add little.*

> *Riversoft, a British software developer, persuaded the retired chairman of Dunlop Corp to be their chairman. Soon after taking office, he called the head of British Telecom and arranged a fifteen-minute meeting where Riversoft presented and was able to make its first significant product sale.*

Help in finding angels.

While the question "How do I find these business angels?" continually circulates and there are lots of answers, it's still true that a large portion of middle and upper-income individuals may easily invest in your company and never think of themselves as angels, just someone willing to take an intelligent risk. You may receive smaller investments and need more of these people than the "whales" that you may have read about, but they will probably be more receptive to you than people who are pitched to day after day, by different entrepreneurs looking for money.

There are a number of books on angel investors as well as websites, clubs, forums and even a magazine. The best information on this attractive source of early capital is a book entitled *Angel Investing* by Osnabrugge and Robinson (see bibliography). *Angel Investing* is a serious study conducted at the Harvard Business School and illustrates the plusses and minuses of this type of funding. A planned *Angel Society's Directory of*

Angel Networks & Early Stage Venture Capital Firms by Grey House Publishing of New York has not yet materialized. The *Directory* hopes to provide coverage of sources to include their mission statements, investment criteria, investment sizes, etc., as well as contacts, addresses, phone and fax numbers, and e-mail and website addresses.

Flocks of angels.

You'll find a number of angel groups or clubs nearby, along with a suggestion that you present your business plan and see if you get lucky. A presentation makes sense but I've never seen much come out of these groups, often the members seem to have their own deals that they're seeking added money for. Even if you don't get a check, they will probably improve your business model by asking intelligent questions and members can refer you, maybe sit on your board, etc. About 170 of these groups are organized in the U.S. Business angel groups can also provide a key source of qualified companies for venture capital firms and, when they do write the checks, provide intermediate capital in a growth stage between the family and friends, and institutional venture capital.

Though business angels are difficult to locate, there are effective ways for entrepreneurs to find them, such as: personal networks; professional networks; snowball effect of early investors; formal matching services; angel alliances; venture capital clubs; the Internet; matchmakers; mailing lists and publications; and investment banking firms. A web search under "angel investors" could identify a number of angel groups as well as lists of angel investors. In regards to the latter, don't get your hopes too high since their Internet listing probably means they're inundated with business plans.

You can find yourself buying lists of angels, looking up websites, and attending meetings, etc., but that may not be your best source. Upper middle-income and middle-income individuals along with the wealthy should be looked upon as your potential pool of angels. These are people who nearly all have invested in the stock market, have experienced both making and losing money on a number of investments, and could be receptive to your business idea. Instead of ferreting out lists of a number of people who have previously made $50,000 investments in young companies you may find that block after block of your neighbors qualify as angels or mini-angels, many of whom will have never been asked to invest this way before, and could jump at the chance. Take the expansive view of who has the cash. If you opt to find these people, Chapter 11 on PR may be of particular help to you as well as Chapter 8 on small stock offerings.

Some angel resources identified by the Ewing Marion Kauffman Foundation include: National, www.investorscircle.net; California, www.angelsforum.com; Mid-Atlantic, www.thedinnerclub.com, and www.angelinvestorfunding.com; Midwest, www.c-cap.net/angels.html, www.prairieangels.com; New England, www.walnutventures.com; New York, www.nynma.org; and Canada, www.mindfirst.com. www.dealflow.com was formed to help angels find entrepreneurs and has a database with a fairly small annual fee attached. www.businesspartners.com is also a matching service.

> *An entrepreneur knew of one angel who he was certain would be the right investor to both fund and help direct his company. The problem was that the angel wouldn't return phone calls. He found out who served as the angel's accountant, worked on him, and had the accountant make a successful introduction.*

The SBA spent a lot of money developing an angel network (ACE.NET, https://ace-net.sr.unh.edu or links from www.sba.gov) and old groups with a similar mission such as the MIT Enterprise Forum (MITEF) are thriving. MITEF puts on lots of seminars to help new businesses. The Technology Capital Network at MIT (www.tcnmit.org) is a database that connects entrepreneurs with funding sources ($300 per year to list your plan). One of the earliest attempts to organize angel investors and put them in contact with deserving companies was begun by the University of New Hampshire's Professor William E. Wetzel, Jr. Wetzel has devoted himself to helping entrepreneurs but he has never felt these organizations have lived up to their potential. He's now a Director Emeritus of the Center for Venture Research at UNH and is possibly the most serious researcher in entrepreneurial finance in the country.

> *"The first thing anyone said to me when I appeared at an angel group was 'You don't expect to get any money out of the people here, do you?'" Judy Howard, the co-founder of Lightwave Technologies on her feeling that this was more of a dinner discussion and social group than a real funding source.*

For $200, the Sausalito, CA-based Angel Capital Network will provide an all-day session on how to make an investment appeal to angels. They teach you to make an executive summary, a 6-8 minute pitch, a 2-minute oral presentation, and they also provide mentoring for your company. You'll find details including a calendar of meetings at www.angelcapitalnetwork.com. Many other groups including most business schools provide similar services.

www.inc.com/finance has a directory of angel investor networks broken down into regions. As an example of what you'll find, in the Pacific Northwest, the site lists the Portland Area Angel Network with contact information including a website, their investment criteria (high-growth industries with a clear exit strategy), number of angels (100) and average investment range ($.5 million to $2 million). Valley Angels in Green Bay, WI nurtures Wisconsin companies. The largest and one of the oldest groups in the country is the Silicon Valley, Band of Angels investment club. The Band of Angels format of listening to pitches from entrepreneurs at dinner has become a standard, as well as the requirement that you need a member to sponsor your appearance. If you make it through an intensive winnowing process to the dinner, a number of companies report they found the cash they needed.

"I need an angel, a good one, not a vulture in disguise." Doug Adams.

Speaking to angels.

Just like making a presentation before venture capitalists, you should be prepared to answer penetrating questions about your business. You can expect that questions from angels may be even more industry-specific and detailed, since several of them may have run companies in your target market. While you need to be able to answer reasonable questions, and you may find that you do beautifully through this interrogation, this still may not be enough. Entrepreneurs know how difficult it is to build a business and they may be looking at you to see if you're tough enough and have the staying power to last through inevitable disappointments and problems. Do you have the fire in the belly to make this company a success and produce profits for these people?

When you access angels you'll find that you're getting nearer to other forms of capital too. These are often well-to-do people with lots of connections. Members of Memphis Angels, for example, have separately contributed funds to a new $20 million biotech venture capital fund in the city, and lead you to the greater venture capital community. A connection to angels could lead you to dozens of other sources of money and techniques for growth.

At the same Inc Magazine website, www.inc.com/guides/finance/capital you'll find a checklist of items you need to prepare before talking to angel investors plus suggestions on many types of business financing. www.angel-investor.com has a free six-page guide to making presentations, written by Tech Coast Angels.

Characteristics of angel investing.

The study by Osnabrugge and Robinson provides a number of statistics on angel investing:

- Business angels are the oldest, largest and most often used source of outside funds for entrepreneurial firms;
- The United States has close to three million angels, investing more than $50 billion in entrepreneurial firms each year [note that this figure differs by half from the NCOE's separate compilation, suggesting that no one knows the right figure anyway]. With the right incentives, this market could become many times larger;
- Angels already fund thirty to forty times as many entrepreneurial firms as does the formal venture capital industry, investing three to five times more money;
- Many of our most influential firms, such as Ford, Apple and Amazon.com, were initially angel-funded. More and more firms over the coming years will also be angel-funded;
- An increasing number of today's most successful high-tech and Internet entrepreneurs, such as former Apple CEO John Sculley, Netscape's Jim Barksdale, and Microsoft's Paul Allen, have partially cashed out and become angel investors;
- Angels fund 60 percent of all new technology firms in the United States.
- There are ten distinct advantages that business angels bring to their investments:

    1. They prefer smaller-size investments than venture capitalists and may fit you better.

2. Usually invest in start-ups and early-stage companies without demanding proven revenues (though a cash stream is always valuable).
3. Make investments in virtually all industry sectors.
4. More flexible in their financial decisions than venture capitalists.
5. Raising funds does not involve high fees.
6. Most angels are value-added investors that contribute their skills along with their money.
7. More geographically dispersed and easier to get to than the concentrations of venture capitalists in Silicon Valley, Boston and New York.
8. Have a leveraging effect by making the firm more attractive to other sources of capital; they lend their own prestige.
9. Often offer loan guarantees if not the outright cash.
10. Not averse to funding radically different technologies.

Since angels have their own investment criteria and behave differently than of venture capitalists, it's vital for you to understand these differences. Many Americans have become angels already by investing a small part of their portfolios in entrepreneurial firms and, if the stock market starts rising again, their numbers may easily double by 2010.

Angel investors have the reputation for being tolerant with young companies, may put more money into them as they progress, and provide invaluable suggestions for growth and development. Angels will often serve on your board or become part of your management team. As America's largest companies continue to downsize, competent people will be out work and they could be your angels, perhaps just seeking an interesting job and hoping to make some money on an investment.

Angels can be more like a partner and less like a demanding shareholder. Since they usually have business experience their comments and suggestions should be taken seriously, unlike freshly minted MBAs are often found at institutional sources of capital.

Realize what angels need from you.

Angels need an exit strategy. Even with their longer holding horizons, a liquidity event should be discussed to show how they can realize profits on their investment. While firms are usually merged or acquired (roughly ten times more often than likely to cash in with an IPO), make sure you consider possible sources of acquisition along with the omnipresent "going public." The horizon for holding an investment varies but is typically counted in years and changes with the fervor of the stock market.

> *A recent $2.4 million angel funding for life sciences firm Cylex followed a $3.6 million round two years before. The company developed tests to measure the strength of a patient's immune system and made their presentation with an FDA approval letter in hand, taking a lot of risk out of the investment. Angels are in tune with markets just like venture capital firms and other investors. When we're facing bear markets, angels are far less likely to invest in riskier ventures, and an appeal to real revenues and markets will prove necessary.*

Angels may relate to your technology quickly but their own investment experience will probably make them more interested in management and particularly in sales. If you haven't recorded any sales yet, or gotten commitments from potential customers, you need to show a dynamite marketing plan that will dispel fears that you haven't done essential homework.

www.techcoastangels.com has a complete guide for submitting an investment proposal to a prominent angel group. Sections on the site include: an overview of how they screen investment opportunities and conduct due diligence; suggestions for a presentation; the types of companies they seek; factors that determine valuation; term sheets; a hypothetical proposal; things to consider in your elevator pitch; a comprehensive guide to delivering a succinct and effective presentation; and the locations where they hold screening sessions.

Where to start.

The Private Investors Network at www.mava.org/pin.cfm is a prominent angel network in the greater Washington, D.C. area that mixes area entrepreneurs with accredited equity investors, through the Capital Access Network. Under the general sponsorship of the University of Maryland, funding ranges between $250,000 and $3 million and the company must be located in the Mid-Atlantic. An application costs $200 and needs to be accompanied by a business plan and certain disclaimers. Details for submission are given at www.rhsmith.umd.edu/dingman/PIN.htm. The Chesapeake Emerging Opportunities Club of angel investors is interested in the categories of: life sciences, Internet companies, telecom and optical-networking. Details can be found at www.ceopportunities.com. In Lexington, MA you'll find the 55-member Common Angels (www.commonangels.com) as well as a raft of individual angels and venture capitalists in and around the Boston, MA area. Angel Healthcare Investors in Newton, MA (www.hcangels.com) placed $7 million with young companies that interested their life sciences, biotech and service-oriented entrepreneur members. Angel Healthcare usually invests along with VC firms and leverages their investments considerably by doing so. A little searching is bound to turn up one of these groups close by.

The California-based Central Coast Angels join with the International Angel Investors to put on programs with technical topics such as nanotechnology as well as help for entrepreneurs. You can check their respective websites, www.ccangels.net, www.angelinvestors.org, or call the offices of InfoPoint, Inc. at (831) 471 1671. www.angeldeals.com seeks to match investors with young companies and charges an annual subscription fee for access. The Angel Investor Magazine website profiled a number of angel investors and suggested differences in each. At this writing the magazine seems moribund, www.angelinvestormagazine.com.

MerchantBanc in New Hampshire holds an Angel Breakfast every six weeks to bring new companies face to face with investors. Steak and Eggs does the same thing in Bethesda, MD. In the United Kingdom, things are more organized. A free 61-page report and listing of angel groups is available from the British Venture Capital Association at www.bvca.co.uk. You'll get a report on how to go about interacting with these groups plus telephone numbers, websites, etc.

Sandra K. Richardson Metier and her husband Douglas formed a software company to help predict future work performance across an enterprise. They had an initial contract with Lockheed Martin and used that connection to show serious potential and used it to help secure angel funding. The Metiers raised $1.2 million from a collection of silent investors and business leaders in Washington, D.C., an industry expert, and from an investment club called WomenAngels.net. Along with the money Metier has been given specific financial and technical expertise plus the inputs of 80 high-profile investors who care about her firm.

SMALL STOCK OFFERINGS

"There is no sucker money out there. If there was, I would have taken it a long time ago." An investment banker at Ferris Baker Watts and a strong suggestion that any funding proposal has to be well thought out, completely accurate, and documented. If you're thinking of taking the route of a small stock offering (SSO), remember that you'll be involved in a highly legal process that subjects you to a host of rules and regulations. Nonetheless, it can have a great number of benefits.

Small stock offerings provide specific solutions.

In the 1980s, the Connecticut State Medical Society wanted to protect cash flow from competition by non-physician HMOs and allow practicing physicians to determine patient care, by creating a statewide physician owned and controlled HMO known as M.D. Health Plan. The problem was that if individual physicians invested, some could gain financially more than others. Another difficulty was that outside investors would want significant control and equity, neutralizing much of their goal. Tom Garvey of TMG Consultants in Merrick, NY, suggested a novel and creative route for physicians. They registered a small securities offering with the SEC and raised the $4.5 million they needed in seven months, entirely from practicing Connecticut physicians. Investors, who were not allowed to buy more than $5,000 and had to be members of the Connecticut State Medical Society, reaped a huge reward on M. D. Health Plan a few years later while solving their problems of control and competition (garveyt@optonline.net).

Portland Brewing in Oregon used four small stock offerings over several years to raise nearly $7 million. Blue Fish Clothing in Frenchtown,

NJ raised $4 million on the strengths of its hand-painted clothing and organically grown cotton. Mendocino Brewing in Hopland, CA, saw its shares nearly double in price but this may have more to do with the company's promise to give a pint of free beer to shareholders each day at the brewery, than the intrinsic value of the stock. Annie's Homegrown Macaroni-and-Cheese sold shares to its customers by placing stock information in each box. Success in raising capital with these kinds of instruments often revolves around affinity groups, either existing or newly-created by your marketing efforts.

If you decide that an SSO works for you, don't dwell on the pace of the stock market. SSOs seem largely independent of either strong or weak stock markets and buyers focus on the company's message more than they worry about a declining overall market. SSOs are original offerings made by filing a registration statement with securities authorities, not reverse mergers into existing listings—shells. Shells can carry a lot of baggage and are not an automatic way to raise money. Capital raises occur when the liquidity that shells represent can be turned into a secondary stock offering, something that requires a lot of publicity or hype as well as cost. Expect to see shells at three or four times the cost of a new SSO.

Examples of how companies used a small stock offering.

1. Floated a small stock offering and used the publicly held shares to acquire other companies.
2. Used an aggressive public relations campaign to attract stock buyers and customers at the same time.
3. Marketed a stock offering to clients, suppliers and distributors and raised the capital they needed from the circle of people who knew their business as well as from strangers.
4. Used the publicity associated with a small stock offering to find strategic partners who both supplied capital by buying shares and set up new marketing channels.
5. Found that shareholders buy 100%-300% more of a company's products than ordinary customers and targeted sales to existing as well as new clients.
6. Gave key employees shares in a publicly held small stock offering and gained not only more loyalty but also paid lower salaries during the lean startup years.

7. Sought a buyer for the company by freely advertising the share offering and specifying the terms they wanted up front.
8. Gained credibility with larger investment banking firms by making a small stock offering and going through the regulatory process before approaching major Wall Street firms.

Private placements and small stock offerings.

A common packaging for a company seeking early funding is the use of a private placement memorandum (PPM). This is little more than your business plan wrapped up with a number of statements that illustrate risk and other characteristics that are designed to protect the principals from lawsuits. A PPM is fast and it is easy to do but it is hardly a marketable instrument. Statistics suggest that as little as one out of every two hundred-fifty PPMs are fully subscribed and it is a difficult item to sell, filled with many restrictions designed to insure that state and federal securities laws are not bypassed. It may be better to take the extra step and register your security with federal and state regulators, something that has become far easier and cheaper to do with provisions designed just for small offerings and newer companies. An SSO is roughly the same as a direct public offering, a DPO, and along the same lines as an IPO. An SSO and a PPM often address the same set of early investors and the same stage of development for a young firm. An SSO differs from a PPM as follows:

1. An SSO can be freely advertised and is not limited on the number of subscribers. While restrictions are sharp on the methods you can use to reach investors with a PPM and the number of investors cannot be above 35, unless they have substantial assets, an SSO eliminates these concerns. In fact, SSOs have been sold through radio advertising, television programs, magazine articles, etc.
2. The typical investor qualifications are eliminated by filing a registration statement. (California and New Jersey retain minimal factors). While the number of "accredited investors" who can participate in PPMs is unlimited, these people have to attest to a net worth above $1 million or joint incomes above $300,000.

3. A registered offering comes with the "seal" of the SEC and State Securities Commissions, at least in terms of qualification. While the regulators don't approve or disapprove registrations, and they don't warrant that the facts are true, they have reviewed them and the filers are liable to criminal penalties if they have made any false statements.
4. Foreign securities agencies usually accept an SEC qualified offering without further problems. If you have a few isolated sales to foreign residents you may find that having a full U.S. securities agency review alleviates most uncertainty about the offering. If this becomes an issue with you, it will be necessary to check with a securities attorney.
5. An SSO offering circular is a readable document with color illustrations and is printed in exactly the same format as an IPO offered by investment banking firms. You will go through an identical review procedure and provide most of the same information that full-scale IPO offerings are required to do. If you've ever slogged through a PPM, too many of those are pretty unreadable and contain legal material that is extraneous for the typical investor.
6. Publicity associated with an SSO provides invaluable marketing and development benefits including the possibility of a buy-out, IPO, merger, strategic partner, increased sales, added personnel, added distributors, etc. Since a stock offering always involves getting the word out with as many potential investors as possible, many of those same people may be new customers, suppliers, employees, etc., that you need to grow your business.
7. Creating a publicly held security gives the company leverage to use its stock for acquisitions and other purposes over and above the money raised. You don't need to have your stock traded on an exchange, but you do need to have a company that will grow and eventually provide liquidity to any company that you bought with shares. Many successful firms have used their stock to buy up assets and grow in this fashion. You effectively "create money" by having an issuable security.
8. Popular forms of registration include Regulation A, allowing the raising of up to $5 million of capital each twelve months and an SB-2, which allows $25 million in market

capitalization and assets. Small Corporate Offering Registrations can be made in multiple states with a ceiling of $1 million, and followed later by other forms of registration. A number of companies have first offered a SCOR, then a Regulation A, an SB-2 and finally, a full-scale IPO, an S-1. If you seek buyers in only one state and you are both incorporated and do most of your business in that state, you may choose an intrastate offering and only have to contend with your state regulators and their rules.

9. The procedure for qualification has been deliberately shortened with SEC comments on the first submission received back in about thirty days. The process will go on from there but need not be lengthy given a well-prepared offering at the beginning.

10. Firms can typically prepare a submission to the SEC fairly quickly, working with company advisors such as the attorney and accountant. While the first-time one prepares a registration statement can be a nightmare, once a person gets the hang of it things go pretty quickly. The most common delay comes about from not having the financial statements ready.

11. SEC attorneys and accountants examine the document in detail (without charge for a Regulation A) and state just what has to be changed to be in full compliance with the laws and regulations. This is an incredible benefit that comes with making a filing since professionals in these fields read every word that you have submitted and indicate just what needs to be changed, substantiated, etc.

12. An SEC accepted document could be legally more protective of the entrepreneur, underwriter, directors, executives, etc. than a PPM, though this is one of many things you need to check over with your lawyer. Your registration statement will go through an extensive review process by regulators while your PPM may never be seen by any professionals outside of those who prepared it.

13. SSOs or DPOs can have wide offering amounts. The Price Club completed a DPO for $71 million while a $100,000 offering for a taco manufacturer was made in Mississippi.

14. A private placement or other form of early stage investment is usually recorded on the books of the investor at cost

regardless of how well the company may be doing. An SSO may allow the early stage investors to record their investment value at the public offering or traded price. (Check this with your own CPA).

15. The ballpark costs of registering an SSO are usually within the budget of emerging high-growth companies:

a. SEC filing fee:	$0 (Regulation A is zero, SB-2 is $92 per million for 2002 under section 6 of the '33 Act)
b. NASD filing fee	$1,000 (computed at $500 plus $100 per million)
c. State filing fee	$1,000 (average, per state where registered, runs from $0 to $10,000)
d. Audit	$5,000-$10,000 (average, required by many states and desirable)
e. Prospectus	$3,100 (average for 1,000 copies. Note: offerings on the Internet can lessen this charge and save postage as well.)
f. Registration Document	$12,000, more or less. We've seen charges for registration statements run up to $140,000 and other instances where the entrepreneur wrote it entirely by themselves.
h. Opinion of Counsel	$1,500
i. Public Relations	$1,500 per month for a minimum of three months.
j. Electronic Filing	$2,500 if required by SEC.
k. Marketing	$5,000-$10,000 (you can spend a lot less or much more, depending on the marketing plan).

Appendix A has a list of the kinds of information that you need to compile for these registrations. A set of slides on The Dirty Dozen, frequent mistakes/oversights of start-up companies helps avoid all too common errors committed by registrants, and is available from Phil Feigen at www.pattonboggs.com.

Bill Rose graduated from the University of Iowa with the conviction that he wanted his own company. Running a profitable record and tape *store near the campus, he sold it and invested the proceeds in a new bagel business. The bagels sold fine and in response to customer's requests, he devised a bagel with a longer shelf life, using Iowa State University technology. He needed capital to expand and talked to his stockbroker about sources of money. The broker indicated that a small stock offering might work and Rose filed one in Iowa and surrounding states. Today, Rose's Uncle B's bagels are the number one branded bagel in supermarket cases nationwide. Getting to a $20 million business took a number of financing steps, including a state-backed industrial revenue bond for a large bakery, but the initial stock sale was the key to his expansion. Rose sold some of his shares to executives of General Mills and Pillsbury in Minneapolis, people in a similar business who understood quickly what he was talking about and felt good about the market he was going after. In addition to their money, these seasoned professionals acted as an unpaid advisory board to help him grow.*

Characteristics of small stock offerings.

- The stage of development of your company is far less important than how you package your concept and deliver the message.
- An SSO is markedly different from an ordinary stock peddled by a retail broker and failure to understand that distinction can lead to big problems in both the short and long term.
- Liquidity is over-valued. People need to know that they should hold on to these shares for a few years while the company grows. Their eventual profit depends on your exit strategy, perhaps an IPO or acquisition.
- Gurus Warren Buffett and Peter Lynch tell people the identical path to making money in the stock market. They both say to " . . . find a product you like and think has a great future. Buy shares in the company that makes it and hold on for the long term." This advice fits an SSO perfectly and is an intelligent remedy for the agony of looking at the stock market pages every day.
- You need a marketing plan that has several different approaches since you can't be sure just what will actually work.

- Treat the stock sale as a "product rollout" and never differentiate the stock from the company message. Always be talking about the products/services and the company and simply let people know about the stock. Don't ever hard sell the stock or over-promise.
- The Internet is a superb vehicle for SSOs, but maybe not the way you think. It's fanciful to think that people will surf the Internet, download your prospectus, read it and send in money. That's not how people act. The Internet is a way to deliver your prospectus cheaply (you don't have to pay for printing or postage) and it is a way to tell the story of the company and its products. The Internet is really a vast incentive system and using it correctly is a key to success.
- Build a team to launch the offering. Get everyone involved and solicit ideas from all your team members.
- Keep the interests of your new shareholders uppermost in your mind. If you treat people right, not only is it ethical, they will do much more for you in the future.
- Companies generally find that shareholders become ardent users of the company's products so think inclusively about the number of your potential shareholders. This is a group that will become free marketing agents for you.
- Don't think that browbeating people on the telephone is the correct way to get your stock sold. People are not anywhere near as receptive to phone solicitations as they used to be and you need to use different communication vehicles. AT&T tells us that only one out of every four calls reaches the intended party on the first try.
- Think about enlisting a professional PR firm or at least being creative in your approaches to people. Advertising works for established products to keep market share and stem competition but PR is the magic vehicle to launch your company and build a market position (see the next chapter).
- Being first with a product or service is often one of the most powerful messages to solicit investors. Even if it is a conventional product think about re-packaging it as something novel.
- Money tends to trickle in at the beginning of an offering period and cascade nearer the end. This may not be the case for you but plan on it anyway. You should try to create some

kind of imperative so people sign up quickly for your shares instead of procrastinating.
- Think "strategic partnering." Many other companies may wish to associate with you for one reason or other and they can bring some heavy capital to the table. It's a lot cheaper to form a relationship with you by buying stock than to try to copy the same idea in-house. Also, a licensing agreement is an expense while a stock purchase is a capital investment and can look much better on a balance sheet.
- Think globally. You may find that people and companies in Italy or Korea may want to buy into your company and intelligent PR can get your message to them.

Types of businesses that have used SSOs.

e-Commerce Provider
Publishing
Physician Care Network
Golf Course
Retail Store
Medical Supply Company
Pharmaceutical Firm
Restaurant
Brewery
High-Tech Company
Energy Equipment Firm
Physician's Hosp. Org.
Commodities Firm
Environmental Consultant
Computer Company
Homebuilder
Musical Producer
Renovator
Auto Dealer
Childcare Center
Water Sports Dealer
Communications Device
Winery
Clothing Manufacturer

Data Mining Firm
Entertainment Company
Graphics Design Firm
Sports Franchise
Automobile Leasing Agency
Biomedical Company
Tire Processing Plant
Engineering Management
Furnace Manufacturer
Coffee Brewing Equipment Manufacturer
Travel Agency
Learning Center
Mortgage and Security Firm
Engine Manufacturer
Electrical Vehicle
Natural Food Supplier
Bakery
Building Supply Company
Skating Rink
Livestock Market
Winter Sports Manufacturer
Resort Hotel
Multimedia Company
Meat Processing Plant

Juice/Beverage Wholesaler	Aircraft Leasing Company
Bioremediation Firm	Communications Supplier
Internet Services	Clothing Retailer
Data Warehousing	Oil Blending Firm
Health Food Supplements	Bank
Physician's Practice Mgmt.	Liquids Processing
Shoe Factory	Environmental Timber
Information Technology	Alternative Energy
Tissue Engineering R&D	

You need to prepare to make an SSO. (See Appendix B)

1. Be ready to be public. Validate all the elements of your business model and think through the requirements of acting like a public company.
2. Plan your public relations. If you don't coordinate your PR effort with your legal, financial and administrative needs you may find that you cannot successfully launch your offering.
3. Build a solid management team. You'll need help during the offering period and investors want to see the short biographies of the people that will be responsible for running the company.
4. Resolve accounting issues early. Financial disclosure is critical to all forms of capital raising and doubly so in a public offering. Check SEC accounting regulations with your auditor. Cheap stock issues can be avoided by careful determination of fair market value when determining option exercise prices. License agreements must be structured with revenue recognition issues in mind.
5. Put your house in order. Put in-place new contracts for management, make certain all share issuances and other corporate actions are fully documented and implemented and review employee stock plans.
6. Determine your capital needs. Be sure to have enough authorized capital to meet your acquisition, option pool and capital needs for at least 24 months following a public offering.
7. Raise money in advance of your needs. The worst time to raise capital is when you must complete the offering

by a specific time; short-term pressures can lead to poor long-term decisions.
8. Examine your board of directors. A public company needs different advice from its board than a private company. Add talent as well as two independent directors for compensation and audit committees.
9. Select your advisors well. Insure that all of your advisors understand both the registration process and your company's vision for growth.
10. Avoid surprise. The worst nightmare for investors is surprise because it damages your credibility. Be up front with your problems since they invariably cause more damage the longer they remain hidden.

Information on SSOs.

The best book available on the registration and sales process for smaller stock offerings is Drew Field's Direct Public Offerings, Sourcebooks, Inc., Naperville, IL, 1997. The author is both a lawyer and accountant by training but his passion is seeing younger companies successfully launched. You'll find a questionnaire on his website at www.dfdpo.com that will help suggest if you're a good candidate for one of these offerings and Drew is nearly always available to counsel entrepreneurs. He notes that "the SEC's latest rules on electronic communications seem to have appropriately dealt with a company's dual use, allowing (even encouraging) information about the business on the home page and others related to purposes apart from offering securities, while having a link to the pages with the announcement, registration, prospectus and purchase order."

The SCOR Report out of Dallas, TX reports the successes and failures of small stock offerings across the country and indicates state hurdles along with suggestions for making registrations. Run by Tom Stewart-Gordon at www.scor-report.com, this is a compilation of do's and don't for entrepreneurs using this instrument. Tom's website provides a source of links for security offerings and provides information on: state security codes and regulations; accounting; attorneys; legislation; banks; entrepreneurial sites (including entreworld's Helping Entrepreneurs Succeed); investor information; SEC links; taxes; SBA; etc. Addresses and telephone numbers of all state securities regulators are at www.nasdr.com. The Corporate Finance Institute in Bethesda,

MD, put together instructions, forms and other material for making a filing in a book on SCOR. Brad Smith in Dallas, TX has filed registration statements for clients and found the process expedient and helpful if done right, but he felt too many entrepreneurs and service professionals alike unnecessarily delay a project (bradwsmith@aol.com). Tom Biggs at Vertex Capital maintains relations with many broker-dealers and sources of capital in a financial consultant's network for startups (Biggs@cfl.it.com).

The SEC has a kit for potential registrants that they will mail you by calling (202) 942 8088 and asking for "Publications" or you can go to the SEC website, www.sec.gov. The Government Accounting Office (GAO) has a free report that was compiled for the Senate Committee on Small Business entitled, "Small Business, Efforts to Facilitate Equity Capital Formation," GAO/GGD-00-190, at (202) 512 6000 or their website, www.gao.gov. The GAO's report covers types of capital, methods of solicitation; rules and regulations; fees; federal securities laws; use of the Internet; explanations of the exemptions, etc.

State filing fees.

State registration fees are a mare's nest of minimums and maximums and usually are based upon a sliding scale depending upon the amount of the offering. Oregon is the lowest cost state starting at $25 and peaking at $500. Texas is the most expensive and costs $1,000 per million of the offering there.

Internet-based offerings.

Wit Brewing made the first Internet offering in 1995 with an appeal to beer lovers. Wit was organized by a former securities attorney and with its early Internet reputation of selling stock, eventually grew to become an investment-banking firm with substantial equity from firms like Goldman Sachs. Wit developed a list of interested investors and had a conventional broker-dealer follow up the leads.

Advantages of a registered offering.

Consider filing a registration statement with the SEC and demonstrate the possibility of funding through a public offering. Tropicana filed an

S-1 for an IPO and was bought out by Pepsi three days later. Hull Financial filed a registration statement with a total company valuation at $460 million and was bought out by Goldman Sachs for $530 million instead.

Sara Lee decided to remake itself into three divisions and focus upon only its largest markets and brands. Their food service unit, PYA/Monarch, was spun-off into a separate company. An S-1 was filed with the SEC for an IPO of $160 million for Monarch that valued the entire company at $800 million. Shortly after the filing, Sara Lee entered into negotiations with the Dutch grocery group, Ahold, and sold the company instead for $1.57 billion. They received nearly twice as much for the company with a direct sale than they would have had with an IPO.

Going through the exercise of preparing a stock registration statement is usually a good idea for a company, even if it isn't the alternative you eventually choose for funding. A stock registration puts your firm "in play" and lets potential investors know not only about your proposition but also the fact that if they don't do something now you will soon be out of their reach. If they don't invest in you or buy you out, it's going to be too late.

A prominent corporate attorney in Atlanta, GA regularly counsels clients to prepare a registration statement as a discipline and exercise in getting together the firm's message and documentation.

You don't have to undergo the agonies of a declining stock market.

While some small stock offerings list on exchanges such as NASDAQ or regional exchanges, our bias is to avoid listing until such time as the company uses the investment funds to develop real revenues and earnings, often a multi-year undertaking. Stock market listing requirements for NASDAQ can be found at www.nasdaq.com. V-One, a leading security infrastructure firm, saw its stock dip dangerously low on NASDAQ despite a string of government and commercial successes. You can't correlate short-term stock market action with the longer-term developments of a company so don't look for logic to dictate prices. An exchange listing for a stock can be a two-edged sword. In bull markets your shareholders are happy and you may be able to use the shares to acquire other companies. In bear markets, shareholders complain and many of your plans may go on permanent hold.

Added SSO approaches.

The Micro Angels in San Francisco use the concept of placing small investors in contact with interesting new companies looking for seed capital. Using a monthly meeting format, they sponsor intrastate and SCOR offerings in the plus and minus $500,000 range. The meetings allow investors to question the entrepreneurs, much like an IPO road show for larger offerings, and provide for a lively exchange of information. Aggregating nearly 500 investors and helping to fund 17 startups through 2002, the Micro Angels are focusing on green and sustainable companies, mostly in California. Check with Mark Perlmutter at www.sfmicroangels.org. Chris Knight runs a securities consulting service for small stock offerings at www.dpocentral.com and many other service providers and broker-dealers have extensive experience with carrying them out. www.threearrowscapital.com has probably made more of these securities filings with the feds than any other broker-dealer.

www.direct-issue.com organized a no-frills electronic marketplace to solicit transactions throughout Europe. While focused on financial experts, it represents a start in widening access to funding.

PR AND YOUR ELEVATOR SPEECH

Amanda Rubinstein appeared on the television show MoneyHunt and made a concerted effort to introduce her kitty litter company to investors. Her special litter helped diagnose urinary tract disorder by a color change. At one of her appearances a few weeks later she was introduced to a wealthy individual who had seen her on the show and was also a cat lover. Within weeks, she had a $3.5 million investment.

What you get from a public relations effort.

PR is potentially the most powerful weapon you have in finding money. It's better than having several venture capitalists as friends or a host of well-meaning advisors. Advertisements occasionally work but they don't have the credibility or generate the interest that a good story can do for you. Ideally, if *The Wall Street Journal, London Financial Times* or the *New York Times* became interested in you and ran a story, you'd reach the widest possible audience of wealthy people in the most credible way possible. A good PR person can be worth their weight in gold and can help you shape your story while putting you in contact with reporters and publications where you have a chance to tell your story. If your budget is limited, you can probably do a lot yourself, often with local newspapers. Community papers are especially eager to run stories about people and new enterprises in their area, particularly if you have something unique. The bigger papers review the smaller ones in their territories and if the story is good enough, the large circulation press will do a story as well.

Keep letting people know what you're all about.

At a nine year-olds' soccer game in suburban Washington, D. C. two of the players' fathers had gotten to know each other casually through their sidelines chatter. At a game one of the fathers wore a shirt that had the logo and name of his company embroidered on the pocket. The other father, a venture capitalist, asked what it meant and gave the entrepreneur a chance to briefly describe his technology and market. Piquing his interest, the venture capitalist suggested they meet the following week and explore detail plans for growth. They met, an investment was made, leading to several more funding rounds, and his company became a fast-growth reality.

Two things are essential for something like the above to happen to you. The first is a way to let people know you're in business. The second is that you're able to explain what you're all about and get someone excited in the few moments of casual contact that most of us can get. If no one knows about you and if you can't articulate your proposition, nothing is going to happen in your search for capital. The first of the two is often a reflection of PR, and maybe as simple as the shirt you wear. The second is how you verbally convey your vision in a short time, your "elevator speech."

One component that we usually find missing from every business growth strategy is the one that may be most important to the young firm, their communications. The development of a profile with all key audiences (a "brand") is just as important for the fledgling company as it is for the giant. No one is going to invest in you unless they learn about your company's potential. How are you going about making this case?

Learn about PR.

Bill Gates, certainly one of the most successful CEOs in the world, always made himself and his staff accessible to the press. Microsoft, at least in the early days, seemed to get consistently positive coverage, a lesson for all of us. While checking out PR firms you will want to learn more about PR generally, and what it can do for you throughout your many phases of business life. PR can help attract capital but also customers, suppliers, employees, etc. One of the first places to learn is your public library, or perhaps your business-oriented bookstore. Marcia Yudkin has a paperback called 6 Steps to Free Publicity and the author is available as a telephone consultant to give you specific ideas for your company. Marcia is at www.yudkin.com/resources.htm and has a five-page listing of resources that includes tens of thousands of media outlets. The following is from her popular book:

Ten ways to be timely:

1. What is new about your business?
2. What is different or distinctive about your business?
3. Do you have an event you could create or publicize?
4. Can you make your products or expertise relevant by piggybacking on current news?
5. Have you done or could you do some research to merit press coverage?
6. Could you sponsor an interesting contest or award?
7. Is there a holiday or anniversary that you could hook onto?
8. Is there a trend in the general population or some particular population that relates to your offerings?
9. Can you suggest a surprising twist on received opinion?
10. Can you provide a pretext for a light, witty report?

The media have become a crossroads for companies and investors to meet, making a growing need to have business news presented in an entertaining fashion. A thesis put forward in the book *The Entertainment Economy* is that all business is, at its core, entertainment. In Silicon Valley, entrepreneurship itself has become a form of entertainment. Are there ways that you can attract attention while remaining credible? A factor in making your company newsworthy is that opinion journalism has become an influential subset of business journalism. Your judgments and suggestions can be informative, interesting and printable.

People want to invest and are looking for ideas.

The responsibility of individuals for their future financial well-being has created a class of Americans who look at companies not simply as makers of products or providers of services, but also as potential investments. The Internet is important to them and to those reporters who need to check facts under deadline. Your website has become essential in communicating news about your company to journalists, investors, potential clients and nearly everyone else. Opening a site with a fast-loading home page to give impatient people the background they need, and separately providing a "journalist's track," is a good media strategy. Stanford University gives a free set of guidelines as a credibility check for a website at www.webcredibility.org/guidelines.

What you need for a PR campaign.

A PR campaign should consist of information that is novel, not hackneyed, while being interesting and deep enough so that it can form the basis for a reporter's story. Since investors come from nearly all walks of life and are difficult to pigeonhole, the widest possible audience is your best bet to get a response. When forming a campaign, ask yourself if your information meets these criteria:

- Could your solution form a precedent for aiding people in other markets?
- Is there a breakthrough that suggests previous beliefs may no longer hold?
- Is there something that could form a trend for the future and suggest to people that they get on board?
- Is there information that teaches a lesson or provides insights for other entrepreneurs or managers?
- Can the essential message be boiled down into a couple of thoughts and sentences so a busy reporter can decide to look further instead of tossing it aside as too cumbersome and confusing? Are your points poignant enough so that people can remember them, possibly much later?

PR validates your story.

In terms of publicity, third-party recommendations carry far more weight than your releases. Simply put, verification in all of your steps by trust-worthy, third-party sources, is highly desirable, but when provided by the press becomes even more valuable. We had two favorable articles in the *Wall Street Journal* and an entire page in the business section of the Washington Post, simply by giving them information on something really interesting. Writing a note to the Post Publisher, Ben Bradley, complimenting the reporter, Bradley wrote back that in all of his years in journalism he could count on the fingers of one hand the number of times he had received a compliment on a reporter's work. Identifying the reporters that work in your area and beginning to track their interests and their styles will go a long way in helping you to shape something that can get printed.

> Breakthrough Software Corporation received dramatic proof of a credibility difference when it spent $6,000 to advertise one of its programs and received 100 responses. A free favorable magazine review of the same program generated 900 responses.

Capturing attention.

Writing in *MarketScan*, Michael Teachout suggests that correspondence that is a bit irreverent has a good chance of capturing an editor's interest. He suggests that providing an edge to your message does the following: (1) gets attention among the thousands of e-mail pitches that a journalist receives; (2) can be intriguing and start a journalist looking into your story; (3) may promote a unique perspective; and (4) humanizes you and the situation, prompting a relationship. The Senior Writer for *Fast Company*, Ron Lieber, says the best PR pitch letter he ever received contained a number of personal notes, invited him to lunch and had a P.S. at the bottom, which researchers say always gets read.

> The Johns Hopkins University public relations office briefed a manufacturing trade magazine about some research being done by a couple of their engineering professors. The magazine ran a story on the work and before long the professors had almost 300 requests for more information. Two of those callers were entrepreneurs who took up the technology and formed a successful company around the Hopkins research, providing a source of income for both the professors and Hopkins.

Yudkin notes, "The makers of the game Trivial Pursuit had no advertising budget whatsoever. Instead, by sending sample games or just the cards to game-industry buyers, celebrities who were mentioned in the game, and disk jockeys, they created a stir that the media had to keep reporting. Consequently, sales reached 1.5 million in 1983, the year the game was introduced."

PR resources.

"Click Press" is an Adobe PDF file that lists active email and URL contact links to editors and reporters in the U.S. for $99. The package provides 2,081 business and consumer magazines, 3,821 national, regional and local newspapers, 304 radio stations and 592 TV stations. You can buy that and many other PR and marketing aids from www.ideasiteforbusiness.com.

North American Press Syndicate guarantees you 400 stories for $3,000, mostly second and third tier publications. If you get heavily into this area, PR Solutions from www.lexisnexis.com provides weekly media updates along with special sections, at hotnewslist.prsolutions@lexisnexis.com. www.getpress.com has a range of inexpensive PR services to get you started.

How to make your firm newsworthy.

PR professionals are your best guides in both forming and executing your campaign. Being on the same wavelength can materially speed things along and save you money. When you're thinking of something that could be the basis of an article, consider the following:

1. Put your story into context. Think it all the way through and see it with the eyes of a reporter or editor. What is the real import of your story and how would it fit the interests of their readership?
2. Don't send information that isn't really newsworthy. Leave the routine items behind and only provide data that can become an interesting article.
3. Quantify your story. If you're talking about growth note the year-to-year change. If you're talking about benefits show the size of the marketplace and estimate the savings/revenues/etc.
4. Make sure that your contact is available right after the story goes out. You will seriously damage your

credibility if a reporter is unable to contact a company spokesperson.
5. Your point of contact should have full information at their fingertips to include fact sheets, references, telephone numbers, etc. to facilitate the work of the journalist.
6. Piggyback your story on other breaking news. If a fire claimed a large building and you have a form of sensor and monitoring system, as an example, take advantage of the opportunity.
7. Go to the reporter instead of to the editor. Reporters want to initiate stories instead of being told what to write—it's an ego thing.
8. Think visual when you're putting out your story. The media needs pictorial content. Try to make an exciting representation instead of just pictures of guys in suits.
9. Generally you should plan on a one-week lead-time for any story except for breaking news.
10. You're more likely to be picked up if you deliver your story in the early morning instead of afternoon and the earlier in the week you can do it the better.

Ben Silverman expands on these principles with "Ten tips from the PR boot camp" that you can read at www.pressaccess.com. As an example, Silverman suggests that it's best to put out a press release in the morning, " . . . but don't do it too early. If you put out a press release at 7:00 AM it may end up being ignored because by the time journalists get through everything in their inbox, there are already 200 other releases that have come after yours. Private firms should wait until after 9:30 AM [a period following a public firm's barrage of press releases]."

When everything else fails.

An entrepreneur had begun his company, E-College, and was succeeding with his technology and getting rave reviews from his first customers. He needed money to build out his concept and venture capital seemed to be ideal. Located in Silicon Valley, he started making the rounds of the many nearby VC firms. Door after door he found closed to him and after many months no one seemed willing to take his proposition seriously. He was sure that his company was going to succeed and that it would be an excellent investment for a VC. He finally found someone else who thought it was a good story, a reporter for the San Jose Mercury News. An article appeared in the newspaper on E-College and that morning the entrepreneur received five calls from venture capitalists who wanted to see his business plan. It wasn't long after that he received the funding he needed, from one of the five who called. Nothing had changed about his business except that PR told his story.

How to place an article and use PR to attract capital.

1. Don't call with your proposal or story, write something brief. Also, it's better to write a personal memo to the journalist than sending a broad press release.
2. Don't call either a VC or publication a few days after and just ask them if they received your proposal or release. It's fine to call if you have additional information to add or simply to make a query about possibilities, but don't needlessly harass them.
3. PR is an ongoing process and one memo/release is not the end of it. Keep looking for news opportunities such as contracts, new partners, etc. Your website is essential since people who have some interest in you will look for more background by going to the Internet.
4. Find speaking opportunities. VCs and other investors will be at trade shows and meetings and you need to become known.
5. Very clever stunts can work. One company hired the shoeshine boy at a hotel to give free shines to any VC or journalist who stopped at their booth, giving them enough uninterrupted time to tell their story.
6. Personal public relations need to be your foundation. You personally have to get out and mingle with people and get your story told, although everyone associated with your company should be an asset as well.
7. Start with the assumption that PR can be your most effective way of getting the attention of venture capitalists and other funding sources and then map out your campaign.
8. Determine the PR channels that you want to use. Who do you want to get to and what story do you want to tell? What

channels are available to you, what affinity groups exist for your company?
9. Direct approaches to VCs are far less effective than referrals or PR that triggers their interest. VCs are inundated with business proposals and simply have no good way of identifying the truly promising ones that show up, so you have to find a more interesting approach.
10. It's unlikely that your technology alone is really what interests most VCs or publications (unless you are truly unique). You need to answer questions about who the players are, any named customers, any prominent investors? The interest will be in how you're solving a problem—what's the benefit that you provide?

How to become a media source

There's no better way to get publicity than to be an expert and a resource that's available to the media when something breaks in your industry. You needn't be concerned that you're commercial, only that you can respond intelligently and with some imaginative insights. Here are a few suggestions from industry experts:

- Write an article about your industry without mentioning your own business. Speak about concerns that are common to everyone and elaborate with authority, citing examples that support your claim.
- Begin a letter-writing campaign to the trade press editors who are responsible for your area of expertise.
- Write a short press release covering initial subject matter.
- Send an audiotape to area radio stations of a staged interview between a staff member (moderator) and yourself.
- Create a press kit that includes all of the above materials and your photo mounted on a resume.
- Create a library of reference materials that can be called upon for adding integrity to your claims.
- Offer to speak at industry gatherings, trade shows and professional associations.
- Subscribe to (and consider paying for a listing in) Experts, Authorities and Spokespersons, a yellow page type of

publication that lists speakers and authorities by category. (Broadcast Interview Source, www.yearbooknews.com)
- Create a press event for your company, inviting prospects to attend a party with refreshments and information. You will be the keynote speaker and will be distributing valuable resource material to attendees.
- Contact local cable television shows and include information on your specific areas of interest, awards and previous press coverage.
- Hire a professional PR person to do all of the above.

Three Dog Bakery placed a tiny ad in a local weekly that was read by a reporter for The Wall Street Journal when he was holed up in a Kansas City hotel room. The reporter visited the store, was intrigued by their canine confections, and wrote a feature story about the concept. They have had a never-ending flow of publicity in various media ever since, helping them to grow from less than $.5 million to $40 million in five years.

www.pressaccess.com has a set of free articles that suggest how best to get your story placed, how to flaunt your small business, PR at conventions, etc. The site is sponsored by LexisNexis and called The Scoop. Recent Articles included Freelancers have the talent and connections to get your story placed and ShowStopper's Tips for Successful PR at Conventions. Joan Stewart has a CD that offers 847 tips on making an event a smashing success, as well as a new e-book How to Be a Kick-Butt Publicity Hound, both found at www.publicityhound.com. Joan also has a free electronic magazine, The Publicity Hound's Tips of the Week. www.edithroman.com is the site for a free news release tutorial including articles that provide tips for appearing on radio talk shows, fax vs. email news releases, publicity for websites, etc.

The business stories you read.

By day, Seth Apple is director of the New York City-based American Jewish Volunteer Corps. By night, he and two friends cook pralines for a nascent candy business they have put together. Testing the product and marketing ideas, they have used the input of focus groups that were willing to try the candy, resulting in modifications to their recipes but moving them much closer to commercial launch. Abby Ellin at the New

York Times writes about people like Apple and countless other budding businesspeople in her monthly column, Preludes, and can be reached at preludes@nytimes.com.

The next time you pick up a newspaper, trade magazine or professional journal stop and think about the stories you're reading. If there's an article in the health section of the paper regarding a new method of reconstructing hips or replacing joints, and a local orthopedist is quoted, how do you think that particular physician happened to become the expert referenced in the story? By accident or design? PR is usually so subtle that readers have no idea that almost every quoted source in both consumer and trade articles comes from a public relations effort.

Press releases.

Marcia Yudkin reports "*Wall Street Journal* Executive editor Frederick Taylor admitted that as much as 90 percent of its daily news originates in self-interested press releases. Yet when the public reads what reporters have done with that information, it tends to trust and respect the material, which rarely happens with advertising."

A story is an essential business tactic.

Tom Davenport and John Beck, two consultants at Accenture's Institute for Strategic Change, have a new book called *The Attention Economy*. Their thesis is that "The scarcest resource for today's business leaders is no longer just land, capital, or human labor, and it certainly isn't information. Attention is what's in short supply." They suggest that when you think about who competes with you, also think of who competes for your customer's attention. A much larger set of competitors will appear through this effort, giving you a better chance to form effective counter-strategies.

Your elevator speech.

Some business experts have called the short verbal presentation an entrepreneur can make describing their company to be the most important part of the whole funding strategy. Instead of a two-hour presentation of your business idea, complete with a slide show, handouts and a balanced question and answer session with your whole group present, you may really only have the length of an elevator ride to get someone interested in putting up cash. Serious investors see lots of business plans and don't have time to examine yours unless you have already stimulated their interest. The point is not to try to make the sale at the first juncture, only to get someone interested enough so that they'll take your call and give you the chance to make a longer presentation at a later time.

Forming your elevator speech.

In your elevator speech, state the problem and your solution first, along with the thought that the market is large and profitable. In regards to the problem and solution, try studying a few 30-second commercials and you'll get the drift. Get a listener interested enough to meet with you and to examine just what you're doing. They may have already made most of their decision within the first 30 seconds of listening to you, but now they need to find out if it is really doable.

Don't focus on the technology, just the end result—that you're running a business not an academic research group. Don't ever say that you have a billion dollar idea or that you have no competition because both are turnoffs to experienced investors and immediately suggest that you don't have a real head for business. Show how early-stage investors will come out on top. Focus on getting to your market, the service or product that you provide, and evidence of customer demand. The same elevator pitch is also useful for obtaining customers, employees, strategic partners, PR, etc.

> *Akamai in Cambridge, MA used a variation of their elevator speech to open the door to Yahoo, an early and very important customer. In a short phone call they told them what they were developing, why they thought it was important to Yahoo, and why they could do it successfully. All skills developed while looking for money.*

You have to keep an elevator speech short.

A practiced elevator pitch potentially has just two sentences: the idea and the evidence that it will work. The purpose is to tell what you do, what's special about your company and why people are going to come to you rather than somebody else. In one sentence, you explain what you are delivering and why. Problem, solution and result, all within a few seconds. The evidence can be as little as a statistic, survey, sale or other indication that you're not just blowing smoke. You're showing a sign that you're serious and worthwhile looking into. While the solution in a toothpaste commercial is obvious, you can go to the drugstore and buy it, your elevator speech has to be more explicit.

After quickly showing your market and solution, describe it as an investment opportunity. Put your listener into the picture in a meaningful fashion. You need to show that this is an open idea and that the listener could benefit by investing. You have to be subtle, because you don't ask for the investment until you feel that you'vee made the sale, but you want to invite the listener to learn more about your company. Ideally, you'll like a chance to make a complete pitch to the person and perhaps their friends, relatives, company, etc., as well. You're opening the door to a dialogue and you're doing it without boring them. If you want to attract capital your energy needs to be in your voice and this comes when you're 100% sold on your own proposition. When this happens, you'll want everyone to invest. How good is your elevator speech? If you can't get someone excited in 60 seconds, it needs work. Also, can you characterize your company as something more memorable than "software" or "biotech" or "retailer"?

Your message has to be distilled down or it's going to be lost. Entrepreneurs often go on and on, "we've got this and we've got that, and we're going to do this and all that" but people have lost interest by the time the entrepreneur has finished.

You say you're going to do that? Well, show me some sign you're serious. It could be someone important who has taken an interest in you, or you've done a deal with somebody, or some other kind of proof in the form of a name or statistic. Premise and endorsement: that's the elevator pitch. Two sentences, and make it really interesting. Accenture Consulting suggests that the elevator speech should take no more than 17 seconds, your only chance to get across your most intriguing value proposition.

Networking.

Susan RoAne, the author of How to Work a Room: The Secrets of Savvy Networking and What Do I Say Next? publishes ten commandmandments for connecting with people that are displayed at her website: www.susanroane.com. She says that everyone has a network already if they look hard enough and that you should start by making lists of the people you remember, old address books, etc. Tom Power at www.ecademy.com shows how to develop your network, and gives special tools at www.insightexec.com.

The managing director of the entrepreneur center at MIT's Sloan School of Management, Ken Morse, teaches presentation skills by offering guidance on networking and even on cocktail-party management, complete with sketches of a typical reception. MIT holds an annual competition for business plans and counts on large numbers of investors and venture capitalists to tune in to the plans and pitches. A number of scientists and engineers have had to learn that long descriptions of technology usually lead to glassy-eyed disinterest and what's needed instead is to get to the benefits right away. What is it that someone will buy? Can you define your market, service and customer demand?

Coaches can help you get ready for presentations. Patricia Fripp is a San Francisco-based executive speech coach who advises her clients to discard fancy Power-Point presentations and tell stories instead. Her terrific website www.Fripp.com is a tour de force of help in making a good and profitable impression. She suggests that people remember what they "see" in their minds while listening, not showy visuals. Other Fripp suggestions include starting by answering the audience's basic question, "Why should I care about your subject point of view?" She tells us to "Make your point of view obvious and compelling. Turn numbing data into exciting pictures of what will change in the listener's life. Help them make the decision your presentation is designed to promote." New York-based Amy Solas gives a workshop entitled How To Win Business, Raise Capital, Sell Companies—A Hands-On Workshop that focuses on making a good presentation, www.solascommunications.com.

RMR Associates in Rockville, MD holds a workshop on delivering your elevator speech. They ask you to picture this: "You're at a networking event. Everyone has a chance to talk about himself or herself. You are next. What will you say? Will you be remembered? Will you get the results, the contacts, and the action you want? Or will your intro fade into the background like so many others?" They promise you'll learn: "How to set yourself apart from others. A step-by-step, foolproof approach to creating the introduction. How to get the audience's attention. How to close your introduction and get what you came for." RMR charges $140 and can be accessed at www.rmr.com. Bob Bailey of ebiz presents workshops on elevator speeches entitled "Does Your Elevator Speech Go All the Way to the Top Floor?" Bob is an expert at sales presentations (ebiz@usa.net).

Packaging and presenting.

David Kirby is a PR specialist who has a unique background, developed in a prominent investment banking firm, for raising capital for entrepreneurial companies. He notes that one of the first things an entrepreneur seeking money needs to do is to re-package his company into the most attractive presentation possible. David isn't talking about bells and whistles but about the words that catch attention and convey meaning. He usually rewrites business plans to put the best and most salable aspects up front before launching an effort to find money and grow the business (www.biz-writers.com). www.capitalsearch.net is a financial public relations firm that looks to connect emerging firms with investors.

Tips and Insights for Putting Your Best Foot Forward with Investors and Corporate Partners is a free 41-page booklet from the Department of Commerce's Advanced Technology Program. Written by Rick King, the guide has sections on: "Storytelling: The Gateway to Business Success; Presentation Tips: Telling Your Story; and Preparing to Make Your Presentation." Access tellyourstory@preflightventures.com (or GPO NIST GCR 02-831). Commerce also has a 260-page book—designed especially for technology entrepreneurs—on business development, fundraising and licensing called *ATP's Commercialization and Business Planning Guide in the Post-Award Period* (NIST GCR 99-779, June 2000).

BUSINESS AND MARKETING PLAN

"At a ham and egg breakfast, the chicken is involved but the pig is committed." Jim Barksdale. Simply, your business plan needs to show how committed you are to making this enterprise work.

The business plan has become a standard.

You're expected to have a business plan. The plan is necessary for communication, due diligence, the consideration of alternatives, establishing milestones and the host of information needs that are required to mate the entrepreneurial vision with the requirements of financiers. Still, the entire business planning procedure is way over-emphasized and spending too much time on making a plan beautiful probably means that you've wasted effort and money. No one funds business plans! People get funded. The plan is simply there to "paper" your proposition so you simply need to write it correctly.

Help in forming your business plan.

A vast industry of assistance for entrepreneurs has sprung up with literally thousands of organizations, websites, classes, forums, meetings, coaching sessions, business plan reviews, funding assistance, etc., that can be researched by budding entrepreneurs. Your local university business school is a good place to start, especially if you find someone on the faculty who is sympathetic to your business model and could even serve as a board member. Inc magazine, with a rich array of resources at its website, www.inc.com, is an excellent start as is the Kaufman Center for Entrepreneurial excellence, www.entreworld.com. University business schools can provide help in many different ways.

Try running your business model past a faculty member or two who are familiar with entrepreneurship, your technology, or your market. www.MoreBusiness.com is a source for sample business plans, etc. Palo Alto Software at www.pasware.com sells packages to help you write a plan, priced at $99.95 for heir basic template and $299 for the Pro Premier. www.bixplanit.com contracts to write business plans with an orientation to investor's interests and www.postidea.com lists your summary for a fee. For consulting and professional services firms, www.practicebuilders.com provides a list of marketing initiatives and growing a practice that's important for a plan and www.Findlaw.com has sample business agreements on line.

The SBA business plan outline is at www.sba.gov/starting/indexbusplans.html as well as links to another 18 sites for business plans including the University of Colorado workshop and template, the Howard University outline and American Express's "Creating an Effective Business Plan." Ernst & Young has a free 20-page guide to business plans at www.ey.com/global and you'll find many other websites as well as books, classes, academic and business resources, etc., that will help you develop your plan. www.bplans.com offers free sample business plans and http://startupbusinessplans.com shows the services of a professional business planning company that helps find funding as well.

Most of the business plans we've seen written entirely by the entrepreneur are frankly awful and show no evidence of any assistance. Generally, a business plan of ten to twenty pages should convey enough evidence to satisfy readers and either tickle their interest and invite them to take the next step of meeting with you, or consign it to the circular file. Throughout the document, try to infuse how well researched the marketing part of your business really is—show that things will sell.

There's value for you as well as for investors in writing a business plan.

By continually planning, simulating, costing and otherwise working out developmental steps in the process of writing and updating your plan, you gradually reduce risk to both yourself and your investors. The more detailed you are—even given the uncertainty in the future of any business—the less risk you present. You can generally expect that any business is going to take longer to get off the ground and cost more than you expect. As a corollary, completing a variety of cash flow alternatives that result from changes in your assumptions can be a valuable aid in obtaining capital. This type of exercise shows a realism that is unusual and also a respect for the investor's capital that is protective. The whole process builds in a number of milestones that can help maintain the equity of the entrepreneur as well as protect the investor, so it becomes a two-way street.

Alba Aleman, founder of rapidly growing Cairo Corporation found that taking her ideas and transferring them to paper transformed the business and changed things for the better.

Guidelines for your business plan.

Open with a real bang. Your first few lines must grab the reader. Too many people try to be dry and logical up front, a major mistake. You have only seconds to engage a busy reader and they will not continue to read on unless they have become taken with something you wrote. You must convey a sense of excitement. Start by answering the question, "what was so compelling that it made you want to go into this business?" The technical analysis comes later. Illustrate your market in the first breath.

Follow the money. Investors want to know how your company will earn a profit and you cannot make them sift through jargon or flip pages in order to find this out. Illustrate where the money stream lies along with how you're going to tap into it.

Hit the hot buttons. Skip the hollow hype and explain in one sentence how your business will stand out from rivals and have a competitive advantage.

Summarize the summary. Some investors prefer a teaser that promises the whole business plan if they're interested, and starts the ball rolling. Write a two or three paragraph e-mail as your first encounter with the investor. Establish that you operate in the areas that the investor cares about, that you have a good management team and a valid growth plan that fits the investor's needs.

Check your numbers. Proofread your document to insure that continuity exists between all parts.

Skip the hyperbole. Get rid of the adjectives! Your audience will be warmed up by facts and turned off by exaggerations. In a study of companies that allowed consumers to configure their own purchases on the Internet (Dell for computers, GM for automobiles, etc.) the findings were that people tend to select more features than they would otherwise—without a hard sell. The low-key passivity of this kind of connection and the sense of control that it gives to the customer, seem to sell more effectively than a salesman's wiles. Provide the facts and the opportunity for people to respond to you. Don't try to force them to do anything.

> *"As I considered my business plan, I also asked myself, 'What is the worst thing that could happen if this doesn't work out.'"* Rebecca Smith in businessweek.com. *"For all of the wisdom that goes along with experience, it is the vibrancy of risk-taking that is necessary to build companies. To be a risk-taker, one needs often—always?—to turn a blind eye to what are undoubtedly truths that those more experienced are trying to convey."*

Help in the process.

www.businessplanarchive.org houses a number of business plans that have been extracted from security filings with the SEC. The outline of these plans is wonderfully rational and following these guidelines will make you look professional when you're seeking capital. The site also has a set of 10 lessons from the Internet meltdown, such as number 1: "Nothing changes overnight. The single most fatal miscalculation investors made regarding the Internet was to massively overestimate the speed at which the marketplace would adopt dot com innovations. That assumption of speed dictated the rapid pace and scale of investment by both VCs and public investors—and the resulting over-investment led to the inevitable bubble and bust. We somehow believed it was different this time. It wasn't. It will always simply take time and lots of it for people to integrate innovations into the way they do things." The rest of the lessons are just a worth reading.

You can adapt a variety of comparable development experiences in terms of time and perhaps capital by examining security filings or perhaps such sources as: *Value Line Investment Survey* and the *Standard and Poor's Analysts Handbook*, publishers of industry-level data. Gale Research puts out the *Encyclopedia of Business Information Sources* and the Funk and Scott, *F&S Business News Index* are also places to start. Associations usually have libraries or in-house studies on the industry you've targeted so a quick call to these professionals may be warranted..

A free booklet, *Scoring Points With Your Business Plan*, from the law firm of Gardner, Carton & Douglas states that a good business plan is a lot like a screenplay. They suggest having a set-up, followed by a first turning point, then a second turning point, the climax, and the resolution of the story that takes place at the end of the movie. Ask for a copy from www.gcd.com and you'll also find references there to another eleven websites for business plan help.

Start with a vision.

Ice hockey great Wayne Gretzky always skated to where the puck was going to be, not where it was then.

How does your business model (plan) fit in with the rest of the world and in what directions do the trends point? Do you have a strategy, a vision that will unfold in the future? Imagining a new competitive space and how you act to influence migration towards that future is critical. You can't influence the evolving industry environment if you don't start with a point of view about how the world can be, how to improve what's available now, how to radically alter things. What insights do you bring (or you need others to add for you) about how these trends will transform industries and customers? What new opportunities are bound to emerge?

Business planning checklist.

1. Illustrate a clear vision of what the business can be.
2. Keep the process simple and straightforward
3. Begin with the customer and the market
4. Understand the competitive environment (demonstrate that you know it cold)
5. Identify the critical success factors for the business
6. Focus on issues of major importance
7. Build on strengths
8. Have more than one route to success

9. Commit to the plan; have action steps developed by those responsible for implementation
10. Monitor performance against goals and objectives; apply flexible control

Non-disclosure agreements.

One of the biggest mistakes entrepreneurs make is to require a non-disclosure agreement before providing your business plan to a potential investor. If your business model is so easy to replicate, chances are that you don't have anything really unique or perhaps of much value anyway. You'll hear the expression "stealth mode" to indicate that mums the word about what you're up to. If you choose that approach and keep things quiet you'll have less and less chance to poll the market and find out if what you've got really has value.

> *Venture capitalist Rob Adams said: "I have yet to see one original idea in a business plan, and I'm talking as a person who has probably read thousands of them . . . ideas are commodities." During a stock market mania in England during the 17th century, one company sold out a stock offering by telling everyone it was revolutionary and a world changing new business technique but it was so secret that they couldn't tell anybody what it was. Guess what happened to the money.*

Your management team is of primary importance to experienced investors.

A business plan in the hands of a veteran venture capitalist, angel investor or other party who is regularly solicited for investment will usually be reviewed in the following manner: The first paragraph of the executive summary will be read and, if it's interesting, the reader will flip immediately to the management section. People invest in other people and they want to know who is playing in this game. Credentials in the form of experience count most, followed by academic achievements for high-technology companies. In particular, show that you have a team together that can execute this business plan (it's okay if you're missing some part of the team as long as you acknowledge what you're missing and indicate you're searching—the VC or angel may have a good candidate for you). If you included all your friends and relatives as executives and board members you're sending out a strong clue that you shouldn't be taken seriously. Also think of showing that you can keep a team together by providing equity incentives for management, board members and employees. SAIC studied their employee turnover and found that those who owned stock in the company had a turnover rate of 5 percent while those with no ownership had a rate of 12 percent.

You can package your business plan in several different ways.

There are several different forms in which to offer your business plan. A private placement memorandum, a registered stock offering, a presentation to a venture capitalist that illustrates their exit strategy, or a presentation to a strategic partner that shows how your company will complement their own business. Each form is going to be appropriate to a different audience. Regardless of the form taken, try to get your essential proposition, your unique solution and market, into the first sentence or two since that is all you can ever count on people getting around to read. Also, consider graphics or some visual way to represent the idea. A modern prospectus that you can pick up from any brokerage firm will usually have a foldout cover that gives you this kind of overview. People respond differently with some of them trusting most to the written work, others to visual representations, still others to a story that you tell them. Give yourself the best chance to trigger interest and the right response by providing all the stimuli that you can.

Show the investor when and how they can make money.

You need to build in a mechanism for investors to harvest their rewards and have a step-by-step plan for achieving an exit. Your liquidity event can take several forms and if you identify these exits it will suggest to potential investors that you're looking out for them. While IPOs are often on the entrepreneur's mind, most successful companies will be merged or acquired. Other companies will buy back shares, spin off subsidiaries, or find ways of raising cash for their early investors. Your business plan needs to highlight the benefits and features that result from an investor's contribution and company growth that results from their stepping up. Things like patents and other intellectual property such as brands can be essential and referencing these as spin-offs or a major focus can help assure the investor that you're building real assets and increasing his wealth.

Demonstrate some financial sophistication.

Knowledge of finance and cash management may be the single most critical area of operations for an entrepreneur to master. Generating revenues and what you do with that money shows any investor how your business plan will unfold in terms that are important to him. Also, incorporate as early as possible to give your company a history (home state is fine, you can re-incorporate elsewhere later if you find you need to).

Even though people are attracted by the vision of the entrepreneur and the prospects for a new company, the business of investing is often done first upon the financial statements, and the more complete (schedules, notes, etc.) the better. It's difficult to look at conventional accounting schedules when much of today's assets are in the form of intellectual property, human capital and other largely intangible or difficult to measure line items, but this is the game required. Robert Howell of the Tuck School at Dartmouth in a *Fortune Magazine* article suggests that the best way to produce meaningful financial statements is to forget many of the old measures and focus on cash.

Paul Broni at Mercury Partners prepares a funding strategy and introduces clients to investors and buyers (www.mercurypartners.com). Broni also has an excellent article "Making Your Financials Add Up" that illustrates how to make your financial projections intelligent and credible.

Get a number of service providers to make suggestions on your business model.

More and more service providers such as attorneys and accountants have found ways of working with smaller technology clients who are seen as low or non-paying clients at the moment, but ones that have terrific potential if successful. Many law firms have technology experts on staff or on call and are actively seeking such clients, usually just for advisory services. Service providers can often introduce you to capital, have capital to invest themselves, and give excellent feedback on your proposal as well. They may make suggestions about marketing your company more effectively and in a different fashion. They'll ask you questions such as can you finance it alternatively? Are tax benefits for investors available?

Bias your investment proposal towards the market you're approaching.

For example, what if you have a chance to make a pitch to a union pension fund? You must know that they want to invest in worker-friendly businesses and are steadily becoming a bigger factor in emerging company financing. If you intend to solicit this money, think of having a company benefits package and deal with employee training needs to show up well during due-diligence tests. A number of venture capital firms and other investors have passed on firms that have not provided equity participation or other incentive program for employees—its absence suggests that you don't know what's important and are seeking to keep everything for yourself. The Director of the A.F.L.-C.I.O.'s Office of Investment, William Patterson, feels that more labor oversight of corporate pension funds might have done much to forestall excesses such as those represented by the Enron pension fund. The boards of some large companies such as General Motors and Eastman Kodak have listened to labor and made changes to align their investments more with these interests, so it pays to be sensitive to such issues.

Prove that you're marketable.

The most important part of your documentation and intellectual property is a set of tests about the market, product, advertising, marketing methods, etc. Take your proposition out of the "good idea" category and put it into the proven and market growth category. This is important for VCs and doubly so in an investment made by a corporate strategic partner. The primary goal of corporations, who research investment and partnership opportunities in great detail, is to reduce uncertainty and verify prior beliefs, so meet them on common ground right in your business plan. Corporate research represents an investment in information and is correspondingly more scientific so statistics and testing have even more credence. Corporate decision-makers who use research to place large bets have to be wary of the inevitable encouraging but false positive results that come their way, and cannot rely on the ad hoc improvisation of bootstrapped entrepreneurs. www.bizminer.com provides industry data profiles on over 19,000 types of businesses and breaks down financial data, industry trends and survival rates, all of which can help solidify your proposition.

The planning process.

Arrange a session with everyone involved in your business to develop ideas about possible sources of capital. Solicit input from everyone and you may be surprised and pleased with the potential new sources of cash suggested that you may have never thought about. Also, when you invite other people to help you with your project you begin to mobilize talent and energy for your company that will benefit you for years to come. This is also the beginning of a valuable company-specific form of network that you can grow with PR, speeches, white papers, organizational memberships, business partnerships, board members, government organizations and bodies, etc.

The marketing plan needs to be especially thoughtful.

A detailed marketing plan should be included in your business plan. The marketing steps permit an investor to "see into" future activities to check the realism of what you're promising and conveys to them a feeling of controlling the investment, as they monitor the fulfillment of the plan. You've got a lot of information and the prospective investor has little. You need to help bridge this divide and level the playing field. When you do this well, you may find the investor more comfortable with you and demand a lower return on his money.

Your marketing plan has to show how your company is going to make sales. Simply relying on partners for distribution or assuming that retailers are going to stock your product is wishful thinking that can sink you (think about how hard and expensive it is to get shelf space in a supermarket). While you may not be able to build a national sales team right out of the box, if you're not making the sales yourself, probably no one else is going to lift a finger to do it for you either. Also, by being intimately involved in the sales process you can follow Dell Computer's experience of being close to the customer—working without intermediaries—and get to know quickly just what the customer wants and what trends are starting. Palo Alto Software at www.pasware.com sells a marketing plan template for $99.95 and a more comprehensive version for $299. www.guaranteedmarketing.com will provide a free initial consultation for creative approaches to marketing and sales and www.marketingtips.com is a source for a succession of marketing ideas. An outline of a basic marketing plan by Carol Ann Waugh is available at www.xcellentmarketing.com/plan and a set of marketing articles and resources at www.mplans.com.

> *Pleasant Rowland, the textbook author who began the American Girl doll company in the mid 1980s, found that interviews with mothers about the idea were universally negative but when the doll was brought out the reaction changed to positive nearly instantly. "Success isn't in the concept. It's in the execution." She began her company with $1 million in savings she had kept from her writings.*

Relationship/charitable marketing.

When Outback Steakhouse opens a new restaurant, they seek a charity or two as an event partner. They produce $5,000 to $15,000 for the charity while generating goodwill for themselves and introducing the new restaurant to other community groups. Several issues of marketing are applicable if you steer towards this approach:

- Relationship marketing maintains a personal relationship with the customer.
- Cross-promoting uses one marketing message to introduce another.
- Morality marketing is a form of communicating business values or unique qualities that includes not only product information but also benefits for a special group of people.
- Direct marketing is used to get into the customer's home or business with a message.
- Premium marketing is the use of a product offered free as an incentive.

- Publicity is stronger when not directly associated with self-promotion.

The Social Marketing Institute at Georgetown University is run by Alan Andreasen, a marketing professor who feels that corporations can benefit from social marketing programs in many ways.

Business strategy and a means to measure your progress.

The strategy and implementation portions of your written document form the core of the business plan. The entrepreneur needs this to control and monitor progress of the venture and to solicit outside financing. Milestones that are specific and verifiable performance benchmarks including completion of research, production of prototypes, tests, and first sale need to be included in your business plan. Predicating ownership on milestones makes it more likely that investment will be secured and that the entrepreneur will be able to retain significant ownership. Specifically, the ability to alter planned decisions and deal with uncertainty in response to new information, reduces the downside risk to the investor as well as the entrepreneur, while maintaining different alternatives on the upside.

> *"If it's neither snow nor rain nor heat nor gloom of night, what the devil is wrong with this place?" Anthony M. Frank, former head of the U.S. Postal Service, and a suggestion that if your plan isn't working, you need a new plan.*

When you build in milestones you create funding options that are valuable in their own right. You give the investor the option to proceed with more money when certain parts of your growth are successful. Realistically, when new technologies are concerned, credible estimates of returns are difficult to make. By establishing milestones and framing them as options, a number of intangible benefits of technology can be spelled out and even separately valued.

> *A survey conducted by Inc Magazine indicated that sixty percent of Inc 500 CEOs did not have a formal business plan before launching their company. The same survey showed that forty-one percent of the group started their companies with less than $10,000 (www.inc.com).*

Consider how your solution is going to fit into customer's needs.

Newer companies find that marketplace barriers—customers that were not receptive or ready—are primary obstacles and needs to be dealt with at the beginning of their plan. Human behavior is much slower to change than technology and considering that obstacle is critical. Harvard Business School Professor Rosabeth Moss Kanter states, "Years of research shows that the innovations most likely to take hold are those that don't demand excessive change from the customer. Incrementalism—represented by the following eight characteristics is key:

- Provable: the product can be demonstrated on a pilot basis. Customers can try it out on a smaller scale before committing to replace everything.
- Divisible: it can be adopted in segments or phases. Customers can ease into it, one step at a time. They can use it in parallel with their current solutions.
- Reversible: if it doesn't work, it's possible to return to life without it. Don't burn down the house to demonstrate the fire extinguisher system.
- Tangible: it offers results that can be seen to make a difference in something that the customer needs and values.
- Fits prior investments: it is an area where there have already been actions or investments, and it builds on them. The product helps make use of "sunk costs," rather than requiring customers to take losses.
- Familiar: it feels like things that customers already understand, so it is not jarring to use (early telephone promoters had to develop the term "hello" to make it comfortable to address someone you didn't necessarily know). It is consistent with other experiences, especially ones that have been successful in the past.
- Congruent with future direction: it is in line with where the customer is heading anyway.
- It doesn't require customers to rethink their priorities.
- Publicity value: it will make the customer look better to itself and others."

Show sacrifices on your part.

When building your business plan, make sure that executive salaries for founders are kept as low as possible. Investors want to see sacrifices and commitment on the part of managers and would hate to think of their funds going to finance a high life-style. Ideally, management rewards should be tied as tightly as possible to the perspective of the investor, showing an identity of interest throughout the life of the investment.

Simulate your business plan and test different assumptions.

When developing financial projections, model these numbers in different ways including: cash flow breakeven analysis; scenario analysis; and simulation, as different means of showing outcomes. As a real exercise, try drawing up your business plan to succeed with no infusion of outside capital whatsoever. Does it break down? What's the difference in steps that are involved? Also, when you're detailing the competition section of your business plan, don't comment negatively on other firms, but indicate the differences between competitors' solutions and yours.

In software there's a unit of measurement called "Simple Matter of Programming" or SMOP. You can roughly evaluate how long a software development project is going to take by how many SMOPs are involved. A simple little thing that will take a team of four programmers six months to complete is one SMOP. Big projects are going to call for multiples of time and personnel, and compute to maybe five or ten SMOPs. If it's not in your main area, chances are that you'll spend your time better by trying to figure out who to partner with.

> *"Although it is popular to think that great ideas start with individuals, most knowledge gets produced in and by communities of practice (COPS). These are teams of people that have worked together over a sufficient period of time to have evolved a deep ability to read each other, to communicate in highly condensed ways, and to know exactly when and when not to trust an opinion from one another. Within such entities, knowledge gets created, and when it does, it flows almost effortlessly."* PARC veteran John Seely Brown writing in the book, Understanding Silicon Valley.

Harvard Professor Michael Porter's emphasis on the value of clusters helped form the impetus for the British government's guidance to regional planning commissions for land use and the necessity to promote these regions as a source of competitive strength. The amount of services and support for entrepreneurs in places such as Silicon Valley dwarf efforts found elsewhere, but you have resources nearby as well and may have either a fully developed or nascent cluster of your own.

Valuing a company.

No one knows exactly how to put a price tag on a company but when you're out looking for money you must value it somehow. A number of books have been published on making these projections and values but none is less than an inch and a half thick, attesting to how many different ways you can do it. Instead of stamping a particular value on the firm, you're better off to forecast your sales and earnings out a few years and give your potential investors a chance to input their own ideas about value. Valuation, like beauty, is in the eyes of the beholder. www.houlihan.com has a number of articles that speak to valuation and the firm itself, Houlihan Valuation Advisors, has a long history of making these complex determinations. Attorney Mark Gross has an article that is relevant to this kind of exercise, "How to Value Your Start-up for Venture Capital" at www.gigalaw.com. M-CAM is a company that uses special software as a base to start a complex valuation methodology. M-CAM started off by asking the questions: "Do you own an asset? Does Anybody care?"

Common planning mistakes.

The typical entrepreneur underestimates the need for capital by a factor of three, as evidenced by several studies. Also consider that the typical firm that receives venture capital financing accumulates an average level of investment of $16 million over a number of years before they ever do an IPO, become acquired or are merged. With this kind of scenario possibly ahead for you, don't give away the family farm since you may easily need more equity rounds than you think. Make sure you're fair to people, but since you can't grow a company to its full potential if you've sacrificed too much equity early-on. If you treat your shareholders fairly, they'll be there for you in the future to help you grow your company and perhaps your next one as well.

Do you really even need a business plan?

While we believe the process has inherent value and most investors want something to study and feel comfortable with, focus on the plan is probably way overblown—except for the marketing plan portion of the document. The author of two widely read books on business plans, David Gumpert, dramatically altered his thinking based upon his own experience looking for money. His latest book is *Burn Your Business Plan! What Investors Really Want from Entrepreneurs* (www.lausonpub.com). Gumpert's new emphasis is upon making sales, obtaining publicity, keeping finances under control and creating a website that communicates the business model (see his *How to Really Create a Successful Marketing Plan*).

Further thoughts on the marketing plan.

If you have sales on the books and show reasonable steps to obtain a lot more, you're well on the way to having a powerful marketing plan. This step is often overlooked or given short shrift in the fervor to craft a business plan and to make forecasts of revenues and profits. If your business doesn't have a proven sales formula you need to put together a knock-your-socks off type of marketing plan. Show investors that you've really thought through all the important steps that are involved in growing your company.

Marketing expert John Ver Steeg suggests that marketing considerations should really help dictate the design of your business plan. His steps are: (1) begin by stating the market problem to be solved; (2) identify the customers, by name and number; (3) determine how much a customer is likely to spend each year; (4) reason out price changes over time; (5) figure out what sales methods are going to work best for your type of customer and your type of product; and (6) determine what marketing methods work for your market.

A marketing plan should be a mini-business plan and have the following general outline:

- An executive summary that indicates both your most powerful avenue to generate revenues and a concise indication of how that fits with the remainder of the plan.
- A current or state of the market section to indicate what similar companies are doing to generate sales and the strategies of the most imaginative and successful ones. You should give some idea of costs, competitors and the general environment for introducing your product or service. Within this section make sure you illustrate who your competitors are and how you distinguish and differentiate yourself.
- Your niche needs to be reasoned out and aligned with the opportunity to make sales. What are the obstacles as well as the things you need to build upon to make a successful business?
- Develop milestones in terms of sales, market share, etc., all numeric measures, so an investor is able to track your progress.
- Illustrate the marketing approach that you have opted for and what you have considered and what you have rejected. State what you expect to do if (or when) some of your marketing assumptions don't work out.
- Delineate the steps that you're going to take to achieve your marketing goals. Show who is going to do what and how much it will cost.
- Put together a revenue and cost projection that ties back into any of the other forecasts that are made elsewhere in the plan.
- Show the controls and management structure that you're going to put in place to monitor this plan and just who is going to be responsible for supervision and reporting.

Your marketing plan should illustrate sources of information on the market and as many tests of your product as you can possibly generate. A focus group could be easy for you to put together, right in your neighborhood. A focus group can be a moderated roundtable discussion with 8 to 10 people who have been recruited to participate in a discussion, usually lasting no more than 2 hours. The moderator will guide the discussion into pre-determined areas and distribute questionnaires, samples or mockups. All with the intent of giving clues and information to help provide more assurance to the potential investor, that you've done your homework. The rate of mail-out questionnaire completion improves dramatically when some incentive is involved. A dollar bill attached has often given positive results in the past.

While a focus on solving problems in one area is the best way to concentrate a potential investor's attention, there is no guarantee that the target market is going to work out once you find funding. Consider showing a number of other ways that your core technology can be applied and other solutions and markets that can be derived from it.

An article by Jennifer Gilbert in Business 2.0 on February 6, 2001, illustrated a number of cheaper ways to market a company. Gilbert notes how Bag Media places messages on paper bags from doughnut and other shops and another firm, Eisnor, created a contest to promote a New York City guide by the New York Times. Resources her article referenced include: www.autowraps.com, www.bagmedia.com, www.innovyx.com, www.eisnor.com, www.javajacket.com and www.tbsmmm.com.

BIOTECH, A SPECIAL CASE

Craig Venter left NIH in 1992 to pursue his own approach to gene sequencing. He formed a collaboration with Harvard professor, Bill Haseltine, who moved from academia to head the start-up firm, Human Genome Sciences. A notable coup for this company, negotiated less than a year after Haseltine's arrival, was a $125 million partnership agreement with SmithKline Beecham. This agreement has been described as "the genomics era's big bang," signaling the recognition by big pharmaceutical companies of the contribution which the new genomics firms could make to the future of medicine.

Biotech exhibits a range of financing problems.

The principle problems in funding technology are the long lead-times, uncertainties, and the size of the expense associated with bringing a product to market. The biotechnology industry is a case in point where the decade-long lead-time and multi hundreds of millions of dollars involved in drug development prove daunting. The job of the entrepreneur is to alter these dimensions by creative thinking and planning. The first task is to segment the development chain and throw major hurdles onto other organizations—perhaps government, university, and corporate labs that are able to finance the work. Another is to segment the chain further by specializing in a sector of the corporate activity such as project management, consulting, manufacturing or marketing. Arranging partnership relationships and creating true virtual organizations are also ways to reduce the efforts to more manageable tasks and should become more important all the time.

"Whereas in the 1970s and 1980s, 80 to 90 percent of all health care-relevant discoveries were made in pharmaceutical companies, in

the 1990s and after the year 2000, 75 percent of all relevant scientific discoveries in health care would be made in academic institutions, government institutions and private or biotechnology companies." Wallace Steinberg, founder of HealthCare Investment Corp.

Since the degree of difficulty in raising capital often rests upon the cyclical strength of the economy and the phase of the stock market, companies with long research lead times that require added funding along the way are playing Russian roulette with their early shareholders. Companies with technological breakthroughs are often the ones that prove most susceptible to the downside of these long lead times, since many steps before marketability may be required to make their technologies usable.

VCs have been deserting the early-stage sector in favor of developed firms. Far more angels are funding biotech startups today than venture capitalists. CellGate Inc., in Sunnyvale, Ca received $5 million in early-stage funding from an angel group headed by a cardiac surgeon who had started and sold a company for several billion dollars. Many of these angels are motivated by a desire to see promising technologies successfully introduced in order to enhance public health, just as much as they are to make money.

Knowledge-based industries require special business models.

The financial profile of knowledge-based industries such as biotechnology is quite different from asset-intensive businesses, like chemicals and autos. Knowledge-based firms tend to have high price-earnings (PE) ratios, low dividend payout ratios, low debt/capital ratios and varying levels of profitability. Asset-based firms are just the opposite. To build value, many traditional businesses today are seeking related knowledge-based services to extend their business model. IBM formed a research division called On Demand Innovation Services as a focus on consulting and support for traditional software and hardware development, a changed emphasis for the big company. IBM also bought PWC Consulting as a further move into higher margin business areas. Chemical companies and chemical-based and consumer-based pharmaceuticals have been moving into biotechnology as a means of looking for better profit margins as well.

A large, old German lathe maker began to offer a range of services and applications following competitive pressures on hardware prices, and now derives over 60% of their total profits from the services. Should you give away automobiles and live on their service?

Your most valuable products may come downstream.

Especially in biotechnology, but in numerous other fields as well, the technology that you start out with is not necessarily the technology you end up with. For Genentech, the real drug moneymakers were not even envisioned when the company first secured funding. Having a number of opportunities early in the game seems to be a wise strategy, although funding will probably rest upon how convincing you are in one major arena. Many of the biotechnology products that are obtaining FDA approval now had their origins in the 1980s and 1990s, so don't kid yourself on how fast you can get something new to market. The process can't be truncated dramatically, particularly the clinical development and the information you have to provide to convince regulators of safety and efficacy. Your life cycle is also going to change. You begin with a research group but then grow into a successive development, manufacturing and marketing group in phases. Medimmune began with an HIV focus that mostly did not pan out but the company developed a drug designed to protect premature infants from a dangerous respiratory virus and that product proved successful.

> "We should all know the cycle by now: You discover monoclonal antibodies in 1975 and announce that they will be the cure-all for everything. By the mid 1980s, you launch the first ones, but your first real surge of product doesn't come out until after 2000. Genomics will be on a similar cycle. We have to go through the maturation period. People tend to be good at anticipation long before things are realities, but there is no doubt it [genomics] will be a huge contribution to the field." George Rathman, founder of Amgen, interviewed in Bio-IT World.

Tying your relationships down.

In biotechnology, to a greater extent than even in electronics, commercial success depends on an intimate and continuing relationship between company-based researchers and academic scientists. Biotechnology's close linkage with the pharmaceutical industry provides a scenario for growth and profitability that isn't wasted on far-sighted entrepreneurs. Big pharma is both a natural customer and a partner for the outputs of biotechnology companies.

> *"The FDA SBIR funding has given us credibility with the pharmaceutical industry and resulted in a productive working relationship between a regulatory agency, big pharma, and a small business." Jim Veale, Lighthouse Instruments.*

Because of the long lead-time to market it's critical to link management and staff to the long-run success of the organization. Although this is done primarily through stock options, competitive cash compensation is also necessary since the time to potentially cash-in the stock is so distant. It's difficult to engage in cash for equity tradeoffs like those used in other technology sectors, because of these time horizons.

> *Amylin Pharmaceuticals of San Diego, CA lost 80 percent of its employees and nearly closed its doors following problems with its first drug. Four years later it licensed the rights to a second drug for diabetes to Eli Lilly & Company in an arrangement that could net Amylin up to $325 million.*

Help in research and in business.

> *Calgene modeled itself on Genentech with the vision of taking genomics into the agricultural sciences. Armed with $500,000 of his own money, Norm Goldfarb persuaded Allied Chemical to put up $1 million and a local venture capitalist put up another $3.5 million. What made this easier to piece together was the memory of the highly successful IPO of Genentech a year earlier and the market's sudden receptivity to concept companies that didn't have a history of sales growth and earnings. Goldfarb had no credentials in the biotechnology industry but he made a telephone call and persuaded an eminent scientist in the field, Dan Cohen of the University of California at Davis, to join and give him the scientific standing he needed to make the company viable.*

Gunnar Weikert of the Swiss-based life sciences venture capital fund, Inventages, suggests that public institutions should perform basic technology development and that investors should only come into the act when the business model is ready for commercialization. He thinks that genomic companies should play an intermediate role in drug development by providing model compounds to large pharmaceutical firms, and stay away from becoming integrated drug companies. Under his scenario, biotechnology groups would become more akin to parts manufacturers for automobiles—part of the supply chain.

> *Lynn Barr conceived the business plan for microsyringe company Endo-Bionics while guest teaching a biotechnology class at Miramonte High School in Orinda, CA. Students identified problems existing in two common treatments for heart disease that the microsyringe might alleviate. The high schoolers also helped identify possible customers for the product, including Medtronic. Subsequently, Medtronic made an investment in EndoBionics and formed a strategic partnership with the company to develop the technology and the market.*

Attracting money.

Barrier Therapeutics Inc. received a $46 million investment from TL Ventures and others by taking over drug programs that were already in clinical trials but had been abandoned by Johnson & Johnson.

> *"The venture capital community is just as diverse as the biotechnology industry and the question becomes one of finding those people who are active players in our niche." Gerard J. McGarrity, Ph.D., Intronn Inc.*

Threshold Pharmaceuticals of Burlingame, CA began with $750,000 of seed funding and incubation from Three Arch Partners, a Menlo Park, CA venture capital fund. The founder of the company was the former chief medical officer of well-known Coulter Pharmaceuticals, where he had developed cancer therapy compounds that work on the metabolic abnormalities of cancer cells. Another $8.25 million was forthcoming soon after, following positive exploration results the company was able to record.

> *Alliance Pharmaceuticals (AP) developed a chemical blood substitute that could deliver oxygen to a patient's tissues but when the market turned soft AP had to borrow $3 million from some shareholders at an annual interest rate of 100% to keep its doors open.*

Synta Pharmaceuticals of Lexington, MA started as a spinout from Japanese pharmaceutical firm Shionogi & Co. Shionogi invested over $100 million in their biotech subsidiary, armed it with a chemical compound library to include extensive Russian and Asian research, and set it to work on novel therapies for cancer and autoimmune diseases. With a set of assets in the form of imminent clinical trials on three lead small-molecule drug candidates, they easily raised $25 million for a buyout when the company was formed and double that a few months later. Funding came from individuals in businesses such as management consulting and ethical drugs as well as venture capitalists. In their second round, money came in from a commodities trader, a newspaper investor, banker and corporate raider.

A number of organizations feel that biotechnology will be the driving force of the 21st century and even when the funding climate proves icy, investor interest can be expected to be at least mildly receptive. In the United States in 2002 there were approximately 1,500 biotech companies and at least the same number overseas. While too few of these are close to generating significant revenues, their promises aren't lost on the investing community.

Biotech financing model.

Early biotech companies that followed Genentech in the 1970s included Biogen, Amgen and Hybritech. The financing arrangements were similar to those that had been used in semiconductors—seed money from family, friends and business angels, then start-up finance from venture capitalists, followed within a few years by an IPO. Because of the importance of academic science to the new biotechnology firms, especially at the start-up stage, most of them were set up around universities. This clustering phenomenon was similar to what had happened in electronics with Silicon Valley and along Route 128 outside Boston. The University of Maryland set up a Center for Advanced Research in Biotechnology located close to NIH laboratories, for example, and became a leader in protein engineering analysis.

The hope of early investors was that biotechnology companies would quickly become full-fledged pharmaceutical firms, displacing the incumbents. Comparisons were drawn with electronics, where new entrants such as Fairchild and Texas Instruments had mastered semi-conductors more successfully than established electronic manufacturers, and came to dominate the industry. But that parallel proved misleading. First, the development of new drugs based on genetic engineering was slower and more uncertain than the optimists had expected. Second, the new firms lacked the skills and resources necessary to take a new drug from the development stage, through clinical trials, manufacturing, and distribution and sales into the market. Third, the established pharmas, as they came to realize that biotechnology was a potentially fruitful method of developing new drugs, took steps to acquire their own capabilities in genetic engineering, either through in-house development or by acquisition.

> *Centocor went through at least 25 separate financings to raise the $1.5 billion it required to develop its drugs before it was acquired by Johnson and Johnson for $4 billion.*

What emerged in the second half of the 1980's was a division of labor between big pharma and new biotechs. Some of the newcomers chose not to develop products of their own, but to become suppliers of platform technologies or toolkits to the existing industry. Others continued to focus on developing products, but instead of taking drugs all the way to the market, formed partnerships with pharmas, often at the preclinical testing stage. Out of 95 biotechnology drugs that entered clinical trials in the US between 1980 and 1988, 44 were developed jointly by pharmaceutical and biotechnology firms, 36 solely by biotechs, and 15 solely by pharmas.

> *Using an application to the FDA under Humanitarian Use Device (HUD) provisions, MDS Noridon was granted approval for its treatment of liver cancers within only one year. Australian firm SIRTex's competing technology used a conventional FDA application for pre-market approval with clinical trials that extended over nearly two decades and cost five times as much as Noridon's solution. Susan Buskirk suggests the creative way that MDS Noridon chose to gain approval maximized their market exposure and profitability. The Humanitarian Device Exemption (HDE) encourages companies to develop technologies*

> that will benefit few individuals (those with orphan diseases) with little profits for the company, unless that company finds its solution extends to other applications.

Altering your business model to save money and speed time to market.

> At a time when biotechs are going hat in hand for scarce funding, Kosan Biosciences received $30 million and has a chance at another $190 million from Roche, if certain milestones are achieved and their polyketide anti-cancer drug, Epothilone D, works. The nice thing about this deal is that Kosan has largely eliminated the expense and risk of developing the drug in return for a generous royalty position, if successful.

Since drug development is an industry that is plagued with high costs, long time horizons, and huge doses of uncertainty, is there a way to deal with the process more efficiently? A solution to this question attempted by Pfizer involves a recently opened Discovery Technology Center in Cambridge, MA teaming academic researchers and small biotechs to develop computerized methods for screening thousands of potential drug molecules each day. Because of the Center's location near academic centers, they find drug companies, biotechs, and scientists beating a path to their doors. By constantly teaming, outsourcing and working with other research entities, Pfizer doesn't have to do everything itself and risks and costs can be at least partially absorbed by others. Biotechnology has a large number of alliances, typically built around large firms and involving many smaller ones. Basic research alliances in these models tend to predominate. Alliances can be quite fluid, shifting or growing in response to the viability of the tested approaches.

Complementary assets.

Sidney Winter of the Wharton School at the University of Pennsylvania, writing in *Managing Emerging Technologies* stated, "It would be hard to imagine a more emphatic demonstration of the relevance of complementary assets than is provided by the biotechnology industry, and its pharmaceutical branch in particular. In the earliest days of the industry, new technology emerged from university laboratories by way of a large number of entrepreneurial start-up companies, usually with university links. The first, and one of the most successful, of these new firms was Genentech, co-founded by Herbert Boyer, the Stanford University scientist who was also co-inventor of the recombinant DNA technology basic to the biotechnology industry. These small companies had R&D capabilities and programs, or dreams, and little else. Some developed new drugs for which they obtained patent protection, but the complementary assets and capabilities required for actually getting new drugs to market lay in the hands of the established pharmaceutical companies. Those companies had the ability to arrange clinical trials, obtain FDA approvals, establish manufacturing facilities and get regulatory approval for processes, and ultimately market and distribute the drugs. The ability of the established pharmaceutical companies to come into the biotech game relatively late, and profit from it, is a strong confirmation of the role of their complementary assets in appropriating the gains of biotech innovations."

> *"Six years after opening its doors, Xanthon quietly closed them for good. Unable to roll out its nucleic acid-identification technology fast enough, and facing an arid private-equity market, the company shuttered its facility in Research Triangle Park, NC. 'They couldn't quite get the product out the door,' said Peter Fair of Aurora Funds, one of Xanthon's initial backers. 'They were having problems with the scale-up of it. They could get the technology to work in the lab, but once they tried to scale it up for mass production it was hard to replicate it.' Asked whether the technology might be adopted by another startup, Fair said it is 'kind of doubtful, only because there are probably other platforms out there at this point.'" GenomeWeb, Sept 23, 2002.*

Biotech requires a link between the ability to discover and the ability to exploit, needing to mobilize players from research, industry and finance. Thematic networks are designed to bring together manufacturers, users, universities, research centers, organizations and research infrastructures—all to optimize scientific networking, coordination, exploitation and dissemination. There are about 600 mid-sized pharmas and 40 global companies upon which over 3,000 biotech companies need to either live off of or work with. Many of those biotechs are former tool companies that have since turned to drug discovery only recently, suggesting a lot of consolidations and changes in business models yet to come.

An integrated approach as opposed to sequential innovation closely combines research, industry and capital early on in development work. Good science is necessary but certainly not sufficient for success in the marketplace. Corporate "apoptosis" speaks to the variety of things that can lead to a firm's death. In biotech, plan early on to form an alliance with patient advocacy groups for the diseases you're targeting, since they could become a source of funding for you.

> *There's a star quality to attracting capital known as the "Hollywood effect" among venture capitalists. Nobel Prize-winning biologist Phillip Sharp at MIT launched startup Alnylam and secured $2 million from Polaris Venture Partners and Cardinal Partners, largely on his credentials. Weeks later, another $15 million came in. You're hard-pressed to beat a Nobel.*

State and regional biotech efforts.

A life sciences incubator affiliated with the University of Georgia in Athens, GA, the Georgia BioBusiness Center, finds it can develop biotech companies in defined niches. They know they aren't going to be the next Silicon Valley but by combining their assets, which include a half-dozen research universities, the federal Center for Disease Control (CDC) and Prevention, and lots of bioscience companies, they have a cluster that attracts new companies, investment and workers. The Georgia Research Alliance has invested $350 million of state funds to develop the industry, including the recruitment of top scientists into endowed positions, and has helped spin-off 75 companies from research done at their cluster of universities and labs. Animal and plant genomics have been a top priority in Georgia (www.ads.uga.edu), but the possibility of bioterrorism and the proximity of the CDC have opened a niche there as well. The state also is putting $400 million from the tobacco settlement into oncology research and to establish a state clinical trials network.

Tampa Bay is trying to organize a biotech cluster and city fathers traveled to and examined Austin, TX as an example of how a metropolitan area successfully nurtured a high-tech sector (electronics) into a major industry. The University of South Florida is at the heart of Tampa's efforts to incubate companies through their Center for Entrepreneurship and it can draw upon its acclaimed Center for Ocean Technology in Saint Petersburg, FL as a biotech base. This Center is joined by the Moffitt Cancer & Research Center, which is actively seeking joint ventures and partnerships with all forms of pharmaceutical businesses in the Tampa Bay area. Moffitt runs 50 labs that need biotech startups to convert their anticancer research into viable drugs and companies. Biotechs in the area have also joined together to support each other and to raise their profile. A biotech coalition called the Gulf Coast Life Sciences Initiative has many service providers such as accountants and lawyers available to facilitate entrepreneurs, as well as to look for money for them.

Also in Florida, the Orlando-based Enterprise Florida is a state/business partnership that promotes incentives and tax credits for biotechnology, pharmaceutical and medical device companies. The Sid Martin Center forms the biotechnology hub of the University of Florida. BioFlorida is located in Gainesville, FL and promotes biotechnology and related research throughout the state.

Boston, with particular emphasis in Cambridge, MA is emerging as the largest biotech cluster in the U.S. Big pharmaceutical companies are leasing space to be next to the biotech companies that are sprouting up along with the world-class research and teaching facilities available in the area. Some estimates suggest that nearly 30% of all commercial real estate in Cambridge will soon be occupied by biotechnology laboratory companies.

Medical Alley is a Minnesota-based organization to aide emerging medical device firms in that state by offering clinical, technical and management expertise services. The organization is designed to complement other investment groups including the Alley Institute, a unit designed to obtain grants for large projects. Medical Alley has been spurred on by a realization, expressed by venture capital principal at Channel Medical Partners, Carol Winslow, "Big companies don't want R&D, they want a product."

The Tennessee Venture Forum had 14 of the 22 presenting companies at their last meeting, offer business models in biotechnology, attesting to the emphasis on the life-sciences in that state. Memphis Biomed Venture Partners is a driving force in the city to develop this area as a new industry, and helped turnout the nearly 50 institutional investors who were in the crowd of 300 at the Forum. Genome Explorations in Memphis is spinning out new biotech companies to focus on specific diseases.

The University of Michigan has teamed with Michigan State and Wayne State to support emerging biotech businesses in a new life-sciences corridor in the Upper-Midwest. The University of Maryland runs a well-developed biotech incubator, drawing upon the proliferation of life-sciences professionals in and around NIH. North Carolina is already home to a well-established biotech cluster, able to draw on both extensive university connections and several large pharmaceutical companies that are housed in the state. Tom Vass is organizing startup investments in North Carolina biotechs, using a network of angel and venture capital investors that are interested in these firms. Vass's NC Biotech Center is accessed at www.corporateinvestmentcenter.com. The Virginia Biosciences Development Center delivers fee-based management services and business support to seed and pre-seed startups in the Virginia Biotech Park's biomedical incubator in Richmond, VA (www.vabiotech.com). A coalition of Carilion Health System, the University of Virginia and Virginia Tech, pairs technology and products with a $20 million commitment, in a business catalyst in Roanoke, VA, the Carilion Biomedical Institute. The Colorado Biotechnology Association accesses resources nationwide to help new companies in that state at its website, www.cobiotech.com.

The State of Missouri is promoting itself as the "BioBelt" and has been building biotech clusters largely around the genomics work of Washington University in St. Louis and in Kansas City. A new $60 million life-science research center is being constructed at the University of Missouri, Columbia, MO and the state has an initiative to raise $800 million on cigarette taxes for life-sciences support.

Pennsylvania started a $20 million life-sciences fund to provide young companies, institutions, or individuals located in the southern part of the state with up to $500,000 in pre-seed or seed capital financing, through its creation, Bio-Advance. The money comes from the state's tobacco settlement and is another example of how serious Pennsylvania has become in fostering biotech companies. Bio-Advance is one of three statewide greenhouse agencies that use tobacco settlement money to nurture local businesses, and has already received a big chunk of money from the state for investment and support in this area. Pittsburgh has a life sciences Greenhouse (www.pittsburghlifesciences.com), helping to provide financing for area firms through the following multiple segments: (a) University Development Fund to commercialize technologies; (b) Pre-Seed/Seed Fund for promising startups; (c) an Industry/University Research Partnership Fund: (d) and SBIR assistance. LaunchCyte in Pittsburgh, PA makes seed money investments from private/public sources and helps investigators begin startup life-sciences companies in the state. The Limbach Entrepreneurial Center was organized in 2000 as an effort to commercialize research from the University of Pittsburgh Cancer Institute.

A life-sciences incubator in Indianapolis will be run by Indiana University to turn promising research projects developed at area institutions into businesses. The incubator draws upon the Indiana Genomics Initiative, Indiana University Medical School, Indiana Proteomics Consortium including Lilly and Purdue, the Regenstrief Institute and the School of Informatics. www.biostart.org lists the services available in Cincinnati, OH to include laboratory facilities, incubation and economic development as well as a very useful set of links for starting a life sciences company.

Upon losing a promising biotech to another state, North Carolina Department of Commerce economic developer Jim Nichols suggested states should: consider strategies for more upfront capital and more private venture capital; work more closely with private venture capitalists; consider strategic investments in training; changes in tax policy; and construction of processing facilities to help lure companies who are particularly close to full commercialization with manufacturing and sales.

While the California Mission Bay area is home to a new UCSF campus that is supposed to serve as a Mecca for biotech companies, those firms aren't aggregating there so far, preferring the Boston area instead. Even west coast success stories such as Amgen have opened new R&D centers near Boston.

A description of thirty state initiatives in biotechnology along with contact information, funding sources, economic benefits, associations and organizations, etc., can be downloaded from the Biotechnology Industry Organization at www.bio.org/govt/survey.html. A consortium of eight Midwestern states formed Bio Mid-America to form and help fund startup biotechs in the region, with details at http://bio.org/midamerica. The Washington Biotechnology & Biomedical Association promotes companies in the Pacific Northwest at www.mightydreams.com. A useful set of funding sources is maintained at the website of British Columbia-based BC Biotech, www.biotech.bc.ca and www.canbiotech.com has an excellent search for funding, training and other services.

The International Northeast Biotechnology Corridor (INBC) is a consortium of more than 750 companies, ranging from Connecticut to Quebec, supporting biotechs in the region. Operating out of Fairfield ME, the INBC hopes to emulate Silicon Valley and put capital together with the outpourings of area research laboratories and entrepreneurs. Dallas is establishing a biotechnology incubator at The University of Texas (UT) Southwestern Medical Center under the Biotechnology Dallas Coalition. UT Southwestern plans to receive equity in lieu of rent and other services they will provide at the incubator. The New York City Partnership and Chamber of Commerce hope to form a major biomedical center around city resources including New York University and Memorial Sloan-Kettering Cancer Center. Columbia University in New York City is one of the three largest recipients of technical transfer licensing fees and terrific management and financial help pervades the whole New York area. Columbia's Audubon Biomedical Science and Technology Park is a form of incubator that has been packed with companies ever since it opened in 1993. NYU, SUNY's Downstate Medical Center and Memorial Sloan-Kettering are all planning separate forms of life-science incubators.

Some of the other communities for biotech include: Bio NC; Bio-Capital; BioCorridor; Biotech Bay; Biotech Beach; Genetown; Pharm Country; BioCanada; BioForest; BioMidwest: BioTechxus; and BioUK. You can find a link to these organizations plus a glossary on biotech and a good deal more at www.biospace.com. The Biotech Industry Organization in Washington, DC organizes investor and partnering meetings with biotech firms all over the world. www.biopartnering.com is an e-network for bio-investing that provides access to various forms of business intelligence.

Overseas opportunities.

The Taiwanese Government is building several industrial parks for biotech firms and providing access to $850 million in government R&D funds along with $4 billion in state and private venture capital, plus a range of support services such as marketing and IT assistance. Genome Canada is a $200 million endowment to boost genomics research in that country. Genome Quebec is investing over $80 million in McGill University for genomic and proteomic research initiatives and to open new business opportunities for discoveries made at the school.

A biotechnology park adjacent to the Weizmann Institute in Israel has given rise to many companies including Biotechnology General and Peptor. Singapore is in the process of making a major investment in biotech support and incubation, a republic that is home to 144 venture capital firms. Singapore is already a favorite base for Chinese and Indian entrepreneurs. In Japan, an exchange known as the "Mothers Market" has been the launching place for several biotech firms. Transgenic made an offering on the new Japanese exchange in December 2002 and fetched an initial price 30% over the offering, even though they had substantial losses. Companies in the Osaka, Japan area have a new venture capital group known as "Bio Sight Capital" with over 2 billion yen for university startups and the Japanese government plans to make hundreds of billions available for investment in the biotech arena generally. www.jetro.org is the site for the Japan External Trade Organization, a Japanese government-supported group that sponsors trips, business forums and other marketing and investment connections in Japan, with special programs in biotech. JETRO's mission statement includes helping small and medium-sized U.S. businesses to develop links with Japan.

German biotechs have concentrated on platform technologies to improve the productivity of research and focus on selling to drug development firms, instead of developing the new drugs themselves. Some observers believe that this approach is well suited to German institutions and traditions, a form of comparative advantage for the concentration of efforts. According to this view, new drug development is a high-risk, winner-take-all business; success with one drug can easily be followed by failure for the next. By contrast, platform technology firms develop more stable or cumulative technologies that can continue to generate revenues and lead to a natural succession of new products and new generations of existing products. Most German firms begin with expertise in one or more process technologies that can be applied to a particular group of common molecular biology research activities. They then hope to expand into related areas, basing their business models on externalities that are generated through the completion of particular projects. The financial risks are lower than in pure therapeutics companies, and there is greater scope for maintaining stability of employment—an important consideration in a country that is not attuned to Anglo-American hire and fire practices. If correct, German biotechs may have a niche and can quickly catch up with the British and Americans. Another new program in Germany has been announced to provide financial and technical support to startups in the field of biotechnology and telecommunications. Two existing German government-funding groups were merged to effect this change. Bavaria has its own money to support companies in their region and, for example, granted $700,000 to a German functional-genomics company through the Bavarian Technology Promotion Program. Germany is also one of the hosts of an annual forum for biotech companies to meet venture capitalists and other professional investors at www.techvision.com.

The French government pledged the equivalent of $148 million in loan guarantees and venture funding for biotech efforts, funds that are eventually expected to leverage billions more. The trade organization France Biotech and a biotechnology entrepreneur group known as "Objectif 2010" have teamed with other French organizations to form the Strategic Council for Innovation, not wishing to be left behind in high-tech initiatives. The French efforts include: government subsidies for entrepreneurs; doubling government research; increasing networking and international mobility; and easing regulatory burdens. The French are spurred on by finding they're a distant second to Germany in biotech and their efforts are targeted to surpass their neighbor by 2006. The French are very serious about this goal and have a separate plan for *Jeunes Entreprises Innovantes* that eliminates corporate income tax for R&D startups that are under eight years of age. They also plan to eliminate taxes on venture capital R&D investments, reduce other social charges and local taxes, encourage researchers to file patents, and promote entrepreneurship for students.

The British government formed an office in the British consulate in Cambridge, MA to promote relationships between biotech companies in the United States and the U.K. government. The idea is mostly aimed at genomics and bioinformatics companies and is based upon the need young firms have for mentoring and support. The director of the office believes many partnerships will be formed as well as mergers and acquisitions and wants to insure that an international perspective on these relationships will be maintained.

In 1993, under pressure from British Biotechnology, the London Stock Exchange (LSE) agreed to make special provisions for biotechnology companies. The listing rules were amended to allow these firms access to the Exchange as long as they met several conditions, not including profitability. A major change in US financing came in 1980 when Genentech and Apple Computers both did IPOs before being profitable, an unheard of offering, but an event that heralded a technological revolution. In 1997, Germany created the Neuer Market to mirror the LSE, for all technology companies. The exchange fell on hard times when markets weakened and was closed but the idea remains viable when and if markets become strong again.

Federal resources.

The Department of Defense operates a Congressionally Directed Medical Research Program (CDMRP) that directs funding for a number of diseases, including a variety of cancers, that is run by the U.S. Army Medical Research and Material Command (http://cdmrp.army.mil). The CDMRP has been responsible for funding hundreds of companies and investigators, from the idea on up, and has awarded hundreds of millions of dollars. Their criteria and method of operating includes: specific Congressionally directed research areas; funds for high-risk/high-gain proposals and the encouragement of innovative approaches; involvement of new researchers as well as those that are established; encouraging consumer participation; using two tiers of proposal reviews as a form of checks and balances; supporting of minority health initiatives; and collaborating with other funding agencies. Access them at their website, http://mrmc-www.army.mil or call (301) 619 7071.

The Department of Defense also supports an unbelievable array of medical commands, offices, initiatives, programs and the like, any of which could be a source of contract or other funding for your related idea. If your focus reasonably fits any of the needs of the military services, a call to their program office would be a start. Some of their most prominent areas of emphasis are: military infectious diseases; combat casualty care; chemical and biological defense; telemedicine; medical information science; information management; and logistics. You can obtain some information on funding by calling (301) 619 2110 or, for small and disadvantaged businesses, (301) 619 2471.

Technical transfer from the NIH and a number of its centers is a big deal and lots of help and money is available, if your solutions are on the cutting edge of science. The main Technology Transfer Office at NIH has a staff of 67, thousands of patents and other assets that you may be able to tap into. Access them at (301) 594 7700 or http://ott.od.nih.gov., but note that the emphasis has been on protecting the rights of the government with commercialization second. You can get information on National Cancer Center (NCI) initiatives from the same website or call (310) 496 7057. Drug discovery and development is at (301) 496 8720 or visit http://dtp.nci.nih.gov. Cooperative Research and Development Agreements (CRADAs) as well as Clinical Trials Agreements and Material Transfer Agreements information is at (301) 496 0477 or http://ttb.nci.nih.gov. (Arcturus Engineering developed a clinical pathology laser microdissection system for cancer therapies under a CRADA that led to several commercial products.) The USDA references start at www.nal.usda.gov.

NCI funding for small businesses is at http://otir.nci.nih.gov/ir/small_biz.html. The Index of Funding Opportunities Available to Industry is found at http://otir.nci.nih.gov/ir/funding.html. Remember, "We're from the government and we want to help you." A new forum called the Council on Private Sector Initiatives to Improve Security, Safety and Quality of Health Care has been lodged in HHS just to help companies navigate through the agencies, programs and funds (www.cpsi.ahrq.gov). NIH and Fisher Scientific donated equipment to a sixteen-wheel mobile classroom and laboratory to demonstrate biotechnology techniques to students and teachers, under a program begun by the Institute for Genomic Research, MdBio and the University of Maryland.

Determine who can make money by investing in you.

A new biotech fund, 5AM Ventures, has been organized with $25 million from Versant Ventures and Bay City Capital, both firms that run substantially larger pools of capital. The feeling is that more money can be made from small seed-stage life science companies but success often propels the venture groups into larger and later-stage investments. The pools in venture capital funds had grown so large that a void was left for startups with all the handholding they entail. Most VCs felt the startups simply weren't worth the bother. The market downturn also made these pools more conservative and less willing to take a chance on young companies. The *San Jose Business Journal* quoted one of the fund managers, Camille Samuels Pearson as saying: "The best opportunity for a 10X [ten times] return is at the very early stages. A lot of other venture firms go for a 5X return but we are trying for a 10X."

Other venture capital firms are seeking good revenue producers that can sustain growth without worrying about the success of one or two research projects. ABS Capital invested in US Pathology Labs after determining the firm offers both a solid growth market and a history of profitability, just the criteria they were looking for. The U.S. clinical laboratory business is roughly a $34 billion market and increasingly sophisticated genetic testing is expected to increase that figure considerably.

> *Commenting on whether Advanced Tissue Sciences will continue in business after selling its artificial skin products to Smith & Nephew of Britain, investor relations director Abe Wischnia said: "This time the company is going to do it in a way that makes money."*

A public biotech firm with a small market capitalization is under the radar screen of the nation's major pension and mutual funds. They can't afford to take a meaningful position when the size of their purchases and sales would be pretty much the whole market. Better to solicit their interest before doing an IPO and appeal to the smaller and riskier side of their portfolios, which they earmark as "alternative investments."

> *By focusing drug development activities on smaller and niche markets, Chicago-based Ovation Pharmaceuticals Inc. raised $2 million in seed funding from several angel investors and one venture capital firm, Highland Capital. Large pharmaceutical companies target the primary care audience but smaller physician specialties such as neurologists, often treat illnesses with smaller markets, and offer a window for drug sales. Both King Pharmaceuticals and Forest Laboratories grew to respectable size by developing as specialty pharmaceutical firms.*

Specialty pharmaceuticals generally have drug candidates well along in human tests and are far less risky for investors. Venture capitalists looking at such firms feel they compress the drug-development process into a suitable time frame, materially reducing the investment risk. Pharmacia spun out an entire division with 900 employees, a break-even cash flow and several drugs in clinical trials that helped its new company, Biovitrum, secure $130 million from investors led by MPM Capital.

A list of venture capital companies that are oriented towards life sciences firms is found at www.biospace.com/articles/072099 page 6, and includes prominent firms such as Venrock, Oxford Bioscience Partners and Kleiner, Perkins, Caufield and Byers. www.bioability.com provides complete biotech planning services and sells specialized directories of venture capital firms, etc. You should also think of the many other companies who see the life sciences industry as a major growth area. IBM sells well over $1 billion in this arena and Hewlett Packard with Compaq closer to $2 billion. If your business model is complementary to theirs, you have a good case to make.

How to analyze a biotech business.

Christine Copple, Ph.D. is the President of ASM Resources, the venture arm of the American Society for Microbiology, and a scientist and business executive (www.asmrusa.com). Christine uses an outline to suggest that a biotech firm is assembling the skills and focus for a successful market strategy, and helps form a reality check for any developing firm. Her format is a set of questions and considerations briefly as follows:

- Selecting a lead product. Simply, where should you focus your energies and resources to give you the best chance for growth? What you may produce or provide include: research tools; drug discovery; bioinformatics; contract; what kind of company are you and what do you have? In biotechnology the several sectors that your research organization; drug development (small molecule entities and biologics).
- *Identify a technical base.* Do you have a platform, a suite of complementary tools, a family of biomolecules or a single biomolecule?
- *You need to know your application profile.* Is it broad and deep, broad and shallow, narrow and deep or narrow and shallow?
- *Product selection criteria.* Cash cow or long-term play? Development investment versus financial market conditions. Development costs versus anticipated return on investment (ROI). Infrastructure creation—now or later. Availability and quality of partners. Dollars today versus dollars tomorrow.
- *Realities of product development.* Do you own the intellectual property? Do you have freedom to operate? Is the technology ready to deploy? If you aren't ready to deploy, what is needed to reach that stage? Will you need additional technology to deploy? Do you have the team that you need? Can you farm out a number of functions? Can you manufacture? Store? Ship? Will you need a deep pocket partner?
- *Focus.* Building your core competency requires: protection for your core IP; file additional IP around products; capitalize on the strengths of the core team; license-in complementary technology; sign up key technology collaborators

(develop new and related IP); and should you have a partner in sales and distribution?

- *Identify the value proposition.* Is this proprietary, sustainable and give you IP? Is there a lack of equivalent alternatives? Is it easy to adopt? Have you built in premium quality, reliability and value? Can you keep high-cost personnel productive? Does this give you reasonable places to say "go" or "no go" in regards to continuance and spending? Does this reduce the time to market?
- *Regulatory.* A hierarchy of regulatory oversight speaks to the expertise you need to have, acquire or partner for. Routine research products with no oversight are the easiest. Human derived products with minimal regulation are next in regulatory difficulty. Medical devices that require moderate regulatory requirements follow. Small molecule entities (SMEs) require high oversight and biologics even higher. Stem cells or gene therapy invite the highest regulatory hurdles.
- *Market size.* Are you North American only? If worldwide are you EU, Japan and the Far East? What about the rest of the world? What are the drivers for your demographic concentration? What complexities of reimbursement, rules, currencies, etc., will require attention?
- *Target market.* Define the audience for your marketing messages and illustrate the primary and the secondary receivers. Your target market may not be the end market. Drivers may be less about the end market than about the target business model.
- *Market demand.* Is this a push or a pull situation? If you have a technical audience realize they may be attracted by elegant solutions. In any sale, getting to "no" quickly is much cheaper and better use of your sales assets. Can you profit from low overhead? Realize that pharmaceutical companies have increasingly dry drug pipelines and that their R&D is going off balance sheet. Can you respond to unmet medical needs?
- *Competitive analysis.* What current companies are in your space and who are the dominant players and which ones are second tier? What about emerging companies and what do you know about their strengths? What about raw

technology and where it may be in the development and adoption cycle?
- *Market access.* Consider: size versus reach; tools at your disposal; staffing needs that have been met and those that haven't; what geographic considerations are relevant; and is culture any kind of barrier?
- *Branding.* If you seek to own the niche: realize this is expensive upfront; you need to validate core competencies including customer testimonials; it will facilitate future launches; and gives you higher long-term ROI. If you partner for instant recognition instead, you will save the upfront expenses but experience a reduced long-term ROI.
- *Customer support.* Do you have it or can you build it? You will need: quality control and assurance; your product should have "crack & peel" ease of use; website with on-line video support; and a live support line. Don't forget that this will be a valuable source of customer feedback to give you ideas for product extensions.
- *Ethics and public relations issues.* A separate effort should be conducted to: find issues that you will be proactive with; develop a corporate ethics statement; realize the audience is no longer just technical and be able to speak to all levels; do contingency planning for both positive and negative events; have an ongoing PR strategy in place; and have a disaster recovery plan.
- *Sales force versus distributors and representatives.* Do you want to build your own sales team? Are your representatives going to be part of a custom network? Will distributors be in the U.S. or worldwide? What is your relationship to big pharma and are they a marketing asset for you?
- *Collaborative development.* Combine your core competencies for "best in breed" results. Look for cross-licensing convenience. Seek synergies for rapid product development and launch. Can you access clinical sectors? Be on the lookout for cross-marketing opportunities.
- *Opportunism and the value of flexibility.* Identify existing or potential bottlenecks and work out solutions. Always listen to your customers. Capitalize on the pull that your partners create, especially when it is often driven by unrelated business needs. Use one of the best tools available, "OTM,"

or "other people's money." Today's deal is tomorrow's validation and you want to use partner money during closed markets.

- *Return on marketing investment.* Try to design market metrics to give you a feel for how well you're doing. Identify and tie costs to specific products. Evaluate the effectiveness of your various strategies. Measure more than just sales. Speak to the awareness of your brand, quality mark and customer loyalty.

"We know the financial community rewards diagnostic aspects of a business model less than the therapeutic portion." Christina Hedberg, ExonHit Therapeutics.

Other assistance

ASM Resources, Inc., holds a biotechnology business boot camp in Washington, DC as a one-day program at a cost of $795. Their stated aim is to sharpen your understanding of: invention disclosures, preliminary patent application filings, and prudent intellectual property protection; steps to verify an early stage biotechnology business concept and solicit seed stage funding; helpful resources for developing business plans that attract capital; regulatory hurdles for different types of biotechnology products; and what academic scientists experience when transitioning to industry. Background information on the camps is at www.asmrusa.com. www.csc.com offers consulting and systems integration to speed the process of biotechnology commercialization.

www.womeninbio.org is a new organization that is sponsoring events and communications to help open more professional and business slots for women in biotechnology. www.lifesciences.com is a reservoir of scientific and business information and sponsors a number of conferences in biotech. The website of Michigan State University at www.msu.edu/user/biomed has a great set of links for entrepreneurs and biotechnology resources (including SBIRs at DARPA, NIH, NSF, etc). www.biotechventures.com is a specialist investment banker with a full range of services including links to universities, healthcare statistics, finance, etc.

The Practicing Law Institute held a two-day seminar in Boston that covered biotechnology patents and business strategies. The $1,395 session splits between patent tactics and various business issues such as valuing inventions, technology transfer, raising private and public funding, government funding, corporate collaborations, M&A, etc. A special session is devoted to certain funding techniques such as off-balance sheet deals known as SWORDS, Lazy Susan agreements, and PIPE transactions for public companies.

www.biotechfind.com has part of its website devoted to BioFinance. David Anderson, Ph.D., MBA, has a book published in August 2001, entitled: *Compound to Capital: Financing Biotech* which is 80 pages long and sells for $1,200. A report that illustrates the history of a number of biotech companies along with an insight into the development of an industry on a state level is contained in "Founders of Maryland Bioscience and Medical Instrument Companies," August 2002. The report is free and, along with a list of seed funding sources, is available from Linda Saffer, Ph.D., at e-mail lsaffer@marylandtedco.org. Guides for life-sciences companies on topics such as strategic alliances, business plans, due diligence and CROs are sold by Drug and Market Development at www.drugandmarket.com. A free guide to Negotiating Pharmaceutical and Biotech Licenses and Other Strategic Alliances was published by the law firm of Kaye Scholer (www.kayescholer.com) and includes sections on: (a) licenses; (b) joint research and development collaborations; (c) equity investments; (d) co-promotion/co-marketing agreements; and (e) manufacturing and supply arrangements. *Bio-IT World* and *Genetic Engineering News* magazines are both heavily weighted towards technology but provide regular insights into funding as well. You can find an excellent list of biotech-oriented venture capital firms at www.bioexchange.com in addition to scientific reports. www.biotech.about.com will provide salary surveys in addition to venture capital sources, business development, and scientific information. www.bioenterprise.com helps access capital while providing equipment, facilities, management support, collaborations and professional services. Most states will have offices and teams that are available to help any biotechnology business initiative. In Maryland, the High Tech Council hired Matt Gardner following his long experience in California and scouting opportunities for Australian biotechs. Meet with people such as Matt and let them know what you're doing, they're paid to help.

Getting your management team right.

Biotechs regularly have turned to big pharma for experienced executives—a trend that was welcomed by investors, who were often uneasy about the continued dominance of founder-entrepreneurs as companies grew. Big pharma, however, tends to nurture corporate managers who may easily be risk averse, used to long time horizons, have access to many supporting services and depend on continuing budgets instead of nursing a front-end investment from a VC.

The top-heavy scientific backgrounds of many biotech managers are not a comfort to investors. While this characterizes good science it does nothing to suggest the company will be well-run. Placing scientists in technical and board positions makes eminent sense but recruitment of CEOS, CFOs, marketing directors, etc., should focus on qualifications predominant in those areas. Many scientists are worried that managers won't understand their vision and are therefore reluctant to surrender power, believing that the science will become wayward under different hands. A number of programs exist to bring non-technical people to a quick understanding in the biosciences and an investment in some instruction could bring people to a more even footing. Stanford University has an on-line track with a certificate in bioinformatics and the University of Maryland has an on-line master's degree in biotechnology management, to name just a few of the programs that are available. Vladimir Makarov has developed new bioinformatics offerings for UC Berkeley and the University of Maryland. S-Star hopes to launch a series of free online bioinformatics courses at www.s-star.org. A set of life science courses including both advanced and basic offerings are provided at reasonable charges from www.geneed.com and www.lifesciences.com. Gene Expression at www.sciencemag.org has a terrific set of links to biotech resources, databases, tutorials, tools, etc. EMBER is the name of a European-wide bioinformatics educational effort that groups the efforts of numerous universities and laboratories, (mabey@bioinf.man.ac.uk).

Most major universities have extensive course offerings in the biotech arena, many offered in an executive fashion or on-line. For people in the sciences already, New England Biolabs of Beverly, MA holds two-week boot camps in molecular biology and PCR. Beginning at 8:30 in the morning and continuing until 10:00 at night, participants conduct dozens of experiments along with the lectures. Knight Science Journalism Fellowships at MIT offer boot camps in the life-sciences for journalists (http://mit.edu/knight-science/). The NIH-NSF Bioengineering and Bioinformatics Summer Institutes Program is a resource for some universities to heighten offerings in those areas. The NIH runs classes in clinical pharmacology and in clinical trials from a theater at their campus in Bethesda, MD and rebroadcasts to several universities.

> *An angel group, Tenex Medical Investors in San Mateo, CA has 90 members and is focused on life science companies. Members come together for dinner, listen to company presentations, and each takes it from there. Oxo Chemie was angel financed in 1986 and the founder of that company along with ten of his friends later financed another company, IntraBiotics.*

APPENDIX A: FEDERAL TECHNOLOGY TRANSFER

What do the following have in common? Disposable diapers, golf balls, eyeglasses and mammogram machines. Answer: all incorporate technologies from federal labs. The diapers use a super-absorbent starch developed by the USDA's Agricultural Research Service. The golf balls incorporate NASA technologies from the space shuttle program that improve aerodynamics. The eyeglasses use "memory metal" developed by the U.S. Navy. Mammograms are now more accurate thanks to a spectrometer developed by NIST.

Instruments for technical transfer include:

- Cooperative Research and Development Agreements (CRADAs)
- Material Transfer Agreements (MTAs)
- Patent licenses
- Technical meetings
- Information dissemination/collegial interchange
- Cooperative agreements.

What is a CRADA? An agreement between one or more federal laboratories and one or more nonfederal parties under which the laboratories provide personnel, facilities, or other non-monetary resources and the nonfederal parties provide funds, personnel, services, facilities, equipment or other resources to conduct specific research or development efforts that are consistent with the laboratory's mission.

Steps:

- Lab scientist finds a prospective partner and works out a draft statement of work (SOW).

- Scientist requests CRADA from applicable laboratory's Office of Research and Technology Applications (ORTA).
- ORTA prepares draft CRADA and obtains legal and programmatic review from the installation.
- ORTA sends draft CRADA to prospective partner and negotiates terms and conditions.
- ORTA obtains approval from laboratory director and initiates departmental review.
- CRADA signed by laboratory director.

Attributes:

- The heart of a CRADA is the SOW
- The government cannot provide funds to a nonfederal entity—other mechanisms exist for that purpose
- Intellectual Property rights in existence prior to a collaboration are retained by the provider, while any rights to newly created IP are negotiated on a case-by-case basis subject to applicable law and regulation

What is an MTA? A short form CRADA solely for the provision of materials and information between a laboratory and a nonfederal party. No collaboration is contemplated.

What is a Patent License? A contractual agreement between a licensor (IP owner) and a licensee granting the licensee the right to use or develop the IP in exchange for a royalty fee or other considerations.

Attributes:

- U.S. industry/small business preferred
- Can be exclusive, nonexclusive (preferred), for specific field of use, or a specific geographic area.
- Substantial royalties return to the laboratory and government inventors
- Licensee must present plans to commercialize the invention
- Government obtains a nonexclusive, royalty-free, worldwide license
- Subject to conflict-of-interest rules

Royalty Income Use. The inventors receive the first $2,000 and

20% thereafter up to $150,000/year of any royalties/payments resulting from commercial licensure.

Each of the agencies involved in the program differ markedly from the others in some degree, and you need to find out those characteristics before going to the time and expense of submitting a proposal. The overall track record of being awarded a grant goes up considerably when you resubmit proposals and also when they are done professionally and with agency sensitivity. People in the agencies will provide you a lot of guidance and will vary in their ability to understand and respond to your proposition. The Director of NIST's program, Omid Omidor, for example, has an MBA, a Ph.D., over 150 scientific papers to his credit, a record as a successful entrepreneur, and can be found at various forums where he provides briefings on the program to prospective grantees.

Legislative history of technology transfer.

1980   Stevenson-Wydler Technology Improvement Act
- Established technology transfer as a government mission.
- Established offices of research and technology applications.

Bayh-Dole Patent and Trademark Amendments Act
- Permitted universities, not-for-profit organizations and small businesses to obtain title to inventions developed with government support.

1986   Federal Technology Transfer Act
- Authorized CRADAs
- Authorized laboratory invention and intellectual property rights to be granted and waived.
- Required patent license royalties to be shared with government employee inventors.

1989   National Competitiveness Technology Transfer Act
- Essentially extended the same technology transfer and CRADA authorities to

> Government-Owned Contractor-Operated (GOCO) laboratories.

1995   Technology Transfer Improvement Act of 1995
- Guaranteed private companies the option of choosing an exclusive license for an invention created under a CRADA.

NIH's technology transfer program has a separate source of information on licenses and technologies accessed on the web at www:

- CRISP Database—nih.gov/grants.
- Pharmalicensing—pharmalicensing.com.
- Technology Exchange—tech-ex.com.
- University Ventures—uventures.com.
- Pharma-transfer—pharma-transfer.com
- Knowledge Express—keonline.com.

The Federal Laboratory Consortium (FLC) is a nationwide network of federal laboratories that provides a forum to develop strategies and opportunities for linking laboratory mission technologies and expertise with the marketplace. Access the FLC at www.federallabs.org and the output of the following agencies: CIA; USAF; Army; Navy; Defense Technical Information Center; Ballistic Missile Defense Organization; EPA; NASA; NSF; TVA; National Science Foundation; Tennessee Valley Authority; and the Dept's of Agriculture; Commerce; Education; Energy, Health and Human Services; Interior; Justice; Labor; Transportation; and Veterans Affairs. The FLC will provide regular information to you on particular technology areas with a subscription through NewsLink at flcmso@utrsmail.com, or help you find a laboratory doing work in an area of your interest by calling 888 388 5227. With 700 research labs and centers and 100,000 scientists and engineers spending a budget of $70 billion, the Feds may have something useful for you.

A comprehensive report on government technology transfer has been issued by the Government Accounting Office, October 2002. The differences in agency programs are illustrated as well as comprehensive statistics at www.gao.gov/new.items/do347.pdf.

The *Advanced Technology Program* (ATP) of NIST offers substantial research funds along with technology transfer in a unique program. "ATP began in 1990 to provide cost shared funding to industry to accelerate the development and broad dissemination of challenging, high-risk technologies that promise significant commercial payoffs and widespread benefits for the nation. This unique government industry partnership accelerates the development of emerging or enabling technologies, leading to revolutionary new products, industrial processes and services that can compete in rapidly changing world markets. The program challenges industry to take on higher risk projects with commensurately higher potential payoff to the nation than they would otherwise. Basically, ATP will fund up to $2 million of direct costs (not indirect costs such as overhead) for the research and development required to create important new technologies. Also, ATP does not fund commercialization activities. ATP does no equity investing, they are grants that cover expenses. It's a great way to get significant funding without giving up a large piece of equity. The three most important factors in an ATP proposal are: 1) Potential for broad economic benefits 2) Need for funding (i.e. been turned down by VCs/other investors) and 3) Commercialization plan. Companies must show that they are able to commercialize the technology once it is developed."

APPENDIX B:
SMALL STOCK OFFERING REQUIREMENTS

List of items needed to file a registration statement with the SEC and NASD (these two filings must be simultaneous while filing with the states can be done later). Send a check to the NASD for filing, zero to the SEC for a Regulation A and $92 per million of registration for an SB-2. A registration fee with the NASD is computed at $500 plus .01% of the gross proceeds of the offering or $100 per million plus $500. The SEC will require two years of audited statements for an SB-2 and three years for an S-1. While the SEC does not require audited statements for a Regulation A, many states will require an audit. You can often file in those states without your audit completed but you won't be qualified until the audit is final and reviewed. It is materially better to file with audited statements at the outset. Each state in which you choose to sell stock will also require a registration statement and a filing fee.

Check the following and provide the items or the information that you now possess. If much of the following appears foreign to you, don't worry, a number of models can be easily accessed. Much of the following you may have in your possession but the list is designed to trigger memory and completeness. Please remember that the basis of SEC registration is "full disclosure." DON'T HIDE ANYTHING. Please also note that the SEC wants to know complete details on ownership to insure that assets and revenues are indeed company property and will not be siphoned off instead of benefiting the new shareholders. You may only make statements of fact or reasonable expectation and sales rhetoric and hyperbole will be required to be struck out of the document by the SEC. While your business plan is designed to illustrate your vision of where you want to take your company as well as its past and present, this is a legal procedure and the task is to successfully take it through those hurdles. Rarely will a prospective buyer ever make his decision to buy or sell exclusively on the basis of your offering document but you do want it to look professional.

Note that service professionals will provide much of the following for you but you need to be familiar with all of the kinds of information and documentation that will be required. Also note that you will be responsible, either through your CFO or CPA, for the financial statements, calculations and accounting registration responses.

- Business plan
- Financial statements
- Date and state of incorporation
- Exact corporate name, address, telephone number, fax and e-mail address
- Employer tax identification number
- Do you have a web site and if so what is the address?
- Articles of incorporation
- Bylaws
- List of investors in the prior twelve months with their home and work addresses; the dollar amount; price and number of shares and basis or means of calculating the price; telephone numbers; identification as to accredited, sophisticated or non-accredited. Services (if any) provided in full or partial compensation for stock.
- List of the board members and management-team with their respective educational backgrounds, home addresses and their employment for the last five years including the month and year. Identification of the CEO and CFO. Also, if they or anyone in their immediate family holds a security license or are otherwise employed by a brokerage firm.
- Stock option plan (if any) and agreement.
- Management's Discussion and Analysis of Financial Condition according to the SEC instructions
- Identification of the corporate secretary.
- Number of shares outstanding and authorized.
- Share and option ownership of management and anyone owning more than 5%.
- The dollar amount that you want to capitalize the company at (for $5 million, what percentage of the firm are you giving up?).
- Size of offering

Employment agreements
Copies of any significant agreements or material contracts including lease agreements
Opinion of counsel
Consent of auditors and counsel
Lock up agreement for management's shares.
Salaries of corporate officers
Shares of stock held by corporate officers
Have any corporate officers ever been involved in security fraud or felonious activity?
Number of employees
Number of square feet occupied and rent or lease terms.
Involvement in any legal proceedings
Plan for use of the proceeds of the offering
Indebtedness to be paid from the proceeds
Plan to acquire any companies
Affiliates
Projections for growth over the next three years and the next five need to be made. Bottom line earnings are expected in those projections. (Note: when you figure the capitalization above, you should be able to demonstrate high compound growth in the value of shares by year five. Venture capitalists are typically looking for at least 30% and you want to give your shareholders equivalent compensation for their risks.) Projections *do not* go in a registration statement, but they do go in a private placement or other form of non-registered business description.
Good color pictures or schematics that can tell the whole story of the company's products/services, etc., in a glance. These can be used in the final printed offering circular.
Added products/services/markets that you're thinking of bringing out in the next few years.
Description of your R&D activities.
Registration in New York State requires the identification of officers and directors to include: place of birth, telephone number, social security number, date of birth and residence for the last five years.
Glossary of technical terms.
List of competitors and the differences between them and your company.

Citations for claims to include the publication or authority and description of the journal or organization.

A canvass of your present shareholders, officers, directors and affiliates to see if anyone is associated in any way, marriage or other relationship, with any member of a broker-dealer, a National Association of Securities Dealers member-firm.

Checklist of items:

Signature page with a majority of board members plus the CEO and CFO as signatories.
Individual state registration letters signed by the CEO.
Samples of standard or special agreements the company is a party to.
Signed underwriting and selling agreement.
Signed employment agreements.
Signed lock-up agreements.
Signed consent agreement of the auditor.
Signed opinion of counsel.
Signed escrow agreement.
Tombstone.
Specimen of security.
Original signature corporate resolutions (form U-2A) for each state filing.
Signed and notarized uniform applications for each state filing.
Residence street address of officers, directors and principal shareholders.
Dilution, capitalization and use of proceeds checked by the CFO.

GLOSSARY

For a comprehensive glossary on investing, with particular reference to venture capital transactions, go to http://vcexperts.com/vce/library/encyclopedia/glossary.asp. The SBA has a link to dozens and dozens of glossaries at www.sba.gov/hotlist/busstart.html including highly specialized listings such as "Glossary of Object-Oriented Terminology for Business, Insurance Glossary, Netlingo Internet Glossary, and Glossary of Leasing Terms" to name only a few. www.geneed,com has a comprehensive Life Sciences Glossary.

Accredited Investor. As defined in rule 501 of Regulation D of the Securities Act of 1933, as amended, an accredited investor means any person who comes within any of the following categories, or who the issuer reasonably believes comes within the following categories at the time of the sale of securities to that person: a bank, insurance company, registered investment company; and employee benefit plan; a charitable organization, corporation, or partnership with assets exceeding $5 million; a director, executive officer, or general partner of the company selling the securities; a business in which all of the equity owners are accredited investors; a natural person with a net worth of at least $1 million; a natural person with income exceeding $200,000 in each of the 2 most recent years or joint income with a spouse exceeding $300,000 for those years and a reasonable expectation of the same income level in the current year; or a trust with assets of at least $5 million not formed to acquire the securities offered, and whose purchases are directed by a sophisticated person.

Business Angel. A high net worth individual with an interest and knowledge in a particular business sector, often because that is where he or she gained personal wealth. Business angels can help a stat-up company with their considerable experience but can also cause considerable harm if they are naïve about the needs of the business. An angel will frequently become an active advisor to the company and often take a seat on the board.

Blue-Sky Laws. Each state has statutory laws governing the distribution and sale of securities. These statutes vary widely in their terms and scope and need to be examined closely before soliciting investment capital.

Bridge Financing. Money that is provided to a company that is expecting to go public, usually within 6 months to 1 year, or is initiating its next stage of financing. It is often structured so that it can be repaid from proceeds of a public underwriting.

Early-Stage Venture. Firms that have a substantial risk of failure because the technology behind their production or the logic behind their marketing approach has yet to be proven. The objective of an early-stage venture is to grow fast enough so that it will be able to go public or be sold to another company.

Equity. Ownership interest in a company or corporation that is represented by the shares of common or preferred stock held by the investors.

Equity Stake. An equity ownership position in the company that is provided to a funding source, usually lenders or other investors, as compensation for providing management consulting, financing, or miscellaneous services.

First Stage. A stage of development in which the company has expended its initial capital and requires funds, often to initiate commercial manufacturing and sales.

Follow-On/Later Stage. A subsequent investment in which the company has expended its initial capital and requires funds, often to initiate commercial manufacturing and sales.

Form S-1. The most comprehensive registration statement to be filed with the SEC by companies that wish to offer securities to the public.

Initial Seed. A relatively small amount of capital provided to an investor or entrepreneur, usually to prove a concept. It may involve product development, but rarely involves initial marketing.

Intra-State Offering. An offering of the sale of securities within the borders of a state in which the company is registered, and requiring state securities agency clearances.

Internal Rate of Return. The discount rate (or interest rate) at which the present value of the future cash flows of an investment equals the cost of the investment. Present vale is the value today of a future payment, or stream of payments, discounted at some appropriate interest rate.

Investment Bank. Usually a registered broker-dealer that undertakes the sale of securities or otherwise seeks to secure capital for companies.

Later-Stage Investment. An investment strategy for financing the expansion of a company that is producing, shipping and increasing its sales volume.

Later-Stage Venture. Firms with a proven technology behind their product and a proven market for it. Their risk is based on a myriad of uncertainties that affect small business, including the feasibility of their business concept. They have a proven technology and a proven market for their product, are growing fast and generating profits, and need private equity financing to add capacity or to update their equipment to sustain their fast growth.

Limited Partnership, A form of business organization that offers limited liability to the investors who become limited partners and, in certain cases, also offers tax benefits. Limited partnerships are often used for certain types of investments, such as those in research and development and in real estate. Limited partners enjoy limited liability for the debts of the firm, to the extent of their investment in the business. Limited partners have no voice in the management of the partnership. They merely invest money and receive a certain share of profits. There must be one or more general partners who manage the business and remain liable for all of its debts. A limited partnership is organized under state statutes, usually by filing a certificate and publishing a notice in the newspaper. The statutes, codified in many states as the Uniform Partnership Law, must be strictly observed. The death or bankruptcy of any one of the general partners dissolves the limited partnership.

Private Placement. An offering of securities that is exempt from federal registration and limited in distribution to certain types of investors. Generally, no more than 35 non-accredited investors may participate in the offering but an unlimited number of accredited investors may be shareholders. Similar to a prospectus, a private placement memorandum (PPM) is usually written and offered to investors along with a subscription agreement.

Prospectus. A disclosure document prepared to provide potential investors with detailed information regarding the purchase of securities, including debt or equity offerings, or limited partnership offerings. As it pertains to a registered offering, the prospectus is part 1 of the registration statement. The prospectus must be delivered before the consummation of any sale pursuant to a registered offering.

Registration Statement. The disclosure document filed with the SEC and state securities commissions in accordance with securities laws.

Restricted Shares. Shares of a company's stock generally obtained in a private placement that cannot be sold to the public without registration of the shares or an applicable exemption.

Second Stage. A stage of development in which working capital is provided for the initial expansion of a company that is producing and shipping and has growing accounts receivable and inventories. Although the company has clearly made progress, it may not yet be showing a profit.

Securities Act of 1933. The basic legislation that governs the offering of securities to the public. The objectives are to (1) require that investors receive financial and other significant information concerning securities being offered for public sale and (2) prohibit deceit, misrepresentations, and other fraud in the sale of securities.

Seed Stage. Companies at this stage have not yet fully established commercial operations, may still involve proving out an idea, and involve continued research and product development.

Small Business Issuer. A company incorporated in the United States or Canada that had less than $25 million in revenues in its last fiscal year, and whose outstanding publicly held stock is worth no more than $25 million.

Third Stage. The stage of business development in which funding is provided for the major growth of a company whose sales volume is increasing and that is beginning to break even or turn profitable. These funds are typically for plant expansion, marketing, working capital, or development of an improved product.

RESOURCES

A Good Hard Kick in the Ass, Adams, Rob, Crown Publishing, NY, NY 2002.
Angel Investing—Matching Start-Up Funds with Start-Up Companies, Van Osnabrugge and Robinson, Robert J., Jossey-Bass, San Francisco, Ca, 2000.
Angel Investor's Handbook, c. 2001, Benjamin, Gerald, Bloomberg Press, Princeton, NJ 2001.
Attracting Capital from Angels, Hill, Brian E. and Power, Dee, John Wiley & Sons, NY, 2002.
Beermat Entrepreneur, Southon, Mike and West, Chris, Prentice Hall Business, NY, NY, 2002.
Beyond the Banks: Creative Financing for Canadian Entrepreneurs, Riding, A llan L. and Orser, Barbara J., John Wiley & Sons, NY, NY, 2002.
Business Promotions Kit, Griffin, Jack, Prentice Hall, Englewood Cliffs, NH, 1995.
Closing Techniques, Schiffman, Stephan, Bob Adams Inc., Holbrook, MA, 1994.
Dive Right In The Sharks Won't Bite: The Entrepreneurial Woman's Guide to Success, Wesman, Jane, Prentice Hall, Englewood Cliffs, NJ, 1995.
Entertainment Economy, Wolf, Michael J., Random House, NY, NY, 1999.
Entrepreneurs Are Made, Not Born. Shefsky, Lloyd E., McGraw-Hill, NY, NY, 1994.
Entrepreneurial Finance, Janet Kihom Smith and Richard L. Smith, John Wiley & Sons, NY, NY, 2000.
Entrepreneur's Ultimate Start-Up Directory: Includes 1,350 Business Ideas, Stephenson, James, Entrepreneur Media, Irvine, CA, 2001.
EVEolution, The Eight Truths of Marketing to Women, Faith Popcorn and Lys Marigold, Hyperion, NY, NY, 2000.
Everybody's Business, Moskowitz, Milton, Levering, Robert and Katz, Michael. Doubleday Currency, NY, NY 1990.
Financing Entrepreneurs: The Anatomy of a Hidden Market, Gaston, Robert J., chapter in *Financing Economic Development: An Institutional Response*, ed. By Bingman, Hill and White, Sage Publications, 1990.
Financing Your New or Growing Business, Alterowitz, Ralph and Zonderman, Jon, Entrepreneur Press, Irvine, CA, 2001.
Financing Technology's Frontier, Shanley, Richard P., John Wiley & Sons, NY, NY 1998
Fundraising: Hands-On Tactics for Nonprofit Groups. Edles, L. Peter, McGraw Hill, NY, NY, 1993.
Getting Attention: Leading-Edge Lessons for Publicity and Marketing, Kohl, Susan, Butterworth Heinemann, Boston, MA, 2000.

Government Giveaways for Entrepreneurs, Information USA, Kensington, MD, 1992.
Guerilla Financing, Blechman, Bruce J. and Levinson, Jay Conrad, Houghton Miflin, Boston, MA 1996.
Guerilla Marketing, Levinson, Jay Conrad, Houghton Miflin, Boston, MA, 1994.
Guerilla PR, Levine, Melvin, Harper Business, NY, NY, 1994.
Guide to Raising Money, Entrepreneur Magazine ed., John Wiley & Sons, NY, NY 1998.
How to Write a Business Plan, McKeever, Mike, Nolo Press, Berkeley, CA, 1999.
Idea Makers and Idea Brokers in High-Technology Entrepreneurship, Carayannis, Elias G. and Juneau, Todd L., Quorum Books, NY, NY 2003.
I'll Get Back to You, 156 Ways to Get People to Return Your Calls and Other Helpful Sales Tips. Robert L. Shook and Erick Yaverbaum. McGraw Hill, NY, NY 1996.
Innovator's Dilemma: When New Technologies Cause Great Firms to Fail, Christensen, Clayton M., Harvard Business School Press, Cambridge, MA, 1997.
Insider's Guide to Venture Capital, 2002, Fichera, Dante, Prima Publishing, NY, NY, 2001.
Living on the Fault Line, Moore, Geoffrey A., Harper Business, NY, NY 2000.
Loud and Clear: How to Deliver Effective Business and Technical Presentations. Morrisey, Sechrest and Warman, Addison-Wesley, NY, NY, 1997.
Management Buy-Outs and Venture Capital, Wright, Mike and Robbie, Ken, Edward Elgar, Cheltenham, UK, 1999.
Marketing Management, Philip Kotler, Prentice Hall, Upper Saddle River, New Jersey 2000.
Marketing on a Shoestring, Davidson, Jeff, John Wiley & Sons, NY, NY, 1994.
Marketing Without Mystery; A Practical Guide to Writing a Marketing Plan. Dirks and Daniel, AMACOM, NY, NY, 1991.
Mastering the Art of Creative Collaboration, Hargrove, Robert, McGraw Hill, NY, NY, 1998.
Mastering the Dynamics of Innovation, Utterback, James M., Harvard Business School, Boston, MA, 1996.
Money Hunt, 27 New Rules for Creating and Growing a Breakaway Business, Spencer, Miles and Ennico, Cliff, Harper Business, NY, NY 1999.
Mystery of Capital, De Soto, Hernando, Basic Books, NY, NY, 2000.
New Partnership, Melohn, Tom, Omne, Essex Junction, VT, 1994.
New Rules for the New Economy, Kelly, Kevin, Penguin Books, NY, NY, 1998.
New Venture Creation: Entrepreneurship For The 21st Century, Timmons, Jeffry, A. Irwin, McGraw Hill, NY, NY, 5th edition, 1999.
Origin and Evolution of New Businesses, Bhide, Amar V., Oxford University Press, Oxford, Eng, 2000.
Pharmaceutical Innovation (The Chemical Heritage Foundation Series in Innovation and Entrepreneurship), Landau, Achilladelis and Scriabine, editors, McGill-Queen's University Press, Canada, 1999.
Power Promoting, Sussman, Jeffrey, John Wiley & Son, Inc., NY, NY 1997.
Product, Partners & Public Health: Transfer of Biomedical Technologies from the U.S.

Government. Ferguson, Steven M., J. BIOLAW & BUS., Vol. 5, No. 2, Washington, DC, 2002.
Publicity Handbook, Yale, David R., NTC Business Books, Lincolnwood, IL, 1996.
Publicity Kit, Smith, Jeanette, John Wiley & Sons, Inc., NY, NY, 1991.
Publicity on the Internet. Steve O'Keefe, John Wiley & Sons, NY, NY, 1997.
Selling with Excellence. McCloskey, Larry A., ASQC Quality Press, Milwaukee, WI, 1995.
Small Business is Like a Bunch of Bananas, Blasingame, Jim, SBN Books, Florence AL, 2002.
Starting on a Shoestring., Goldstein, Ph.D., John Wiley & Sons, NY, NY, 1995.
Starting Up, Rye, David E. and Hickman, Craig R., Prentice Hall, Englewood Cliffs, NJ, 1997.
Start Up Marketing: An Entrepreneur's Guide to Advertising, Marketing and Promoting Your Business. Nulman, Philip R., Career Press, Franklin Lakes, NJ, 1996.
Strategic Partnering: How to Join Forces with Forces With Other Companies. Silver, A. David, McGraw-Hill, NY, NY, 1993.
The Support Economy. Zuboff, shoshana and Maxmim, James, Viking Press, NY, NY, 2002.
Tao of Sales; The Easy Way to Sell in Tough Times, Behr, E. Thomas, Element Books, Rockport, MA, 1997.
Technology Licensing: Corporate Strategies for Maximizing Value. Parr and Sullivan, John Wiley & Sons, NY, NY, 1996
Telemedicine, Field, Marilyn J., ed., National Academy Press, Washington, DC, 1996.
Term Sheets & Valuations—An Inside Look at the Intricacies of Venture Capital Term Sheets & Valuations, Wilmerding, Alex, et al, Aspatore Books, Boston, MA 2002.
Total Exposure, Carlson, Gustav, AMACOM, NY, NY, 2000.
Trademark: Legal Care for Your Business & Product Name, Elias, Stephen and McGrath, Kate, Nolo Press, Berkeley, CA, 1999.
Understanding Silicon Valley: The Anatomy of an Entrepreneurial Region, Ed Kenney, Martin, Stanford University Press, Palo Alto, CA, 2002.
Unleashing the Killer App, Larry Downes and Chunka Mui, Harvard Business School Press, Boston, MA, 1998.
Valuing a Business, The Analysis and Appraisal of Closely Held Companies. Pratt, Reilly and Schweihs, Irwin, Chicago, IL, 1986.
Valuing Small Businesses and Professional Practices. Pratt, Shannon P., Business One Irwin, NY, NY, 1993.
Wharton on Managing Emerging Technologies. Day, George S. and Shcoemaker, Paul J. H., John Wiley & Sons, NY, NY 2000.
Where to Go When the Bank Says No: Alternatives for Financing Your Business, Evanson, David R., Bloomberg Press, Princeton, NJ, 1998.
Winning Angels: The 7 Fundamentals of Early Stage Investing, Amis, David and Stevenson, Howard H., Financial Times Prentice Hall, NY, 2001.
Word on Business, Luesby, Jenny, Financial Times, London, Eng, 2001.

Working Capital: The Power of Labor's Pensions, edited by Fung, Hebb and Rogers. Cornell University Press/ILR Press, 2001.

World Class Selling: How to Turn Adversity Into Success. Mortel, Art, Dearborn Financial Publishing, 1991.

Young Entrepreneur's Guide to Starting and Running a Business. Mariotti, Steve, Random House, NY, NY, 2000.

Zero-Resistance Selling. Maltz, Maxwell, M.D., Prentice Hall Press, Paramus, NJ, 1998.

INDEX

A

Abingworth 64
ACE.NET 160
acquisitions 105, 126, 169, 228
Akin Gump 99
Alabama A&M 95
Albany NanoTech 85
American Express 58, 128, 196
angel 12, 20, 45, 46, 47, 57, 63, 67, 73, 93, 98, 106, 113, 131, 147, 149, 156–166, 157
angel network 160, 164
Asia Venture 87
Asian Business Association 72
AT&T Small Business Lending Corp. 58
Axxon Capital 73

B

Babson College 91
Ball State 123
Barcelona Science Park 91
barter 102
Barter Systems 102
Baylor University 122
Bio-IT World 215, 236
BioVenture 98, 148
Black Entertainment Television (BET) 58, 72, 113
bootstrap 12, 13, 45, 55, 78, 204
borrow 46, 218
Boston Globe 49, 113
broker-dealer 177, 179, 247, 250
Buffalo, University of 98
Business 2.0 49, 113, 212
Business Journal 182, 230

C

Cal Tech 90, 124
California, University of 22, 84, 91
Cambridge 20, 53, 54, 62, 64, 83, 95, 119, 139, 191, 220, 223, 228, 254
Canada 143, 160, 226, 252, 255
CAPCO 109
capital-connection.com 113
Cascadia Revolving Fund 67
Case Western Reserve 92
catalyst 34, 224

chamber of commerce 118
Chase Manhattan 151
Chicago, University of 92, 123
China Venture Capital Association 66
Christensen, Clayton 9, 97, 254
clubs 63, 126, 158, 159
CMGI 60
Colorado 108, 119, 196
Colorado, University of 196
Columbia University 68, 224, 226
commercial bank equity 77
community college 93
Connecticut 69, 166, 225
Connecticut, University of 69
corante.com 113
corporate diversification 53
customer funding 52

D

Dayton, University of 122
Defi Investment 65
Deloitte 8, 10, 126
Discovery Technology Center 220
Duke University 91

E

ecademy.com 124
Edinburgh, University of 90
eGrants 126
elevator speech 132
EMBER 237
Emerging Venture Network 72
endowment 71
Entrepreneur Magazine 124
ESOP 54
ethnic group 71
Ewing Marion Kauffman Foundation 73, 113, 144, 160
Export incentive 60

F

Fast Company 184
female entrepreneurs 73
Files, Jennifer 107
finance association 58
Financial Times 30, 33, 83, 113, 180
Florida 8, 95, 222, 223
Florida, University of 88, 95, 223
forbes.com 113
Foreign government 82
Fortune Magazine 26, 202
Fortune Small Business 113, 121
forum 73, 98, 117, 119, 125, 155, 160, 223
France 71, 91, 228
franchise 78, 174

friends and family 1, 45, 46, 56
FutureDex Magazine 113

G

Gates Foundation 70
GE Capital 58, 151
Geneva, University of 91
George Mason University 122
George Washington University 73
Georgia 126, 222
Georgia Tech 61
Germany 83, 87, 227, 228
government grant 1, 79
government incentive 86
government specialized 87
government technical transfer 81, 82
grants 107
Greenpeace 36
guarantees, loans 46, 59, 60, 163, 185, 228

H

Harvard Business School 15, 32, 123, 158, 207
Haynes & Boone 99
Hearst 154
Hispanic Business Magazine 72, 113
Hispanic-Net 71
Home Office Association of America 125
Homeland Security Agency 69, 130
Houston Technology Center 122
Howard University 196

I

Imperial Bank 58
In-Q-Tel 69, 148
INBC 225. See also International Northeast Biotechnology Corridor
Inc Magazine 17, 112, 121, 162, 195, 206
incubator 18, 23, 44, 53, 54, 60, 61, 66, 72, 83, 92, 123, 151, 222, 224, 225, 226
independent broker-dealer 76
Indian Venture Capital Association 66
Indiana University 225
Indianapolis 125, 225
Indus Entrepreneurs, The. See also TIE
intellectual property 48, 52, 53, 84, 92, 95, 96, 97, 102, 126, 130, 134, 202, 203, 232, 235, 240, 241
International Northeast Biotechnology Corridor (INBC) 225
intrapreneurship 54
investment bank 1, 19, 20, 47, 76, 77, 94, 105, 112, 113, 120, 134, 159, 166, 168, 169, 194, 250
Investors' Circle 67
Iowa 59, 85, 109, 171, 172
Iowa State 172
Israel 65, 87, 100, 226

J

Japan 227, 233

Jewish community business network 72
Johns Hopkins 18, 84, 184
joint ventures 62, 78, 223

K

Kansas Venture Capital 108
Kauffman Center for Entrepreneurial Leadership. See also Ewing Marion Kauffman Foundation
Kentucky, University of 92
King's College 92
Korean Biotech Investment Capital 65

L

labor union 75
Latin Business Association 72
LBO 45
leasing & factoring 58, 102, 103, 248
licensing 8, 23, 34, 36, 62, 81, 82, 84, 95, 149, 154, 174, 194, 226, 234
Local Living 117. See also Business Alliance for Local Living Economies (BALLE)
Los Alamos 81
Louisiana 109, 122
Luna Innovations 84

M

Making It (television show) 72
MarketScan 184
Maryland 18, 36, 60, 65, 85, 90, 91, 123, 124, 164, 218, 224, 236, 237
Maryland, University of 224, 230, 237
Matrix Ventures 107
MBO 45, 54
McGill University 226
mentor 67, 106, 158
Mercury News 107, 113, 187
Miami, University of 95
Michigan 84, 92, 119, 223, 235
microfinance 110
Milken Institute 72
Mindspring 61
Minnesota 90, 100, 223
Minnesota, University of 88, 90
Minority Business Development Agency (MBDA) 72
Miramonte High School 217
Missouri 109, 224
MIT 13, 26, 81, 89, 119, 160, 193, 222, 237
Money Store 58
Montana 109, 135
mutual fund 48, 55, 101, 104, 231

N

NASA 69, 81, 82, 122, 239, 242
National Association of Women Business Owners 73
National Foundation for Women Business Owners 73
National Institutes of Health 17, 230. See also NIH
National Science Foundation (NSF) 88. See also NSF

National Social Venture Competition 68
National Technical Information Service 41
Native American 71
Navigator Technology Ventures 83
NCOE 109, 127, 157, 162
New Hampshire, University of 160
New Jersey 8, 35, 65, 79, 85, 97, 125, 168
New York Community Investment Company 67
New York Times 34, 113, 180, 189, 212
non-profit technical transfer 83
North Carolina 26, 77, 83, 85, 86, 102, 106, 224, 225
North Carolina State (NCS) 102
NSF 237, 242
NYU 226

O

Oak Ridge 81
Oregon State 108

P

Pakistani investment 71
PARC 54, 208
partnership 7, 8, 33, 53, 61, 66, 68, 71, 73, 103, 108, 123, 145, 149, 153, 155, 203, 213, 217, 223, 243, 248, 250, 251
patent 26, 27, 34, 35, 36, 53, 54, 81, 83, 96, 221, 235, 241
Pennsylvania 9, 19, 84, 220, 224
Pittsburgh 224, 225
political 100, 101
Practicing Law Institute 235
Price Waterhouse 93, 136, 142
Private Investors Network 164
public sector pension 75

R

regional funds 68
religious & nonprofit 28, 74
Rensselaer Polytechnic Institute 61, 98
Retirement Systems of Alabama (RSA) 75
Rice University 122
Richmond, VA 126, 224
Riegle Community Development and Regulatory Improvement Act of 1994 108
Rochester 92, 108, 158
rollout 51, 66, 173
royalty financing 110
Rural Development Fund 67
Rural Entrepreneurship Initiative 108
Rutgers 82

S

San Jose Business Journal 230
SBA 24, 80, 81, 160, 176, 196, 248
SBDCs 114, 115, 116
SBIC 45, 70

SBIRs 18, 34, 45
SCORE 80
SEC 46, 78, 166, 169, 170, 171, 175, 176, 177, 178, 198, 244, 245, 249, 251
seed & venture funds 217, 218, 224, 231, 235, 251
self fund 57
Seton Hall 73
shareholder capitalization 104
Silicon Valley Community Venture (SVCV) 67. See also SVCV
simple products 97
Singapore 226
Slater Center 68
small stock offerings 77, 160, 166, 168, 172, 176, 178, 179. See also SSOs
SmartStart Venture 98
SMOP 208
SMU 122
social investing 101
South Carolina 85
South Dakota 85
South Florida, University of 222
South Korea 53, 87, 152
special interest 104
spinout 34, 81, 90, 218
Springboard Enterprises 73, 98
SSOs 167, 168, 170, 173, 174, 176
Stanford Research Institute (SRI) 89. See also SRI
Stanford University 7, 10, 66, 81, 84, 88
startup 18, 22, 23, 31, 34, 47, 51, 53, 64, 66, 84, 90, 91, 95, 102, 109, 114, 118, 120, 122, 149, 156, 167, 221, 222, 224
states and counties 59, 84
SUNY 226
Sweden 91
Switzerland 91

T

Taiwan 49, 65, 226
teaming 68, 107, 220
technology transfer 34, 82, 83, 84, 85, 92, 94, 115, 123, 126, 229, 235, 239, 241, 242
Tennessee 223, 242
Texas, University of 226
thinking outside the box 105
Toastmasters 117

U

U.S. Army 25, 28, 47, 52, 69, 229
U.S. Navy 239
U.S. Robotics 145
UC Berkeley 68, 237
UCSF 225
UFJ Capital 65
UK 33, 34, 52, 53, 54, 83, 90, 91, 139, 254
university angels 93
USDA 87
utilities & coops 109

V

Vanderbilt University 84, 92
vendor financing 96
venture capital 129–144
Virginia 60, 73, 75, 80, 82, 84, 100, 110, 117, 126, 224
Virginia Tech 84, 224

W

Wall Street Journal 92, 113, 180, 183, 189, 190
Washington Post 113, 183
Washington University 224
Watts, Ferris Baker 166
Wayne Brown Institute 113.
Wayne State 223
Weizmann Institute 226
Wellcome Trust 91
Wharton 19, 114, 123, 220, 256
Wisconsin 71, 75, 161
Wisconsin State Employees Retirement System 75
women business owners 72
Women's Technology Center 73
Wootton High School 94

Y

Yale 93, 255
YoungBiz Inc. 94

ADDENDUM

p. 36—Hale and Dorr launched a free magazine called IP at www.haledorr.com.

p. 58—In the United Kingdom, the Small Firms Loan Guarantee Scheme guarantees loans from banks and other financial institutions (www.sbs.gov.uk).

p. 60—Information on European angels and networks can be accessed at www.eban.org.

p. 60—Otherwise known as "credit enhanced notes" the Oklahoma Capital Investment Board uses a tax credit-backed guarantee to borrow from banks, and the Oklahoma Development Finance Authority issues reserve fund-backed notes.

p. 61—The Decision Point is a novel new venture to provide an incubator setting through the web. Joining with the Canadian Technical Alliance (www.cata.ca), www.thedecisionpoint.com gives business resources, advice, marketing information, etc., to replicate much of the physical incubator experience.

p. 68—Other social venture and social economics websites include: www.sirolli.com; www.culturalcreatives.org and www.barkingowl.com.

p. 74—The Ms. Foundation for Women has distributed over $10 million to women's economic development organizations, and dates back to the 1980s in efforts to funnel foundation money into the area.

p. 87—The Arkansas Development Finance Authority contracted with the U.S. Partnership for State Investment to promote and pool venture capital investments in that state, following a model developed in Oklahoma where seed and venture investors team with public investors at the state level.

p. 91—University of California Discovery Grants funded over 1,000 industry/university research projects totaling $225 million since 1996.

- p. 94—The Colorado Enterprise Fund along with Ms. Foundation's Collaborative Fund helped launch a high school offering of entrepreneurship courses in Denver in 1997 known as B!ZWORK$.
- p. 94—Junior Achievement is the country's predominant organization to introduce youth to the business world. The U.K. launched an effort to promote entrepreneurship among youngsters with an active mentoring program (www.shell-livewire.org/mentor).
- p. 110—The microfinance movement had its start in 1976 when an economics professor in Bangladesh, Muhammad Yunus, loaned $27 to several stool makers in a tiny village to buy raw materials for their output, and launched Grameen Bank.
- p. 119—The Mosh Pit in Baltimore, MD places student-developed business plans against each other for a $10,000 prize, but with the additional requirement that they recruit a stellar virtual management team, adding a realistic element of negotiation to the process.
- p. 124—StartupNation.com has a radio show along with information on elevator pitches, etc.
- p. 172—Native Americans can find support at www.ncaied.org as well as research hosted at the universities of Arizona and New Mexico (including extensive work from Harvard University and the American Indian Studies Center at UCLA). A strategy paper on Canada's National Aboriginal Business Association is available at www.innovationstrategy.gc.ca along with a lengthy set of links throughout Canadian education and other links.
- p. 194—The slowed economy of 2003 has opened many PR doors for entrepreneurs who otherwise couldn't afford substantial up-front and continuing fees from major PR houses. You might check with area PR firms to see if they'll cut you some slack while you're seeking funding (partly to pay their eventual bills). In Boston, Clarke & Co. was happy to help startup ZForm with initial help at a much reduced rate. In Methuen, MA, Sentrepity Associates provides expert help through a group called "MassWit," a division of the WorldWit global online community for women in the technology field.
- p. 204—After exhaustingly researching a market for hypoallergenic cleansing products, Amilya Antonetti and her husband sold their home, borrowed $120,000 from the SBA and established "Soap Works" in San Leandro, CA. The company now does $5 million in annual revenues and has developed nearly a cult following for their products among a growing number of clients.

p. 209—"The automotive cluster centered on Detroit, Michigan began in earnest when Ransom E. Olds began mass producing the Oldsmobile in 1901. After a fire destroyed his factory, Olds put all his resources into producing the 'Curved Dash Olds' (the only vehicle saved from the fire). The cluster grew around a number of entrepreneurial firms, including Olds, Dodge, Cadillac, Ford, and Chrysler, that quickly developed over the next several years. For example, before building its own model, Dodge built transmissions for Olds and engines and axles for Ford. Likewise, the original Cadillac was produced by Henry Ford's former partners using an engine design that Olds had rejected. As the industry matured and consolidated with the formation of General Motors in 1908, expertise in automotive engineering and manufacturing concentrated in the region." From A Governor's Guide to Cluster-Based Economic Development, www.nga.org.

p. 225—The Canadian Government is promoting biotech growth with money, incubators and other resources as well as an active venture capital community (check www.canbiotech.com).

p. 236—BioProcess is a new magazine that helps bridge science and business and provides an excellent Glossary of International Biotherapeutic Regulation.